URBAN AMERICA: INSTITUTIONS AND EXPERIENCE

Urban America: Institutions and Experience

Michael Lewis

Associate Professor of Sociology
University of Massachusetts

John Wiley & Sons, Inc.
New York · London · Sydney · Toronto

Library of Congress Cataloging in Publication Data:

Lewis, Michael, Oct. 2, 1937-
Urban America.

Bibliography: p.
1. Cities and towns—United States. 2. Social institutions—United States. 3. Sociology, Urban.
I. Title.

HT123.L4 301.36'1'0973 72-10944
ISBN 0-471-53380-7

Printed in the United States of America

10 9 8 7 6 5 4 3 2 1

This book is for
Brooklyn and the other
boroughs of my experience

Preface

This book evolved from my troubled feelings about the cities of contemporary America. I grew up in New York which, in this century, has become synonymous with the best and worst of the urban experience. It is a city that I love, but today it is also a city that exhausts me physically and emotionally when I am within its environs . . . a city whose daily agonies distress me even when I am an observer from afar. I have come to know Chicago—that hard-bitten sophisticated city surrounded by prairie innocence—Boston, Los Angeles, Philadelphia, Washington, and a number of smaller urban communities. None is a place of ease, a place where the promise of an American life well-lived is easily realized. The urban communities of the American present, whatever else they may be, are places in which daily life can just as easily be characterized by its problems as its rewards, and perhaps even more so.

I have written this book because I believe that if this balance between rewards and problems is to be reset in favor of the rewards, then we must know better the sources of our present disappointments in urban life. In the pages that follow I apply the tools of the sociologist to this task. I bring to the reader a disciplined view of urban America, a view that hopefully will demonstrate the power of sociology to illumine, in a manner equally accessible to students and professionals, the social logics that determine the quality of our contemporary urban experience.

I have tried to cover as much of the contemporary urban scene as has seemed relevant to my purpose. This is important because it is *my purpose*—my concern about creating a better understanding of our urban discontent—that organizes this book, not some standard conception of what a text in urban sociology ought to be. Because of this, the book does not attempt to develop a comprehensive urban sociology. There are approaches to the analysis of urban America that receive scant attention here—the ecological approach and the demographic approach, for example—although they have been extensively used in other volumes. My neglect of these analytic concerns is not an oversight. It reflects a conscious choice to approach the study of urban America from the perspectives and only the perspectives that I personally have used successfully in my own research and teaching. I do not deny that the concerns I have omitted are important in their own right, but they have not been important in the development of my own sociological understanding of urban America.

I hope that the materials developed in this volume have something to *teach* about the character of our urban present. Stated another way, I hope that this book really is a *textbook* and not just a book containing sociological information about cities. I have attempted to write in the same way that I teach. I take students seriously and I believe that they should be treated without condescension. If there are parts of this book that are difficult (and I believe there are) it is because I have concluded that simplification would only misrepresent issues that are, in reality, difficult for anyone to comprehend. To misrepresent reality in the guise of simplifying it is to be guilty of miseducating one's students, a pedagogical and intellectual error that a serious teacher cannot excuse. When the going gets tough I hope that my readers will exert the necessary intellectual effort to create their own understandings of the issues in question. I hope that I have given them reason to do so.

Beyond this I hope that this book will be read critically. Ideas in print can be intimidating to the point where readers accept them simply because they are in print. I hope that no reader of this book will too easily accept its contents. As a teacher I prefer serious argument to passive acquiescence; as the author of a book intended to teach, I hope for the same response.

In preparing this book for publication, I have benefited considerably from the support of colleagues, friends, and family. I am grateful for their counsel, criticism, and encouragement. For efforts in behalf of my work I thank Bernard Farber, Myron Glazer, Lewis Killian, Eleanor Lewis, Charles Page, Jon Simpson, Hans Speier, Gordon Sutton, and Alexander Vucinich.

Michael Lewis

Northampton, Massachusetts, 1972

Contents

A POSTSCRIPT

Chapter 1
Introduction: Choosing A Perspective

PROLOGUE

We live in the midst of an *urban epoch.* In American society at least, our lives are increasingly affected by the values, norms, and conditions that are characteristic of city life. For some more consciously than others, for some more completely than others, but for nearly all of us—"urbophiles" or "urbophobes"—the city has become the focal point, the dominating entity, of modern life.

It is remarkable how little understood this phenomenon really is. In spite of the many books published and the plethora of papers appearing in scholarly journals, in spite of a journalism that finds the city and its impact irresistible, we seem limited in our ability to adequately describe the urban experience—much less to analyze its sources and consequences.

In this book an attempt will be made to further our understanding of modern urbanism. It is a task hopefully undertaken with no illusions. Our approach disclaims the attempt to develop a conceptual framework applicable to all things urban. Confronted by the variegated phenomena labeled urban, we retreat from attempting to make definitive statements about their nature. Although as social scientists we should be parsimonious in our treatment of these phenomena, we believe that there are few ahistorical general principles to be discovered in the study of urban phenomena; and, consequently, the search for principles that have such general explanatory powers is likely to produce few intellectually satisfying rewards.

This book attempts to make a contribution to the study of modern urbanism by demonstrating how a sociologist might investigate an important case in point—the social life of *contemporary American cities.* The reader can expect two kinds of payoff from his investment in time and interest in this book. First, he should come away from it with an understanding of *American urbanism* that he did not have prior to reading the book. Second, he should gather some insight into how a sociologist can approach the *intellectual and value problems* associated with contemporary urban life.

Finally, this book proceeds on the assumption that an urban sociology must not be a formal sociology; that it must not be an overconceptualized approach which, in its ahistorical abstractness, divorces itself from urban realities. The sociology of cities we are proposing is a historically specific sociology. The remainder of this introductory chapter is devoted to an elaboration of this position.

THE TEMPORAL AND CULTURAL SPECIFICITY OF URBAN PHENOMENA

Americans have what might be termed a "common sense" image of the city. It is an image that derives from *direct* experience with large metropolitan centers in the United States, from *indirect* or edited experience gained through the depictions of urban life in the mass media (television, radio, and newspapers), or from a combination of both. In this image the city is a place where large numbers of people—in the hundreds of thousands or even in the millions—live and work. The city is a place where buildings reaching skyward abut each other in order to accommodate the residential and vocational needs of the multitudes that inhabit it. It is a place of bustle—something is always going on. Great transactions involving astronomical sums are made in the city as a matter of course. Great commercial and industrial empires are housed in the city—as are the nerve centers of the complex communications networks that span not only our own nation, but the entire world as well. The city is "where it's happening;" it is the container of artistic triumph, of unparalleled delights beheld in the concert hall, the theater, and the galleries. But the city is also a "cold, heartless place." The multitudes living in such close proximity to each other rarely know very much about their neighbors—nor do they seem to wish to. City dwellers constitute most profoundly the "lonely crowd" where each man goes his own way in anonymous desperation. The city also houses the poor and the socially disinherited—the new ethnics (the blacks and the Spanish speaking) and the old ethnics (the orientals, eastern and southern European immigrants and their descendents)—struggling, all too often in vain, for their share of society's rewards. And nowhere else in society does one find such large numbers of individuals with derelict tastes: the hippies, the homosexuals, the winos, and the addicts. Because of all this the city is finally an arena for violence in which every stranger threatens. Thus, the common sense image is one in which the city houses both the best and the worst of everything in outsized proportions.

For the moment let us put aside any questions we might have about the accuracy of this image. Completely accurate or not, it does represent the common contemporary apprehension of the city. And it is an image of considerable force in the lives of modern men, attracting many to our urban centers while repelling many others.

In other times and other places, however, this "common sense" image would, in varying degrees, be inappropriate. The modern common sense image of the city is culture bound and temporally limited. In Greek antiquity, for example, it would be difficult to find any collectivity likely to generate a similar image. To begin with, the Greek city was comparatively diminuitive when one considers relative size. Very few settlements exceeded 5000 people. Athens at the height of its dominion during the age of Pericles (461–431 B.C.), numbered approximately 40,000 citizens and approximately 150,000 inhabitants. Relatively few inhabitants of any Greek city could claim rights as full citizens. The settlements usually referred to as city-states were essentially theocracies. Thus, while others might live and labor within the bounds of the settlement, only those initiated into the unique *city-religion* could claim the rights of full participation—the legal protections accorded the goods and, indeed, the lives of the citizens. Thus, although the Greek city had its share of the disinherited, their struggle for acceptance was rigidly proscribed by theological sanction. They were not, as are our own urban poor, seekers of the fulfillment of an officially proclaimed right to citizenship.

Unlike the image we have of today's city as the hub of worldwide communications networks, the cities (or settlements) of Greek antiquity were often isolated from one another. Most of these settlements, instead of facing outward, faced inward in preoccupation with their own religious ritual and customs. Today, in collecting the wisdom of the world, the modern city attracts the new and the different whereas ancient Greece resisted as alien (with force when necessary) those ideas that came from beyond the bounds of its domain. For example, the citizens of each city strove mightily to protect their own gods and dogmas from contamination by outsiders. Only citizens could participate in the sacrifices and other rituals of the civic-religion. The mere presence of a single outsider on a ritual occasion was believed to be a contaminant.

This closure may also be seen in another circumstance. Although the Greeks developed a far flung and sophisticated commerce, the apparent motivation for such activity did not stem from the desire to partake of the world's goods and ideas. Athens a city noted for its commerce, engaged in trade because such activity was seen as contributing revenue to the city-state. The Athenian citizenry, however, was not interested in the expansion of commerce for its own sake. *Citizens* themselves did *not* engage in commercial enterprise but left it to noncitizens and foreigners. Their revenue accrued from licenses and fees charged to those engaged in intercity trade. Thus, even where there was an apparent cosmopolitanism resulting from extended commerce, the citizenry removed itself from direct contact with those activities that might bring new ideas into close proximity.

Because of its obvious nature, we need not dwell on the difference in the technologies that characterize the epochs we are comparing. Because of it, however, the different physical appearances of the ancient Greek and modern American cities is apparent. The use of animate sources of energy limited the physical scale of the Greek "walking" city. The circulation of the population of the cities was governed by the range and speed of human and animal locomotion. The meaning of geographic distance changes according to the speed and efficiency of available transportation. Five miles traversed on foot or on mule-back is a much greater real distance than is the same geographic distance traversed by automobile or electrified tram. Thus the effective physical sprawl of the Greek city was controlled by limited means of human circulation. Beyond this the absence of frame technology in construction precluded extensive exploitation of verticle space in the Greek city, in spite of the sophistication and aesthetic value of antiquarian architecture.

Finally, because of the fear of foreigners and narrow parochialism of the ancient Greeks—a major factor differentiating their cities physically from our modern city image—was the need for self-defense. The heart of the ancient city was usually built on a hill where inhabitants could take refuge in case of an attack; in the same spirit, the lower towns (that is, the areas generally inhabitated by noncitizens) were cradled within extensive walls. Our modern image of the city hardly conjures up visions of the fortress, while the cities of ancient Greece were fortresses before they were anything else.[1]

1 The material in the proceeding discussion is based on more detailed accounts found in the following volumes: G. Glotz, *The Greek City and Its Institutions,* Barnes & Noble, Inc., New York, 1929; Kathleen Freeman, *Greek City-States,* W. W. Norton

If we juxtapose a picture of the *medieval* European city with our image of the modern city, our notion of the cultural and temporal specificity of urban phenomena becomes clearer still. During the 9th century A.D., after the glory of Rome, departed from the earth, cities took on the characteristics of small fortresslike settlements. The major function that sustained these enclaves was administration of ecclesiastical dioceses. The agriculturally based societies that surrounded these settlements had little functional use for them; they were, for example, neither politically important nor critical to the rural economies that predominated; they played no role in commerce as we understand it, for such commerce was almost nonexistent. Consequently, their populations were small and extremely homogeneous. Few if any of these settlements were inhabited by more than 3000 people and practically all of the inhabitants were dependent on the church for their well being. The excitement of the marketplace was missing and whatever "culture" they evidenced in the form of arts and letters was in the possession of a small minority of church functionaries. Except for the dominating cathedral, the physical apparatus of these settlements was in no way memorable. Neither their architecture nor their building technology was outstanding. They were monastic communities turned inward behind their protective walls, the very antithesis of our image of the city.

Within three centuries, however, the medieval settlement had changed significantly. Areas such as Flanders and the north of France saw the development of the commercially dominant "commune cities." These cities had full communal autonomy with their own laws common to all inhabitants within their territorial limits. Dominated by the commercial guilds, these settlements constituted themselves as markets luring both people and goods within their walls. The monastic quality of the ninth century A.D. settlements had given way to a measure of secularization and heterogeneity although religious feeling still maintained strength. It was in these cities that the serf could win his freedom by remaining within the settlement for a period of one year without detection by his liege-lord. It was in these cities that the bourgeoisie (burghers) became a group of economic and social

---

and Co., Inc., New York, 1950; N. D. Fustel De Coulanges, *The Ancient City: A Study On the Religion, Laws, and Institutions of Greece and Rome,* Lothrop, Lee and Shephard Co., Boston, 1873; Ralph Turner, *The Great Cultural Tarditions: The Foundation of Civilization, Vol. II, The Ancient Cities,* McGraw-Hill Book Co., New York, London, 1941; Jean Comhaire and Werner J. Cahnman, *How Cities Grew: The Historical Sociology of Cities,* Revised Edition, The Florham Park Press, Inc., Madison, New Jersey, 1962.

significance. While the clerics remained within these settlements, they ceased to dominate them and the proportion of the population dependent their offices declined considerably.

In spite of these developments, however, these settlements still differed considerably from our modern "common-sense image" of the city. They never approximated in size the great modern cities. For example, Bruges and Ghent in Flanders held less than 100,000 and 50,000 inhabitants each. If these cities were more open to the total European environment than their predecessors had been, they were—if only because a relatively primitive communication and transportation prevented it—hardly the repositories of the multifaceted cultural amalgam we perceive our cities as being. Although they were relatively secular and although anticlericalism was strong in many of them, it was nevertheless true that a religious ethos grounded in Christianity permeated the characteristic "urban" cultural complex. Even the commercial guilds—which were strongly opposed to clerical power—generally legitimated themselves in terms of Christian belief. If their commerce brought with it a certain heterogeneity of population, certainly this mixture of population—of workers, burghers, clerics, etc.—is hardly comparable to the class, ethnic, religious, racial, and occupational mix that we conceive of the modern, particularly the modern *American* city, as housing. Finally, walled as no modern city is, the thriving medieval settlement of 12th century Europe was yet a fortress.

Thus, we may conclude that although these later medieval settlements—generally called cities—were more developed (more socially elaborate) than those city settlements they succeeded, they were considerably different from our image of the modern American city.[2]

Other examples of settlements generally accorded the name city may be briefly cited in order to show how temporally and culturally specific is our common sense image of what is urban. We need only to examine the "cities" of colonial America—Boston, New York, and Philadelphia—those direct ancestors of the major metropolitan centers on the eastern seaboard, in order to further sustain this point. The 18th century American "city" did have many of the characteristics that we commonly recognize as urban. First, the city settlement was a commercial center. Boston, New York, and Philadelphia (as well as

2 Material in the proceeding discussion is derived from more extensive and detailed accounts in the following works: Henri Pirenne *Medieval Cities: Their Origins and the Revival of Trade,* Princeton University Press, Princeton, 1925; Robert E. Dickinson, *The West European City: A Geographical Interpretation,* Routledge and Kegan Paul, Ltd., London, 1951; see also Comhaire and Cahnman, cited earlier.

cities of less contemporary importance such as Newport and Charlestown) all functioned as *entrepôts* for a flourishing trade with Europe and the West Indies. In each of these ports, industries related to this trade were to be found in some abundance. At mid-century, flour processing and sugar refining were thriving endeavors in New York. In Philadelphia leather tanning and sugar refining held sway—as did rum distilling and sugar refining in Boston. And while shipbuilding never really caught on in New York, it was a major industry in Boston and Philadelphia.

Second, this development of commerce brought with it a concomitant development of social stratification and inequality. At the bottom of the stratification ladder were the black slaves, the indentured servants, and the common laborers—impoverished, with little or no education, often mistreated by those in whose service they found themselves. At the top of the ladder were those who were successful in commerce—reasonably well educated men and women who could afford to affect the presumptions of European culture. In the middle were the shopkeepers and artisans of little wealth but possessing such skills as to allow them to maintain their independence by continuous honest labor. Such inequalities as these often bred discontent—much as they do today—and even violence. Those on the bottom bitterly resented their condition, while those on the top, jealous of their advantages, feared the resentments of the others.[3]

Third, such cities as Boston, New York, and Philadelphia were not without their characteristic forms of the arts and letters—not without a cultural life, which was a mixture of the peculiarly American (or colonial) with the influences of the 18th century European salon. In New York, the least restrictive of the city settlements, men and women, usually of the aristocratic groups, could and did busy themselves at balls, dancing schools, concerts, and the theater. Boston, where the Puritan morality prevailed, was not so jovial a place, nor was Philadelphia, where the antifrivolous precepts of strict Quakerism, though failing, did limit the acceptable forms of diversion. These cities housed a growing intellectual and educational establishment. Boston, in particular, developed a public education system unparalleled for its time in western society. Science seemed to find fertile ground in Boston

3 Such fears at times were translated into mass hysteria as in the case of the so-called "Negro conspiracy" in New York during 1741. As the result of a series of robberies and the stories of a white servant girl, the militia was called out to round up Negroes who might be involved in conspiracy against whites. As a result of unfounded rumor 13 Negroes were burned, 8 were hanged, and 71 were expelled from the city.

and from that city residents made numerous contributions to the *Philosophical Transactions of the Royal Society* in the English motherland. In both Philadelphia and Boston there was extensive publication of theological as well as secular literature.

If, however, the 18th century American "city" had characteristics similar to those that we recognize as urban, it possessed them on so diminuitive a scale as to belie the perceived similarities. In terms of sheer size, these "cities," using contemporary standards were little more than small towns. In 1720, the estimated population of Boston was 12,000; by 1742 it was a little over 16,000 and by 1775 it had not grown much beyond that. New York had an estimated population of 7000 in 1720; in 1742 it was estimated at 11,000 and by 1775 it was estimated at 25,000. Philadelphia had an estimated population of 10,000 in 1720, an estimated population of 13,000 in 1742, and by 1775 its population was estimated at close to 24,000.[4] Thus, even though these "cities" possessed easily recognizable urban characteristics, they could not possibly have done so on the large scale which is itself a significant part of our common sense image of the city.

Aside from the fact that the colonial industries operated on a limited energy base (no electric power, for example) they simply could not employ the multitudes we are accustomed to associating with the urban industrial complex, since the multitudes did not exist. That the populations of these "cities" were characterized by social cleavages and that the concomitant inequalities of these cleavages often led to resentment and violence cannot be denied. However this does not mean that these phenomena had the scale and qualities that their contemporary counterparts often possess. While it is possible to isolate three basic economic strata in the colonial cities—the impoverished laboring people, the independent tradesmen and artisans, and the successful merchants—no such simple classification would suit the cities of 20th century America. In today's cities we are confronted with multitudes whose hyphenated identities often crosscut their economic stratification: the Italian-Americans, the Spanish-Americans, the Jewish-Americans, the Afro-Americans, each group within the city possessing its own characteristic economic distribution; and the measure of discontent bred of ethnic competition (for years ethnic identity has been a major factor in determining access to particular kinds of

4 Population estimates for colonial cities are not very reliable. Different sources often cite varying estimates. Irrespective of the accuracy of these estimates, however, it is clear that even the major colonial "cities" were quite small by contemporary standards.

job opportunities) and racial discrimination have resulted in violence on a scale scarcely imaginable in the colonial "city." Incidents of mass violence and hysteria can be found in the colonial city, but nothing existed that approximated the persistant tensions and sense of prolonged crisis that we identify with our modern cities.[5]

Finally, the quantitative as well as the qualitative gap between the arts, letters, and sciences practiced in the colonial and the modern city is so great that to consider them similar in both eras is to falsify reality. It is possible within a relatively few pages to describe in some detail the contribution all the colonial cities together made in these areas. On the other hand, volumes are necessary to describe the organization of such endeavors in one modern city, let us say New York. If it were possible to cite nothing else in this connection, we need only remind ourselves of the vast storehouses of information—the libraries, the government agencies, the museums, foundations and universities that are located in today's cities. The most urbane colonial would be astounded were he to suddenly be confronted by the vast intellectual resources of the modern city.

Although the 18th century colonial city seems more like our common sense image of the modern city than do the Greek city-state and the medieval fortress city, nevertheless, it was sufficiently different (on so many levels) to indicate the phenomenological variability of those social systems that are usually identified by social scientists as urban.[6]

All that we have described thus far has occurred in the past. The story is not so very different, however, when we look at cities of the

5 In this light it should also be noted that for a considerable period during the eighteenth century the colonial "cities" were not open to all comers. Boston, New York, and Philadelphia strove to restrict the settlement of newcomers to those ot backgrounds similar to the original European settlers and those who might otherwise give indication of their economic independence and good health.

6 The above discussion is based on more detailed materials to be found in the following sources: Carl Bridenbaugh, *Cities in the Wilderness: The First Century of Urban Life in America, 1625–1742,* Capricorn Books, 1964, Original date of publication 1938; Christopher Tunnard and Henry Hope Reed, *American Skyline: The Growth and Form of our Cities and Towns,* Mentor Books, New York, 1956, Parts I and II. Original date of publication 1953; Morton and Lucia White, *The Intellectual Versus the City: From Thomas Jefferson to Frank Lloyd Wright,* Mentor Books, New York, 1964, pp. 18–31; Jean Gottman, *Megalopolis: The Urbanized Northeastern Seaboard of the United States,* The M.I.T. Press, Cambridge, 1961, pp. 17–213 especially; Sam Bass Warner, Jr., *The Private City: Philadelphia in Three Periods of its Growth,* University of Pennsylvania Press, Philadelphia, 1968, pp. 3–45 especially.

present that developed or are developing in places other than in the United States or Wstern Europe. While the cities of Southeast Asia, Africa, and Latin America approach our urban image in scale, they differ considerably in a number of other dimensions. The "cities" of these areas are extremely important in the great transformation from rural agrarianism to urban industrialism, which is now almost a universal process among the underdeveloped societies of the world. In many respects they represent the stages on which the great dramas of political and economic modernization are played. As such they are settlements in which the confrontation between tradition and modernity is direct—so direct, in fact, that it has physical as well as social manifestations, which may be witnessed on a day-to-day basis.

In Southeast Asia, for example, cities are in reality two cities: one harbors the modernizing elites (those who look to the West for their models of commerce, polity, education, leisure, and religion) as well as western Europeans, the remnants of the colonial period; and the other harbors the masses who cling tenaciously to an indigenous preindustrial culture. Physically the indigenous or older segments of these cities are characterized by a curiously involuted pattern of narrow streets hardly passable by automobile. These are the quarters of men on foot where *time* is not yet a factor in a rationalized market economy and consequently where the absence of efficient circulation of people, goods, and services is not considered to be a major problem. On the other hand, the new sections have often been planned with rational economic endeavor in mind.

In the industrializing nations, those who cling to indigenous tradition bring more than a touch of rural life into the environs of the city. Quite often they conceive of themselves as temporary residents of the city and they nurture those customs that tie them to the places they regard as their real homes—the villages of the countryside.[7] In Latin America the rural migrants recreate neighborhood arrangements (barrios) that reflect their kinship-based rural origins. New arrivals invariably seek out "their people." In the favelas of Rio de Janeiro, and the vecindad of Mexico City, extended kinship with its associated patterns of mutual aid predominates. This pattern is repeated in the old African city where tribe and kinship lineage often determine the residence of the rural migrant. And in India, where residence has often been determined by the tradition of caste, many of the urban

7 This phenomenon does occur in the modern American city. It can be observed among Puerto Rican, Negro and mountain white migrants to the cities. However, it never occurs on as great a scale in these cities.

poor—casual laborers, for example—shuttle back and forth between the city and the rural villages of their birth.

Cities in the developing nations confound our commonsense image not because they are diminutive, not because they are bereft of the excitement we have learned to expect when many people live extremely close to one another, and not because commerce, industry, literature, and art are missing, but because they are the containers of both a viable past and a viable present. The basic conflicts of cities in developing nations not simply the struggles of individuals and groups to maximize their benefits in a socal system to which they are committed, as they are in the modern cities of our image, but rather they are conflicts between those who would move their societies into the modern world and those who, though seeking some of the ephemeral benefits such modernization might bring, are committed to a way of life which the ascendency of such modernism would no doubt destroy. The city of our experience is most likely to be "*today*" and "*tomorrow*"; the city in the developing societies is at once "*yesterday*," "*today*," and "*tomorrow*"![8]

The preceding discussion by no means catalogues *all* the variations of phenomena which are customarily grouped together under the urban rubric. But even this brief hopscotch through "urban" history should serve to suggest that *the city* is not a stable concept marshalling a series of clearly defined and essentially culture-free empirical referents. *The city* is not timeless; and the key to an understanding of contemporary American urbanism cannot be found except in the analysis of that urbanism itself. For *the city* is not itself a *specie* whose universal essence may be abstracted from comparative and historical study, but a series of discrete species, each possessing its own social life.

THE HISTORICALLY SPECIFIC SOCIOLOGY OF URBANISM: A RATIONALE AND A PARADIGM

Given the highly variable nature of that which we facilely term "urban" it would seem that any attempt to generalize about such

8 The discussion presented here is based upon more detailed accounts in the following sources: Gerald Breese, *Urbanization in Newly Developed Countries*, Prentice-Hall, Inc., Englewood Cliffs, New Jersey, 1966; Gideon Sjoberg, *The Preindustrial City: Past and Present*, The Free Press, New York, 1960; Norton S. Ginsburg, "The Great City in Southeast Asia," *American Journal of Sociology, LX* (March 1955), 455–562; Richard M. Morse, "Latin American Cities: Aspects of Function and Structure," *Comparative Studies in Society and History, IV* (July 1962), 473–493.

phenomena; to discover timeless or a-historical principles which explain urban phenomena—would be nothing short of a fools errand. It would be a fools errand because one can only generalize about social facts which belong to the same empirical class and as we have seen, the term, urban, does not establish a distinct class of social phenomena. The evident variability in the referents of the urbanisms of different times and different places must undermine any confidence we might have in those explanatory principles which some might argue are universally applicable. *What we need is not a general ahistorical urban sociology but discrete sociologies of historically specific urbanisms: sociologies of urban phenomena which by virtue of their manifestation at a given time and in a given cultural setting possess demonstrable unity.* In the remainder of this chapter we will detail a further rationale for this position and set out the plan of inquiry into contemporary American urbanism (or paradigm) that organizes the materials to be developed in this book.

There is a tradition in sociology that links social analysis with the desire to reconstruct human society. In this view of the sociological enterprise the analysis of the arrangements men and women have made to order their collective existence can and should be conceived of as a tool for *improving* the serviceability of such arrangements. This tradition has found eloquent expression in the works of such stalwarts as Auguste Comte, Karl Marx, Lester Ward, Robert E. Park, Ernest Burgess, Robert MacIver, Robert Lynd and Gunnar Myrdal—to name but a few. And if more proof of this strain in sociology and social science in general were needed, we would point to the numerous instances of "applied" social research in our literature as well as the publication of several journals (*Social Problems, The Journal of Conflict Resolution, TransAction* or as it is presently called *Society, The Journal of Social Issues,* for example) devoted to research and theory as they are related to the issues and problems of society in our time.

That there is a counter tendency in sociology toward formalist withdrawal from society and social issues cannot be denied. Nevertheless, there is a historically demonstrable relationship between sociology and social reconstruction (reform or revolution). And it is a relationship to which we should give explicit recognition, for it suggests an epistemological basis (a rationale) for the position taken in this book on the viability and necessity of an historically specific sociology of cities.

If we recognize and accept as valid this connection between sociological analysis and social reconstruction then it is not enough for sociologists to contribute to the development of a formal conceptual framework far removed from the "nitty gritty" of real society. It is not enough for them to create new system-utopias of concepts and categories in which, by deduction, it can be "proven" that the social world is orderly and that social processes operate rationally. If such models as these are to be judged a contribution to social science, we ought to find them illuminating the understandings we have of the social logics we find operating in concrete social systems which we can locate historically and culturally. If we recognize the connection between analysis and social improvement we should, moreover, demand of these models that they provide some analytic basis for a reconstruction of social arrangements; a reconstruction which maximizes personal fulfillment for ever increasing numbers of people.

What constitutes a reconstruction of social arrangements that maximizes the potential for human fulfillment (or, in other words, for the improvement of society) is a value problem. Various and competing conceptions of a reconstructed social future each have their proponents among us. We have no objective criteria, therefore, by which to judge that a given parcel of research or scholarship has unequivocably contributed to the reconstruction or improvement of society. What constitutes improvement from my point of view may not constitute such improvement from yours. However, on the assumption that social "improvement" proceeds best from insight into conditions as they *are* (conditions presumably in need of change), we should judge the work of a sociologist—at least in part—by the insights it generates into some segment of the reality experienced by men and women in contemporary society. This may be termed the *pragmatic test* that, given the relationship between sociology and the will to "improve society," becomes a principle of criticism within the discipline.[9]

When the "*pragmatic test*" is considered with particular reference to the study of American cities and contemporary urban affairs, the

9 This epistemic view of social science has major implications not properly within the purview of this text. While it deserves considerable attention in general, it will only be noted briefly here. If social science is intimately bound to the "improvement of society", there *is* always an implicit assumption—sometimes explicit—in the work of the social scientist: that present conditions, whether economic or political, whether qualities of a nation, state or a city, are at best only imperfect prefigurations of a possible future. Thus, the social scientist is more often than not (and more often than he himself realizes) a social critic. As such, both he and his discipline are politically relevant in a manner in which no physical scientist and his discipline are relevant—merely by the everyday practice of his discipline. This may explain why social science is often regarded with suspicion and hostility by laymen. Explicitly or not—effective or not—social science and social scientists represent to the layman disdain for all that he holds sacred.

following argument would appear to be compelling. If an important part of the sociology of cities is to provide an analysis of conditions *as they are* so that the quality of urban life may ultimately be improved, it is clear that the investigator must study *American cities as they are* in the here and now. He must analyze the *existing* alignment of urban institutions—and the existing events which comprise the contemporary urban experience, these together constituting the present upon which an improved future must be built. It will accomplish little if he attempts to generalize about all cities in all epochs and cultures. To do so would mean operating at a level of abstraction so removed from the events, experiences and institutions of American urbanism that the resulting analysis would shed little light upon the imperfections which inhere in this urbanism. If such a scholar were successful in developing analytic generalizations about all cities in all times it would be a success at cost to the development of grounded analyses which have the potential for pointing the way to a more serviceable urban future. Americans are discontented in their urban existence and our aspirations for a more serviceable urban future will only be advanced when we are able to provide the analytic intelligence necessary for a diagnosis of the sources of this discontent. Only if we are in possession of such a diagnosis can we shape a better future in a manner capable of nonutopic realization. Thus we eschew the quest for ahistoric generalization and proceed with historically specific analysis. We intend to know the present so that the future will better serve us.

Before proceeding to develop the paradigm (or plan of inquiry) that informs this book, the meaning we are giving to historical specificity in social analysis, implicit to this point, needs to be made explicit. We mean by *historical specificity* an assumption by the scholar that the phenomena he is analyzing are part of a particular configuration of events, experiences and institutions, these together constituting epoch (or particular historical period). He holds that any explanation of such phenomena must be made in terms of this mix of events, experiences, and institutions as opposed to some ahistorical universal principle, law or theory. As such, his explanatory effort will be little removed, methodologically speaking, from the phenomena itself.

The scholar working in terms of this assumption, to the extent that he is conscious of his epistemological position, *does not*, as some would argue, *abandon* the possibility of objective generalization in social science. He merely argues that such generalization contributes most to the understanding of social phenomena when the temporal and cultural universe for which it is applicable is clearly specified. If the phenomena one is interested in can only be analyzed in terms of *their position* in a particular configuration of events and institutions, then it follows that whatever the explanatory statements derived from this analysis they can only be pertinent within the limits of the *epoch* (or period) from which they are drawn. There is, of course, nothing contrary to generally accepted methodological canon of social science in such specification. It is considered exemplary for a social scientist to indicate the universe for which his findings are relevant. Most often, however, this refers to a specification of a universe much more limited and of a different order than an historical *epoch,* for example, all college students in the United States, or all divorced women—an empirical class within an epoch. Nevertheless, this principle of *epoch* delimitation is entirely consistent with accepted (indeed encouraged) social science practice.

It should be noted that the scholar committed to the historically specific perspective does not actually deny the possibility of transhistorical generalization in social science; he simply holds that such generalizations must of necessity be at such a high level of abstraction that for most of the problems that social scientists are expected to provide intellectually satisfying, and increasingly, practically applicable analyses, they are of little explanatory use. C. Wright Mills, a proponent of this perspective in social science, has written the following in criticism of "high level" generalization:

> *The basic cause of grand theory is the initial choice of a level of thinking so general that its practitioners cannot logically get down to observation. They never . . . get down from the higher generalities to problems in their historical and structural contexts . . . One resulting characteristic is a seemingly arbitrary and certainly endless elaboration of distinctions which neither enlarge our understanding nor make our experience more sensible.*[10]

This book is inspired by the sociological tradition that links the analysis of social affairs and arrangements to the improvement of the human condition in society. For this reason do we deny ourselves the questionable luxury of contemplating the "higher generalities" such as they are with respect to urban affairs. We take it as *first principle* that sociological scholars have a special obligation to bring their analytic intelligence to bear on the problems of their time and place.

10 C. Wright Mills, *The Sociological Imagination,* Oxford University Press, New York, 1959, p. 33.

No one can guarantee the success of such an effort. Perhaps ours is as much a fool's errand as those efforts that are inspired by the quest for universally valid ahistorical principles of sociological explanation. That the effort should be made, however, seems beyond question. All one needs to do is to read a newspaper, watch the evening news as reported by Walter Cronkite, John Chancellor, or Harry Reasoner, or simply walk around one's own city to know why.

We conclude this chapter with an exposition of an historically specific paradigm for the sociological study of cities. A paradigm may be defined as a codified guide to inquiry in terms of a given theoretical and/or methodological perspective.[11] The paradigm consists of a series of questions or problems that are derivable from the basic assumptions of the perspective being employed and that may be taken as the organizing questions for the scholarship one is undertaking. As presented below, our historically specific paradigm for the sociology of cities will consist of the general statement of perspective and the basic problems of this book as derived from that perspective.

I. *Statement of Perspective*: The historically specific sociology of cities is based upon the following assumptions:
   A. The most meaningful and useful analyses of cities and the urban experience are made when the historical and cultural settings of these cities are taken into account. It is assumed that generalizations derived from the sociological analyses of urban phenomena are applicable *only* within the temporal and cultural boundaries of a given epoch (or historical period).
   B. There is an historically demonstrable relationship between sociology and "social improvement." It is assumed that this relationship is legitimate and that the sociological study of cities presumes the need for improving the lot of men in urban society.

   Consequently:
   C. We assume it is necessary to study *cities as they are;* which may be understood as the analysis of urban institutions and urban experience characteristic of a given historical epoch. Such an analysis is undertaken with the intent to illumine the *urban social logics* of the epoch in question. The intellectual payoff comes in the successful illumination of these logics.

11 For a statement on purposes of a paradigm, see Robert K. Merton, *Social Theory and Social Structure,* revised Ed., The Free Press, Glencoe, Ill. 1957, p. 55.

II. *Basic Problems Derived from the Perspective*

A. *Choosing the epoch for analysis*:

Consistent with the "pragmatic test" (as elaborated in our discussion of the rationale for an historically specific sociology of urban communities) the analyses presented in these pages will attempt to diagnose the sources of discontent in modern American cities. By modern American *cities,* we mean all those extant communities in the United States that are incorporated municipalities, irrespective of their size.

All too often sociological as well as popular concern for contemporary urbanism has neglected small and middle-sized municipalities because the problems and discontents of the large metropolis have been so compelling—because urbanism in the conventional consciousness has been defined in terms of the metropolis. If we are to make any headway in making urban life more humanly serviceable, we shall have to devote systematic analytic attention to the variety of incorporated municipalities which characterizes the American present.

B. *The dimensions of inquiry*:

In order to engage in a systematic inquiry into contemporary American urban communities we shall focus our efforts on two levels. To begin with, we will attempt to shed some light on the *universals and variations* in the structure of American urban communities. We shall attempt to make more substantial the reader's understanding of how various municipalities are characterized in terms of their institutions (their polities, economies, family systems and educational systems). In doing so we shall be addressing the basic problem of trying to understand just how American urban communities are "put together." This form of inquiry may be termed *institutional analysis.*

We choose these particular institutional orders for sustained analysis because as we shall make clear in the following chapters they appear to be the major components of the structure of contemporary urban communities.

While it is indeed true that the structure of a community has a great deal to do with the quality of social life within that community, we must also take note of the fact that from the point of view of those living in the community the quality of life is not experienced and interpreted in structural or institutional terms. People are not generally concerned with the polity of their community but rather with specific political problems. Few are conscious of the economy as a component of community structure, while many are concerned with economic problems of one form or another. Thus in order to understand the discontents of contemporary urban Americans we shall have to take a systematic look at the manner in which they *experience* their communities. In doing so, we shall focus upon those problems which seem to trouble contemporary urban Americans most—the problems associated with *race, poverty, law and order, and justice.* At a later point in this book we shall indicate why these particular problems seem most salient in framing the contemporary urban experience.

With regard to both the institutional and experiential levels of inquiry we shall, wherever possible, analyze the implications of variation in community scale for the manner in which the phenomena under investigation are made manifest. While in some instances community scale (or size) will probably have little or no impact, we take the position—in the form of a working hypothesis—that scale has significant implications for community structure and the character of experience within the community.

In sum, this is a book of sociological diagnosis. It attempts to unearth those social logics that characterize contemporary American urbanism in a wide variety of its manifestations, in search of the underlying sources of our present state of discontent where the quality of urban existence is concerned.

Before proceeding to the substance of our inquiry, there is one final concern that, because it informs this work, should be made explicit for the reader. It has become fashionable for many of those who are vitally concerned with improving the human serviceability of our urban communities to decry the intellectual analysis of urban affairs as an excuse for inaction on problems which seem perfectly obvious. Analysis, it is often suggested, is a mask for apathy or the unwillingness to put oneself wholeheartedly into the struggle for positive urban change. The author of this book rejects these assertions as unfounded and misdirected. The issue is not whether we act. The record indicates that we do act—the urban scene is a veritable clutter of action programs—but whether we act *intelligently* in the pursuit of positive urban change. To respond to the obvious need for improvement in an untutored and unselfconscious manner is to heighten the potentiality for counterproductive effort and, consequently, to sustain those very conditions that we intend to remedy. Analysis *is* action. It must precede intelligent programatic efforts and it must continue even as we attempt to translate our programs into social reality. It is both a source of strategic adequacy and the agent of self-correction. If we fall into an uncritical acceptance of every well-intentioned program for maximizing the human serviceability of our urban communities, we will surely squander our energies and very probably defeat our own purposes. Thus the dichotomy between action and analysis is false, and in our ardor for change we should take care not to allow our emotions to tyrannize our intelligence.

PART ONE

Contemporary Urban Institutions: Their Characteristics and Alignment

In this section we propose to examine the nature of urban institutions in contemporary American cities. In order that there be no misunderstanding between author and reader, we will clarify what is meant by *urban institutions* before we proceed.

As used in this book, an *institution* exists within a given social system where there is a normative pattern that generally elicits *behavioral conformity* on the part of the actors who are within the boundaries of that system. Failure to conform to the patterned expectations is generally regarded by actors within the system as constituting deviance deserving strong moral censure at the very least, and, in some cases, the exercise of legal sanctions.

The institution consists of both *ideal* and *actual* aspects. The normative pattern describes a series of related *ideal expectations* to which the behavior of the actors within the system is the *actual* (*imperfect*) approximation. Behavioral manifestations in terms of the normative pattern may either be individual/idiosyncratic or collective/organizational (that is, behavior may either be the result of individuals acting alone or in concert with one another).[1]

Modern societies are characterized by an alignment of the following institutions:

1. *The polity.* The pattern of values and norms and related behaviors that defines the exercise of legitimate *social* power. Social

1 For a discussion of the concept of institution see Marion J. Levy, Jr., *The Structure of Society* (Princeton, N.J.: Princeton University Press, 1952), pp. 102–193; Talcott Parsons, "The Position of Sociological Theory," *American Sociological Review, III* (April 1948), pp. 156–164.

power means the ability of an actor or group of actors to evoke a desired response from an alter actor or group regardless of alter's intentions. Social power is legitimate when the values and norms of the society sanction or justify its possession and exercise by a given actor or group of actors. It is illegitimate when there are no positive sanctions or justifications.

2. *The economy.* The pattern of values, norms and related behaviors that defines the processes of production and exchange of goods and services within the society as well as across its borders.

3. *The family-kinship system.* The pattern of values, norms, and related behaviors that defines those interpersonal relationships that are legitimatized by reference to a biological relationship (assumed common descent) and regularized, sanctioned sexual cohabitation (marriage).

4. *The educational system.* The pattern of values, norms and related behaviors that defines the processes by which new members of the society become competent to participate in the social life of that society.

5. *The religious system.* The pattern of values, norms and related behaviors primarily oriented toward placing humans in relationship to the ultimate and essentially insoluble mysteries of the cosmos.[2]

These are the constituent institutions of modern society and it may be argued that they are also urban institutions. On the assumption that cities are subunits (or subsystems) of their host society, that which is characteristic of that society as a whole will also be characteristic of the cities—allowing for some variation deriving from "local circumstances." Thus, the institutional makeup of the city should be identical to the institutional makeup of the society.

We will examine the polity, the economy, the family, and the education system, each in turn. In each case we will state the normative ideal and analyze just how urban behaviors approximate such expectations. Where it is relevant to the understanding of urban institutional characteristics, we will focus upon problematic conditions. For the most part, however, the reader should approach the following chapters

2 There are other quasi-institutions that exist in modern society. These are referred to as quasi-institutions because, although they have many of the facets usually associated with institutions, they do not have all of them. A good example is *science,* which can be described in terms of values, norms and related behaviors, and which enforces negative sanctions on deviants. Nevertheless, the normative pattern of expectations and the associated sanctions are only valid in connection with a very small segment of the population who have, of their own volition, made themselves accountable according to the values and norms of *science*.

of Part I as systematic analyses preparatory to the understanding of urban problems. In Part II of this volume we shall have more to say about the major problems of contemporary urban life. By understanding the nature of urban institutions in contemporary America, the reader should be in a position to fully comprehend the analysis that constitutes Part II, particularly that which is developed in Chapter 7.

Chapter 2
Ideal and Actual in the Urban Polity

THE IDEAL IN THE URBAN POLITY

The American urban polity is a normative derivative of the national (or societal) polity. Those values that justify the exercise of social power in the nation (or society) as a whole of necessity justify its exercise within the city. And if the norms for political behavior diverge on occasion at the municipal level from those at the state and federal levels, they do so in a manner consistent with national political values and *ideally*—that is, *normatively*—the urban polity has no characteristics that can be said to be completely independent of the national (or societal) polity. Indeed, given the legal primacy accorded the federal Constitution in American society, it is impossible for it to be otherwise. Political values and norms on the municipal level that contradicted those codified in the Constitution would sooner or later cease to exist in any viable form. In concrete terms this, of course, means that the values of *representative democracy* that inform the national polity must also be characteristic of the urban polity. Thus, it is quite simple to describe the urban polity in *ideal terms*.

Ideally, within the cities the sole source of social power is the citizenry. Those who exercise power must, theoretically, do so by mandate of a plurality of the citizenry. Lest we oversimplify, let us examine this notion a little more closely. To say that those who exercise power do so on mandate of the plurality is not to maintain that each holder of public trust from dogcatcher to Mayor is *directly* responsible to the citizenry. In public bodies ideally representative of the entire citizenry, there are two kinds of responsibility to the public will.

First, there are certain individual wielders of legitimate social power who must test this privilege of power-holding periodically by decision of the electorate. Among those who must submit to this periodic test are those whose offices are elective as well as those whose privileges of power are dependent upon those who hold elective office. Ideally, those who are privileged to hold these positions wield power as the result of a direct mandate. When that mandate is withdrawn they may no longer wield power legitimately. There are, however, limits upon the expression of public will even as there is direct responsibility to it. For example, the mandate is given to any respective office holder for a *specified period,* that for all intents and purposes is unchangeable.[1]

Thus, those who attain positions in which they are directly responsible to the urban body politic are protected from quixotic changes in its mood and loyalties. It is this norm of virtually guaranteed tenure in office for a specified period of time that theoretically allows an individual to exercise power creatively, or, in other words, to lead. Without such a guarantee the exercise of leadership would be severely limited. An act immediately unpopular, but in the long run beneficial to the citizenry, could in such a circumstance result in a loss of office. Without the "guarantee" one could only expect extreme timidity on the part of those to whom power is directly mandated, timidity to the point where popular prejudice and uninformed self-interest might prevent the solution of crucial problems.

The second type of responsibility to the public will that legitimizes the exercise of social power in the cities may be labeled *indirect* or *secondary*. In such cases those who exercise power are not required to seek a renewal of their mandate from the public at regular intervals. Instead, they are expected to conform to standards of performance that the public, through legislative assent, has recognized as necessary for the good of the city. As long as those standards are approximated in performance, those who wield validated power are entitled to do so—provided, of course, that the public continues to recognize the legitimacy of the standards in question. In most instances these standards effectively limit the exercise of power to relatively narrow functional concerns. More often than not, the positions of power that can be designated in this manner are those that involve little or no policy determination with regard to the city system as a whole. The

1 The *term of office* (the period of the mandate) can only be changed by basic reform in the structure of the polity. Such reform—referred to in the urban context as *Charter Reform*—can and does occur. However, the process of such change is such a complex one that it is unlikely that it would occur because of dissatisfaction with the performance of a particular officeholder. Of course an officeholder might be removed from power before his term is up as a result of recall proceedings or forced resignation. The former is so difficult a procedure that it is almost never successful while the latter is usually associated only with those whose tenure is dependent upon elected powerwielders.

police, firemen, building inspectors, health officials, and indeed, dog catchers are all excellent examples of functionally delimited power positions in which incumbents are responsible to the public by virtue of their accession to those standards of performance that, in theory, the public has endorsed.

The American urban polity is characterized by a tension between those who lead and those who are led. Social power, as exercised by those who lead, is always limited (theoretically at least) by the expectation of accountability to the public will. As we have seen, such accountability takes two forms: (1) direct submission of one's record for periodic electoral review, and (2) responsibility to publicly sanctioned sandards of performance in positions of indirect accountability. Thus, in theory, there exists a distribution of power in which everyone possesses some share of the currency (social power). No individual in such a system can exercise total power over the other participants in it, and no one in such a system can be totally without social power.

Effective *exercise* of power in the urban polity is quite another matter. The large number of actors wield very little power as *individuals* on a day-to-day basis—and then only in functionally specific situations, that is, as teacher or fireman, for example. More important, few individuals are ever able to affect politics by virtue of their idiosyncratic efforts. Acting alone rarely results in any far-reaching changes, a circumstance reflected in the euphemism heard so often, "you can't beat the system." Thus, the characteristic mode of non-governmental expression of power in the city takes the form of a proliferation of voluntary associations. Such associations consist of individuals of similar interests and persuasions who come together in the hope of multiplying their individual effectiveness. They band together in the attempt to have their concerns written into public policy or to have those who exercise power in government do so in ways favorable to their concerns.

Some associations such as political parties subscribe to *general* and, more often than not, vague principles for political action in the public interest. In reality their *raison d'etre* is the exercise of power itself (quite often in behalf of interests that run counter to the well-being of the city as a whole). Once established in the polity they tend to become relatively permanent. For as long as there are prizes to be sought in the arena of public power, there will be organizations, the sole purpose of which is the attainment of advantage in pursuit of these prizes. Other groups, also of a permanent nature, are organized to perform what might be called "surveillance" activities. *The Citizen's Union* and *The League of Women Voters* are examples of groups committed to the protection of the interests of the entire community by examining actions that are being taken by the municipal government and informing the general public of their character.

Still other groups are organizations representing relatively narrow but permanent interests in the community (that is, the ongoing interests of stable segments of the community). Among these interest groups one finds labor unions, businessmen's groups, professional associations, religious groups, and even groups of people with the same ethnic or racial backgrounds. There are, finally, those associations that emerge in response to some newly perceived need in the community, some grievance against those who exercise power in the name of the municipality, or in behalf of an innovation or reform of the polity. Such groups usually remain viable until the issue at hand has been resolved, either in victory or defeat. Citizens' groups and neighborhood associations are the most typical of these organizations.

Each of these organizations is recognized as a legitimate participant in the polity—as a sanctioned competitor for power—as long as its leadership and membership endorse the basic validity of the "rules of the game." For as long as a politically oriented voluntary association accepts the basic premise of *peaceful* pursuit of public support or legal redress, its right to propagate its purpose is theoretically unassailable. If, on the other hand, its activities include the disruption of normal processes of urban life or, indeed, the evocation of violence as strategies to achieve its purpose, such an organization will lose its sanction as a legitimate participant in the unceasing power game of the urban polity.[2] It is only through a mutual respect for "the rules of the game" by competing parties that their conflict does not become so intense and irreconcilable that the orderly social processes of the city are disrupted.[3]

2 The line between "legitimate" pursuit of purpose and "illegitimate" pursuit of purpose is not always clearly discernible. For example, a favorite tactic of organizations identified with the Black protest in the cities is the *demonstration.* Demonstrations, or collective expressions of grievance, essentially serve the function of calling the attention of the general public to those conditions the demonstrating group would like to change. However, they do this in so striking a manner—for example, the *sit-in* or *boycott*—that order is disrupted and violence is often evoked. As a matter of fact, such organizations occupy a somewhat ambiguous position with regard to their "legitimacy" as competitors for power within both the national polity and district urban polities.

3 A case that illustrates this point took place in Chicago during the Democratic National Convention of 1968. When both those who were protesting the political orientation of the Democrats and the Chicago police refused to abide by the "game rules," violence ensued that not only took a heavy toll in casualties, but also thoroughly disrupted the life of the ctiy.

Controlled, or "limited" conflict is thus the "normal" state of affairs in the urban polity. The city as a community is so heterogeneous that the interests of some groups are bound to conflict with those of another at any given time.[4] Playing by the rules is, however, only one mechanism for limiting or controlling the conflict within the polity in which conflict is virtually inevitable. The city is not only quite heterogeneous, it is also a system in which there is a high degree of internal differentiation. There are in any city multiple organizations, each primarily oriented toward different functional problems, indeed, different aspects of these problems in the life of the city system as a whole. Not only does each institutional order represented in the urban system have its own distinct organizational characteristics as opposed to the others, but even within a single institutional order there is organizational differentiation (for example, in the economy there are manufacturing as well as distributing organizations, management groups, professional groups, labor groups, and consumer groups). Concomitant to such organizational differentiation is the fact that every individual who is a *full* participant in the urban social system must, of necessity, undertake a *number* of roles and occupy a *number* of statuses in various organizations or groups. This last circumstance is itself a key mechanism limiting the extent and intensity of conflict in the polity. Let us examine the dynamics of this phenomena: the greater the number of distinct roles and statuses an individual plays and occupies, the more diffused will be his "self-interest." The more diffused his self-interest, the less likely is he to commit himself totally to a given cause in which a struggle for power is being waged. To the extent that this is true, the probability that any given cause in the polity will mobilize a segment of the population at such a high affect level that it will be willing to break the "rules of the game" is considerably reduced.

Perhaps a concrete example will bring this point home. Let us take the case of a hypothetical man by the name of Thomas Mercante. Mr. Mercante lives in a large metropolitan area with a population over 1 million. He is 40 years old, and married with three children who are still in school. Mr. Mercante is Italian-American and quite proud of it. He lives in a neighborhood referred to as "Little Italy" and is the secretary of a group called the Italian-American Improvement Association. A skilled machinist, Mr. Mercante is a section foreman at a large plant involved in the manufacture of truck bodies. Like many

4 For a discussion of the effects of heterogeneity within urban populations, see Louis Wirth's classic treatment of the problem in "Urbanism as a Way of Life," *American Journal of Sociology, XLIV* (July 1938), 1–8.

others in his neighborhood, he attends church regularly and is an active member of the Knights of Columbus. He is a member of the local Democratic club and he works hard to get his friend Joe Palombo reelected to the city council every two years, although his interest in national politics is minimal. Mercante is a man of many roles and statuses and, consequently, of many interests, not all of them always pointing in the same direction. The countervailing pulls upon him resulting from the differentiation of the urban system can be seen in the following possible political situations.

(1). The Italian-American Improvement Association wants to keep the local playgrounds open until midnight during the summer months. The city administration claims that it does not have the funds necessary to accomplish this. Joe Palombo, the local councilman, does not want to buck the mayor on the issue and thus embarass his party. Tom Mercante is caught with divided loyalties. As a leader of the Improvement Association, he supports their position; he believes that opening the playgrounds would give the neighborhood youth a place to play, free from the flow of traffic and the negative influences of the street. As a member of the Democratic Club and a loyal supporter of his friend Palombo, however, he does not want to press the issue too hard.

In this situation Mercante must ultimately choose among three alternatives: (1) he can decide that the Improvement Association's position is so important that he must press the issue, come what may; (2) he can decide that his loyalty to Palombo must supersede all else and thus he will refrain from pressing the issue, probably giving up his leadership in the Association; or (3) he can support the Association's petition in a relatively unobtrusive manner, thus protecting his conflicting statuses at the cost of abdicating a real political role for himself. In any case, his interests in the situation lead in different directions and so his action, whatever it is, will doubtless be taken with great caution and certainly with less ardor than might be expected were there no personal conflict involved.

(2). His church and the Knights of Columbus are supporting a referendum favoring the use of tax monies to support parochial school programs. The position taken by most figures in his political party is in opposition to the referendum. To further complicate matters, most co-workers at his plant are bitterly opposed to the plan because—right or wrong—they feel that the hard-earned money that they willingly contribute to a public education system would be siphoned off from the public schools to support a private school system should the referendum pass. They believe this would be detrimental to the public schools that their own children attend. They do not wish to support a school system in which they have no interest.

Again Mercante must choose among conflicting interests. As a parent with children in the parochial schools, and as a faithful supporter of his church, he is inclined to support the referendum. On the other hand, his party leaders feel that the referendum plan is generally unpopular and his fellow workers are adamant in their opposition. He must choose and because his interests are diffused, he will be less sanguine about his position and choice than he might otherwise have been if his differentiated roles and statuses did not create a personal conflict with regard to this particular issue.

Other situations of countervailing interest could be hypothesized on the basis of Thomas Mercante's differentiated roles and statuses. The two examples we have chosen clearly communicate that differentiation as a characteristic of the urban social system may clearly inhibit the ardor of political combativeness. Differentiation is thus a control mechanism that ideally encourages *limited* political conflict and consequently operates to maintain stability in the polity itself. If the *heterogeneity* of the urban social system fosters political conflict, differentiation and its concomitant—diffused self-interest—mitigates against irreconcilability and disruption of the day-to-day life of the city.

At the outset of this discussion of the urban polity we noted that, normatively speaking, it is a derivative of the national polity of the United States. At this point, we should like to note another aspect of dependence that is characteristic of the urban polity, an essentially *structural one*. When the architects of American democracy worked out the delicate balance among the political units of this country (so delicate that it is still a matter not completely resolved), they allocated certain rights to the federal level and others to the states, but they specifically omitted any allocation of rights or charter to the cities. We need not go into the reasons for this but we must recognize the extremely important contemporary implications of this peculiarity of American history. Because of this bit of history, municipalities in American society have no political independence except as they are able to achieve it through the power game played with the state governments who are their prime adversaries. Every municipal polity in the United States is in some measure dependent upon a higher-order polity—most often the state.

When, for example, a municipality seeks relief through the courts against the state, it cannot claim that—as a municipality under the American system—it has a certain basic *sovereignty* that justifies its position. The fact of the matter is that cities possess no such sovereignty, and relief in the courts will be forthcoming only if it can be established that the state is violating one of its own legal formulas for delegating *its authority* to municipal government. Thus it is that cities are not completely free to solve their problems even when their governments would do so in ways thoroughly consistent with the normative prescriptions of the national polity. It may not, for example, be possible for a city to improve its school system simply because as a political entity it does not have the power (that must be delegated by the state) to change the nature of the tax system used to fund the schools. The quest by municipalities for greater control over their destinies—or the struggle for *home rule*—is one of the major structural issues of contemporary urbanism in need of resolution. Indeed, some would argue that the achievement of *home rule* (or *municipal sovereignty*) is the key to the solution of all the other major urban problems. Without it, they would argue, the cities must depend upon state governments that show little sympathy for the cities and little understanding of their problems.

Before turning to the *actual* characteristics of the American urban polity, let us briefly recapitulate what we have described as its *ideal* qualities:

1. The urban polity is normatively and structurally dependent upon the national or state polity.
2. The values that justify the exercise of legitimate power in the cities are the values of *representative democracy* that justify the exercise of power in the national polity.
3. The urban polity is a system in which there is a distribution of power so that no individual can be all powerful and no individual, theoretically, can be completely powerless.
4. The nongovernmental exercise of power in the urban polity tends to be most effective when it is collective. Organizations representing various interests are considered to be legitimate competitors for rewards in the polity as long as they abide by the rules of the game in peaceful pursuit of their purposes.
5. *Heterogeneity* of the urban social system virtually assures conflict in the polity; at the same time, the internal differentiation of the urban social system ideally mitigates against the possibility of that conflict becoming unlimited and disruptive of the day-to-day life of the city.

THE "ACTUAL" IN THE URBAN POLITY

Describing the *actual*—or the behavioral aspects of the urban polity—is far more complex a task than specifying the "ideal"/normative aspects. While the normative expectations for the polity remain relatively stable, the behavioral approximations of these expectations display considerable variability. A systematic accounting of urban political behavior (collective as well as idiosyncratic) must contend with (1) variations in formal governmental organization and (2) variations in the actual distribution of power (or in the *power structure*). Let us examine each in turn.

VARIATIONS IN GOVERNMENT STRUCTURE Although the formal polity of each American city is characterized by a government consonant with the values of representative democracy, there is considerable leeway in the manner in which these values are actualized. In some cities the organization of the formal polity closely approximates that of the federal level. There is in such "strong mayor" cities a clear separation of powers between a strong executive (the mayor), a legislature (the city council or board of aldermen chosen by district, at large, or in some combination of the two) and an independent judiciary. In other cities (the "weak mayor" system), there is a separation between mayor and council, but the executive has very limited administrative powers. In still other cities, in which a board of commissioners is elected (the mayor being the first among them), the separation of powers is ignored to a large extent. While there is an independent judiciary, each commissioner oversees the administration of a particular department of the executive, for example, the police, fire, and sanitation departments, and the board of commissioners *collectively* legislates the city's ordinances and acts upon budgetary matters. There are others in which we find the council-manager form of organization where the elected mayor is simply the chairman of the city council (whose members are usually elected at large) with no real executive powers. The council has appointive and legislative powers and may therefore affect the quality of city administration. On a day-to-day basis, however, executive powers are delegated to a professional administrator or city manager whom the council has appointed. In this form of urban government, the manager is presumed to have a professional competence (rather than a political one) that qualifies him to administer the affairs of the community.

But these types represent only one aspect of variation in the actualization of representative democracy. There is real variation in the degree of centralized authority characteristic of different urban polities in the United States. In some cities a single government structure has authority (direct and indirect) in a wide range of functional areas; the schools, the police, fire, sanitation, parks, transportation, water and energy, buildings, zoning, and welfare departments, all in one manner or another integrated into a single governing organization. In other cities, authority in these functional areas is diffused; the schools are governed by a board directly elected and presumably independent of the general politics of the city administration, sanitation may be administered by independently constituted "sanitary districts," parks by an independently elected park board, and transportation by an incorporated public authority having the power to determine policy without responsibility to the city government, for example. Finally in some instances, certain functions occurring within the city limits may be administered solely by, or in conjunction with, units deriving their authority from a higher order polity. For example, police functions may be shared between the city police department and the county sheriff's office (Chicago, located entirely within Cook County is a case in point). In some cases, public health, housing, and welfare functions are administered by county authority with the concurrence of state and federal agencies.

Although it is not strictly a matter of governmental organization, mention should be made of the variations in the role of political parties in the municipal polity. In many cities political parties constitute the primary "building blocks" of the public sector of the polity. They are the organizational *clearing houses* that function to provide the city with a steady supply of public men whose qualifications for office, if generally less than ideal, usually attest to their adequacy. Such parties are usually local affiliates of the two major national parties. Characteristically, where the urban polity is primarily organized in terms of partisan (or party) politics, one party is usually dominant; that is, is a majority party that is generally in control of the formal machinery of the city government. Such domination, however is never complete—partly because the majority party would not have it that way.

In a partisan situation, the power of the dominant party can only be legitimized by victory in an electoral contest. *This means that there must always be an opposition if only to be periodically and assuredly defeated.* The only way to make certain that there will always be a viable minority party willing to contest—even when it is a hopeless cause—for power, is to make losing a relatively profitable (politically speaking) venture. Thus, in order to keep your opponents in the game when they have no chance of winning a popular (or electoral) decision, you must assure them of a share of power usually in proportion to their demonstrated electoral power. In cities where this is the case, there exist arrangements between the majority party and the minority party that in effect add up to a system "proportional representation" in the municipal government, although there is no formal legal requirement for this. In New York City, for example, where for over 20 years prior to the election of the then Republican Mayor John Lindsay, the Democrats maintained what seemed to be an unchallengeable electoral dominance, Republicans received a regular share of patronage appointments and some Republican candidates for the local judiciary regularly ran unopposed receiving Democratic endorsement.

In other cities, however, political parties do not participate directly in the electoral process, or if they do, they do so covertly. These are the cities in which elections are supposedly nonpartisan and where party labels are theoretically irrelevant. Underlying this system is the assumption that nonpartisan elections will encourage better qualified, more honest men and women to enter the public life of the city or, conversely, that highly trained and talented individuals often find the etiquette of party politics to be petty and corrupting, thus tend to focus their energies upon private achievement rather than public service. The assumption is that by eliminating party loyalty as a test for public office, many more of these people will be encouraged to serve. This works better in theory than in practice. There is, for example, little to distinguish among those who have governed "nonpartisan" Boston and "partisan" New York.

THE PATTERN OF VARIATION IN GOVERNMENT STRUCTURE All of these variants of representative democracy do exist in American cities of one type or another. Confronted with these differing organizational possibilities in the urban polity, one is prompted to ask if there is not a pattern to their appearance. Do these variations occur in a random manner? Are they simply the products of local historical idiosyncracies? Is there some underlying tendency that distributes these organizational forms in some intelligible pattern?

The study of local government has long been a prominent concern of American political scientists. Thus we turn to them for answers to these questions. On the basis of their published materials, a number of patterns emerge although the definitive work on comparative urban government has yet to be done. John H. Kessel, in a study published in 1962, classified 2970 communities according to size.[5] He then tabulated the frequency in which each form of government organization (mayor council—commission—council/manager) was found in each of his classifications. A very large majority, approximately 67 percent

5 John H. Kessel, "Government Structure and Political Environment," *American Political Science Review, LVI* (September 1962), 615–620.

of the governments in the smallest cities with populations between 5000 and 10,000, had mayor-council governments, approximately 28 percent had the council-manager for, and approximately 5 percent had the commission form. Among the cities in the next class, those with a population between 10,000 and 25,000, the mayor-council government was again the most frequent (approximately 50 percent), the council-manager form followed (approximately 40 percent), and the commission form was the least frequent (approximately 10 percent). Among the four middle classifications of cities ranging in size from 25,000 to 500,000, the council-manager form superseded the mayor-council form as the predominant one with the commission form placing a distant third. Among cities with populations between 500,000 and 1 million, the mayor-council form displays a striking predominance (approximately 73 percent), followed by the council-manager form (approximately 27 percent). No commission governments were found to exist in this classification. Among the largest cities with populations of over 1 million, the only form of government found to exist was the mayor-council type.[6]

Thus the pattern may be described as follows: mayor-council government is most popular in both very small cities and very large cities, while the council-manager form seems to be more popular among the middle sized cities. The commission form is a poor third in the small and middle sized city classes and does not exist at all among the very large cities. Indeed, the commission form seems so unpopular (its highest frequency, approximately 17 percent, is among those cities between 250,000 and 500,000) that it may, in fact, be written off as an insignificant variation in urban government.

We can elaborate upon this pattern somewhat. There appears to be a high degree of positive association between the council-manager form of government and nonpartisan electoral systems and a negative association between mayor-council forms and nonpartisan systems. Wilson and Banfield report that 84 percent of 1756 council-manager cities elect on a theoretically nonpartisan basis. Conversely, they report that only 44 percent of mayor-council cities elect on a nonpartisan basis.[7] The political scientists generally indicate that the

6 A later tabulation and analysis using slightly different population classifications generates essentially the same results. See Carl A. McCanders, *Urban Government and Politics,* McGraw-Hill, New York, 1970. McCanders' tabulation is based on 1966 data available in the *Municipal Year Book* of 1968.

7 Edward C. Banfield and James Q. Wilson, *City Politics,* Vintage Books, New York, 1963, p. 151.

council-manager form of government is favored by the native-born, the better-educated, and the more affluent middle class.[8] As the argument goes, these are the people who, in search of efficient administration, seek to professionalize and, consequently, depoliticize urban government. To the extent that this is true, we can expect those communities in which this so-called middle class predominates to be partial toward council-manager government. Thus, whatever the population size, wherever the native-born middle classes predominate, wherever they have effective control of the political apparatus, the probability of the council-manager form existing will be relatively high. For example, wherever you find a bedroom suburb, you stand a good chance of being correct if you predict existence of the council-manager form of government.[9] We suggest further that the probability of finding the council-manager form is high in certain specialized communities such as the following: *college communities, public administration centers, entertainment and recreation centers,* and *financial and real estate centers* or combinations of these. Conversely, we expect that the probability of finding the mayor-council form high in those specialized communities such as manufacturing and transportation centers, in which the middle class is underrepresented and the working class and identified ethnic groups are likely to be overrepresented.[10]

We are not in a good position, empirically speaking, to examine the pattern of centralization versus decentralization of governing powers within municipalities. Charles Adrian, long a student of urban government, maintains that independent departments are found in relatively few cities with over 50,000[11] population. Thus we may argue that the larger cities tend to have centralized organization to a greater degree than do the smaller ones. But this is only a very rough approximation of a distinctive pattern. Adrian is talking about the decentralization that occurs as a result of the *weak* mayor-council form (where the

8 See for example Charles R. Adrian, *State and Local Government,* 2nd ed., McGraw-Hill, New York, 1967, p. 224.

9 For a discussion of middle class political participation in the suburbs see Scott Greer, *The Emerging City: Myth and Reality,* The Free Press, New York, 1962, pp. 138–167; see also Leo F. Schnore, *The Urban Scene,* The Free Press, New York, 1965, pp. 184–200.

10 See Albert J. Reiss, Jr., "Functional Specialization of Cities," *Cities and Society: The Revised Reader in Urban Sociology,* ed. Paul K. Hatt and Albert J. Reiss, Jr., The Free Press, Glencoe, Ill.: 1951, pp. 555–575.

11 See Charles R. Adrian, *Governing Our Fifty States and Their Communities,* McGraw-Hill, New York, 1963, p. 97.

powers of the mayor are quite limited). Impressionistically, it would seem that even large cities with strong mayor-council governments suffer to some extent from decentralization of organization. Certainly this is true of New York City where although the mayor and borough presidents appoint the members of the Board of Education and maintain some budgetary control over the school system, the Board is a deliberative body legally responsible to the State. In contrast, the Transit Authority operates with nearly unbridled independence; the Port Authority as a public corporation often pursues policies that are in opposition to those agencies under the mayor's control.

Let us restate the pattern teased out from admittedly sparse evidence. The council-manager form seems to predominate among middle sized cities while the mayor-council form seems to predominate among the largest *and* smallest cities.[12] Nonpartisan elections appear to be associated with the council-manager form while partisan elections seem to be associated with the mayor-council form. The council-manager form is in turn associated with those polities dominated by the native-born, better-educated, affluent middle class, such as those in the bedroom suburbs and those more likely to exist in certain specialized communities. Finally, neither population size nor characteristic political dominance and associated functional community specialization are perfect predictors of government form and electoral process.

VARIATIONS IN THE DISTRIBUTION OF POWER Knowledge of the variable nature of urban government does not, of course, constitute all that one needs to know about the behavioral (or *actual*) dimension of the American urban polity. Govenment, or the formal, public, decision-making and policy-executing body, is *not* the equivalent of the polity itself. There are the voluntary associations and the interest groups whose roles in the exercise of legitimate power must be considered. Moreover, we would be remiss if we did not give some consideration to individual (or idiosyncratic) exercise of power. Thus, in its behavioral dimension, the polity may be conceived of as a system in which the government is a major operating factor, but certainly not the only one, and perhaps not even the most crucial one. The urban political system of which we are speaking consists of multiple operating units—government, interest groups, and voluntary associations, for example—represented in action by specified individuals bearing their standards and existing in a series of networks so that the operations of one unit are likely to have implications for others in the system.

12 We may ignore the commission form because of its numerical insignificance.

The various interests of the units in the system are not always in harmony. Indeed, as we have seen above, the heterogeneity of the city virtually insures conflicts among them. The units are thus often engaged in competition with one another for the power to "market" their interests; in one instance to make them public policy for the entire city, or, in another to insure for themselves unhindered maintenance of their interests. In each case, therefore, a particular urban polity can be characterized by its *distribution of power* in which some units (and, therefore, some individuals) are better able to serve their interests than others.[13]

It is no easy task to discuss the variety of ways in which power is distributed in urban polities. For while there have been studies—some of them quite sophisticated—attending to the problem of power distribution in urban communities, they have all been subject to methodological and substantive criticisms that render them less than definitive. There is very little, if anything that can be said *with certainty* about the varying distributions of power in American urban communities. Nevertheless, since our treatment of the urban polity as an institution would be sharply truncated without such a discussion, we will proceed with it, exercising the caution that these criticisms dictate.

There are two basic models of community power distributions. The first, the *elitest model* has as its basic supposition that in each community there is a coterie of men—some in government, but more often than not without public office—who represent the dominant interest groups and exercise an inordinate degree of influence over the creation and, indeed, the execution of public policy. They constitute in the community what C. Wright Mills felicitously termed the *power elite*.

13 Most of us are familiar with a popular conception that comes close to this academic notion. It has become part of our everyday experience to be concerned about (or at least cognizant of) the *power structure*. This somewhat mythical term has become part of the American vocabulary in conjunction with the heightening of community conflict, particularly in the area of race relations and, more generally, in the confrontations between the "haves" and the "have nots." Most often invoked by those who are challenging the status quo, it conjures up an image that is based more upon assumption than empirical fact. The power structure is conceived of as a network of groups and individuals, more or less organized, who have a common interest in maintaining the status quo in a community and the power to market this interest. The power structure (or *the establishment*) may consist of individuals and groups of varying importance and potential for effect; but in the eyes of those pushing hard for change it is ultimately a monolith possessing all the powers of impediment to their cause. The power structure conception is not an exact approximation of our concern with the distribution of power within urban polities; it excludes certain groups and individuals—the protesters or users of the conception themselves—who we would include as part of the distributive system.

The second, usually offered in opposition to the first, is usually called the *pluralist model.* While not denying that power is distributed differentially within the community, those who hold this position reject the notion of a single dominant group of individuals who exert influence upon community affairs in very large part. Instead, they argue that power differentials exist relative to specific issues and not across the board; that *depending on the nature of the issue,* (urban renewal, education, business incentives, for example) a particular group representing certain interests will have disproportionate influence while others for one reason or another will have little or none. The alignment of influentials versus noninfluentials is relatively unstable, changing according to the issue at hand.

There are studies of American communities that tend to support one or the other of these models. On the elite side, for example, Floyd Hunter, in his landmark study of Atlanta, Georgia, found that 40 men —most having ties to dominant business interests, only four holding formal public office—constituted a policy-making elite for the entire city.[14] Although every member of this elite was not equally involved in every incident of policy determination (some were "out front" on certain issues while others voluntarily took less public roles), and while the 40 power leaders could not be described as a closely cohesive group, there were a number of cliques or "crowds" into which the leadership group seemed to be divided; Hunter concluded that the 40 did constitute a *general policy-making elite.*

Perhaps the most notable example of research purporting to demonstrate the *pluralist* model of community power/distribution is Robert Dahl's study of New Haven, Conn.[15] While a "political stratum" of individuals intensively involved in the city's "political subculture" could be identified, Dahl stated that the most prominent characteristic of the power distribution was the extent to which influence was specialized. The system he describes is one that is characterized by "dispersed inequalities" of power, one in which there are different sets of leaders representing different social strata (and, consequently, different interests) exerting disproportionate influence in one policy sector or another. The three sectors specifically analyzed are party nominations, urban renewal, and the schools.

Both the Hunter and Dahl studies were undertaken in cities of size-

14 Floyd Hunter, *Community Power Structure: A Study of Decision Makers,* University of North Carolina Press, Chapel Hill, N.C.: 1953.

15 Robert A. Dahl, *Who Governs: Democracy and Power in an American City,* Yale University Press, New Haven, Conn., 1961.

able populations—Atlanta (approximately 500,000) and New Haven (approximately 150,000). Although Atlanta is an extremely important regional city, neither of these cities is considered a major national metropolis such as New York, Chicago, or Los Angeles. Banfield, in studying power in Chicago[16] found a situation somewhat different from those of Hunter and Dahl. He found that the Democratic party was by far the dominant repository of power in the city's polity; that the leaders of the party could, if they so desired, operate as a thoroughgoing power elite. At the same time, however, these party leaders did not choose this course; instead they made policy decisions in response to what they determined to be the most representative community position on any given matter before them. Indeed, so important was their reading of community desires on a controversial issue that they encouraged disputing elements to mobilize as much pressure as possible in behalf of their respective positions. By so doing, the professional politicians could gauge the relative strengths of the various positions by determining which position attracted the most intensive support and act accordingly. In this system, the *power to decide* evidently resided with an *elite*. At the same time, however, the system can be seen as *pluralistic* for on any given issue the decisions of this elite depended upon a specific configuration of support and opposition toward alternative positions.

The differences in these findings and others similar to them need to be evaluated if we are to come to any conclusions—no matter how tentative—about variations of actual power distributions in the American urban polity. Essentially, there are three possible ways of interpreting these differences. We could, for example, argue on behalf of either one of the models, *elitest* or *pluralistic,* claiming universal applicability for either one of them, while discounting contrary empirical findings as the products of an ill-conceived and, therefore, biased methodology. Or, if we are less sanguine about one model as opposed to the other, we could argue—again on grounds of methodological inadequacy—that neither position has demonstrable validity in empirical research. We could, finally, accept the methodological criticisms of such studies but, nevertheless, maintain that the differences in empirical findings are not so much a function of research bias as they are reflections of actual variations of power distributions in different kinds of urban communities. If we choose to adopt the first interpretation, we would conclude that there are no variations in the power distributions of American urban communities—they would all be

16 Edward C. Banfield, *Political Influence,* The Free Press, New York, 1961.

elitest or pluralist in nature. If we choose the second alternative, we would conclude that no empirically based judgments about urban power distributions can be made at this time and that any model or position must remain in a purely hypothetical state. If we choose to embrace the third interpretation, we would maintain that actual variation does exist and that tentatively, at least, we could begin to characterize the pattern of this variation.

All three of these interpretations must take account of the major methodological criticisms that have been leveled at the empirical studies of community power. In general, such studies have been undertaken by practitioners in two disciplines, *political science* and *sociology*. Walton, in an interesting paper, has suggested that there is an association between the discipline of the investigator, the method of his investigation, and the nature of his findings.[17] In his investigation of 33 different studies, he found that sociologists tended to employ the *reputational* method in isolating the characteristic power distribution of a community (such as Hunter) while political scientists were more likely to employ the so-called *decision-making* methods (such as Dahl and Banfield). When the *reputational* method is used, informants in a given community are asked to identify the most influential members of that community irrespective of any particular issues. When, on the other hand, some variant of the decision-making method is used, the researchers, using a wide range of materials from recorded observations to documents, attempt to reconstruct the involvements of individuals in the political process linking them to specific issues in the community.

Walton found that not only did sociologists favor the reputational method over the decision-making method, but also that in so doing they had a pronounced tendency toward identifying a monolithic power distribution in the communities they studied, whereas the political scientists who characteristically used the decision-making approach tended to identify a pluralist power distribution in the communities they studied. In the face of such findings, one can justifiably begin to question the validity of the empirical results derived from the use of either method. There certainly seems to be some justification for arguing that the results are, more than anything else, a function of the methods used in arriving at them. In this light the substantive criticisms of the methods employed are important to note. Those who have been critical of the reputational method generally indicate that the method is more likely to discover perceptions or

17 John Walton, "Discipline, Method and Community Power: A Note on the Sociology of Knowledge," *American Sociological Review, XXXI* (October 1966), 684–689.

beliefs about individuals in the power structure rather than the actual power distribution. Asking a panel of citizens "who wields the most power here?" in no way guarantees that the reports will be valid. *Moreover, unless the reports are tied to behavior which can be perceived by the investigator,* even an essentially valid report must be interpreted as tapping the *potential for power* rather than its *actual* exercise—and the potential for power does not necessarily imply that it is or will be regularly exercised.[18]

An even more striking criticism of the reputational approach raises the issue of the assumption that seems to underlie it. Such criticism holds that the reputational method stands on the assumption that the real power distribution in a community is not accessible to direct observation, that reconstructing the involvements of various individuals in the process of public decision-making on various controversial issues will not reveal the actual power distribution in the community because that distribution is essentially covert, and that those who are publicly involved are more than likely fronting for unidentified persons and interests. This assumption, it is argued, insulates the results (usually in support of the elitist model) of reputational studies from empirical contradiction. If the same community were studied by the decision-making method, and if the results of such a study did not support the elitist model, the proponents of the elitist model could argue the contradictory findings away by maintaining that the decisional research had simply failed to tap the "real," secret distribution of power. Thus, the critics argue, the reputation method, with its quality of systematized gossip, its we-know-what-the-public-thinks-now-tell-us-who-*really*-runs-things, is definitely biased, *establishing only what the researcher* assumed to be true in the first place.

On the other hand, there have been criticisms of the decision-making method which seem just as compelling, if not more so. It has been argued, for example, that the decision-making method is no less a servant of pluralist assumptions than the reputational method is of elitist assumptions and that decision-making investigators (overwhelmingly political scientists), assuming what Dahl has called "dispersed inequalities" in the community polity, use an approach that, in its focus upon overt action in connection with discrete issues, can only serve to sustain the original presupposition.[19]

18 Robert A. Dahl, "A Critique of the Ruling Elite Model," *American Poltical Science Review* (June 1958), 463–469.

19 See Thomas J. Anton, "Power, Pluralism, and Local Policies," *Administrative Science Quarterly, VII* (March 1963), 425–457. See also William V. D'Antonio, "Review of Polsby: *Community Power and Political Theory,*" Social Forces, XLII (1964), 375.

Still another criticism of the decision-making approach focuses upon what seems to be its inherent incompleteness. Such criticism accepts the notion that power is exercised when public decisions are made and that, as a consequence, those who are involved in making such decisions are the possessors of power with regard to the particular issue in question. Nevertheless, so the argument goes, the method of linking individuals to the decision-making process can fall short of characterizing the actual power distribution in the community if it ignores the fact that power, perhaps in its most profound sense, is also exercised by those who determine the *scope* of decision making. *Thus there may be individuals in any given community who exercise sufficient power to block any particular problem or interest from becoming a public issue about which a policy decision has to be made.* If this is true, then public decision-making process alone would lead to an inaccurate characterization of the power distribution in the community, a characterization that takes no cognizance of power public in its implication but not publicly exercised.[20]

In each case noted above there is some merit. And given the inherent problems in both the reputational and decision-making approaches, it would probably be wise for any researcher who seeks to characterize the power distribution of a community to employ some aspects of both methods. Since the bias of each approach seems to go in the direction of supporting polar opposites, it may be argued that used together the biases might cancel each other out, revealing the characteristic power distribution with a higher probability of validity. This, however, is not a problem which ought to concern us to any great extent in these pages.[21] What seems to be clear on the basis of the criticisms we have presented is the necessity of rejecting any commitment to one model of community power—*elitest* or *pluralist*—as opposed to the other. In the face of the criticism it is difficult indeed to be either a sanguine *elitest* or *pluralist* (at least on empirical grounds). This leaves us with two alternatives: we can relegate each model to the hypothesis, maintaining that the existing studies prove nothing one way or the other; or we can argue that in spite of the problems with method, the differences in findings do reflect (tentatively) different types of power distribution in different kinds of communities. This position would argue

20 See Peter Bachrach and Morton S. Baratz, "Two Faces of Power," *American Political Science Review, LVI* (December 1962), 947–952.

21 The issue is not insignificant. However, in the context of trying to depict the variations of behavior in the urban polity, to explore the methodology of community studies in great detail would take us too far afield.

that the elitest and pluralist models simply do not have universal validity for the range of American communities that are experientially included under the urban rubric. Instead of arguing the universal validity of one model versus the other, it might be claimed that both are essentially valid, although in a limited manner.

On the face of it, given the telling criticisms of method, one is inclined to endorse the former position relegating each model to the hypothetical realm and leaving the question open. Nevertheless, reasonable argument can be made for the latter alternative, maintaining that the model represents coexisting realities across the range of American communities. It seems eminently reasonable to maintain that the power distribution of any community will take its form as a function of the matrix of certain demographic, economic, and social factors which are characteristic of the community. Let us make an argument in behalf of such a position.

When a community is *relatively homogeneous*—characterized by the economic dominance of a single specialization (personal services or transportation for example) by relatively few distinct ethnic groups making essentially the same (although competing) claims upon the formal policy apparatus of the community, a population size which is not so large that it demands a highly complex range of public services (that is, from health to transportation and communications) the type of power distribution most likely to appear will approximate the monolithic elitest position. When, on the other hand, a community is *relatively heterogeneous*—characterized by a complex relatively unspecialized economic base, by many ethnic groups making competing claims upon the policy agencies of the polity, by a complex social class system complicated by cross-cutting differences in life-style so that it is really difficult to speak of class interests and their clearly defined place in the polity, and by a population so large that the city government must manage, or at least regulate, an elaborate repertoire of services—the type of power distribution most likely to appear will approximate the *pluralistic model.*

In the relatively *homogeneous* community, the elitest distribution is most likely to exist because (1) there are fewer bases for persistent competition within the polity, (2) there are fewer problems of urban management whose solutions are likely to stimulate controversy, and (3) the well-being of the community depends most directly on a limited economic base. Those exercising power in the economy, and those holding the highest managerial posts in the dominant industry (or their designates) will invariably possess the potential for influence disproportionate to their numbers. In sum, homogeneity means fewer problems and fewer bases of power with the likelihood that, in the absence of a highly competitive polity, an elite with influence in the community at large will emerge from the single most important interest in the community. Whether or not that elite takes action uniformly on all issues is of little relevance.[22] Given its association with the basis for the community's well-being, it is not farfetched to suppose that there are few decisions of any consequence to the community taken without reference (even though it may be implicit) to the wishes of its members.

In the relatively *heterogeneous* community, the *pluralist distribution* is most likely to emerge because (1) *there are multiple bases for competition.* (The economy is so differentiated as to engender persistent conflicting claims on the part of its constituent units—that is, the claims of various ethnic and racial groups, the claims of management and labor, the claims of producers and consumers—and there is the factionalization of class interests on the basis of life style differences); and (2) *the sheer size of the population generates complex service problems* for example, transportation, communications, education, sanitation, health, the solutions for which often tend to be controversial.[23] Moreover, the complexity of many of these problems demands the full-time attention of professional experts. For this reason alone, if for no other, it could hardly be expected that an elite of amateurs could possess the knowledge necessary to make reasonably intelligent policy decisions about such complex affairs necessary to the continued functioning of the community. In sum, the large heterogeneous community has more complex problems that must be solved and a greater dispersion of interests seeking a political voice. Thus the polity is likely to be more volatile or, conversely, less stable than that of the homogeneous community—a condition one would expect to impede the emergence of a community-wide power elite.[24]

22 One of Dahl's criticisms of the elitests is that they are unable to prove that the hypothesized elite regularly prevails on key political issues. See Dahl, "A Critique of the Ruling Elite Model," p. 464, cited in footnote 18.

23 A good example of this can be found in the recent traffic history of New York City. In order to relieve congestion in Manhattan, changes in the flow patterns (two-way streets to one-way streets) were proposed and stringent restrictions on parking were put into effect. These changes engendered stiff opposition from such disparate groups as diplomats, physicians, and businessmen. As a result of this opposition, some of the changes were temporarily rescinded.

24 For a formulation that supports the position developed here, see Paul E. Mott, "Configurations of Power," *The Structure of Community Power,* eds. Michael Aiken and Paul E. Mott, Random House, New York, 1970, pp. 85–100; also see Morris

No matter how plausible this argument is, however, it still remains to be seen whether or not there is any empirical support for it. A systematic test of this thesis is yet to be undertaken.[25] Given the reasonableness of the argument—sociologically speaking—it would seem the better part of wisdom to endorse the probability of real variation in power distribution according to type of community rather than simply maintaining that one of the two alternate models—elitist or pluralist—while presently unsubstantiated may ultimately be proven to have universal validity.

In summary then, we have suggsted that as far as power distributions in urban communities are concerned, there is no good empirical evidence to support the primacy of either the power elite or the pluralist position. Instead of allowing the question to remain open, thereby implicitly endorsing the possibility that ultimately one of these models will be proven valid for all urban communities in the United States, we argue that, methodological criticisms notwithstanding, the differences in results from one study to the next reflect real differences in power distributions. Furthermore, over the long run the more *homogeneous* the community the greater the probability for the emergence of a unitary (or monolithic) power elite; while the more *heterogeneous* the community, the greater the probability that a pluralist distribution of power will emerge.[26]

CONCLUSION: IDEAL AND ACTUAL IN THE URBAN POLITY

It must be apparent to the reader at this point that the urban polity is a many-splendored thing. Indeed, when confronted with the variations in governmental organization and power distribution, one is tempted to maintain that to speak of an *urban polity* in the singular is to be

Janowitz, "Introduction: Converging Perspectives in Community Political Analysis," *Community Political Systems,* ed. Morris Janowitz, The Free Press, Glencoe, Ill., 1961, pp. 13–19, especially pp. 15–16.

25 One study known to this author comes close to making such a test, but the phrasing of the hypotheses is ambiguous and it is difficult to interpret its results. See Claire Gilbert, "The Study of Community Power," *The New Urbanization,* ed. Scott Greer et al., St. Martins Press, New York, 1968, pp. 222–245.

26 A single-community study that describes the political impact of heterogeneity in great detail is Wallace S. Sayre and Herbert Kaufman, *Governing New York City: Politics in the Metropolis,* The Russell Sage Foundation, New York, 1960.

guilty of gross oversimplification. As far the actual (behavioral) dimension is concerned, there are multiple polities on the American urban scene as there are varying social, economic, and demographic characteristics of American cities.[27]

In concluding this chapter, let us briefly recapitulate what it is that we have been laboring with thus far.

RECAPITULATION On the *ideal* level, the normative basis for urban polity in the United States is universal in that it is equally applicable to political behavior and organization in all American cities. *Ideally*, the American urban polity is a normative derivation of the national polity. The values that justify the legitimate exercise of power in the urban polity are the values of *representative democracy* that also justify the exercise of such power in the national polity. Ideally, the urban polity is a system in which power is shared by both individuals and organizations and, while the distribution of power may be unequal, theoretically no individual or organization may be all powerful and no individual or organization may be totally bereft of social power. Controlled conflict based upon the interplay of heterogeneity and differentiation is considered normal and desirable. Beyond normative dependence, the urban polity is structurally dependent upon the higher order polities of the state and the federal system.

On the level of the *actual* or behavioral approximation of the values and norms of the polity, there is considerable variation. There is, first of all, variation in the forms of government organization so that the mayor-council form is most often associated with partisan political process while the council-manager form tends to be predominant, along with nonpartisan political process, particularly in middle-sized cities where the native born, affluent, and relatively well-educated middle classes are the most significant population group. Beyond this, there is also variation in the extent of centralized control over government functions. There is a tendency, it seems, for the larger cities with strong mayor-council governments to be more highly centralized than other forms of urban government. There is, also, an apparent pattern of variation when power distributions in various urban communities are considered. We have come to the tentative conclusion that the characteristic power distribution of a community is a function of the

27 The reader is reminded that we are employing an experiential rather than a *formal* conception of the city. American cities are those communities that, more or less, fit the layman's common sense conception (see Chapter 1) and that fall into the range of communities which social scientists, using one criterion or another, label *cities* in American society.

degree of heterogeneity or homogeneity that characterizes it demographically economically, and socially. Those urban communities tending toward relative homogeneity are more likely to evidence disproportionate control by what we may term a unitary (or monolithic) power elite. On the other hand, those urban communities that tend toward heterogeneity are more likely to evidence a specialized (or pluralistic) distribution of power.

The fact that there is considerable variation in the actualization of the urban polity is of major significance for an accurate understanding of the social logic of contemporary urban life. In seeking the underlying logic by analyzing events in the context of institutional alignments, care must be taken to see the events in terms of the *actual* as well as the *ideal* dimensions of the institutions. The implication to be drawn from this may be stated as follows: since the actualization of the urban polity is variable, both in terms of formal government political processes and the more general power distribution, the social logic of those events that are primarily political in nature must also be considered as variable. Simply, as urban polity varies, so does the social logic of urban political events.

As simple as this idea may seem, it is nevertheless true that it has been largely ignored. In general, when urbanists speak or write about the politics of the city they overgeneralize. They do so because they are not sufficiently aware of the need for refinement of the meanings of the term *urban*. Time and time again, as we shall see, there are indications of considerable variation in the actualization of urban institutions and, consequently of the social logic of the American urban experience. Sensitivity to such variation has, above all, profound implications for reform and social improvement. To speak of "the urban crisis" is to oversimplify, to imply that there is a crisis experienced equally or nearly equally in all of our cities. To conceive of an *urban crisis* in the singular is to imply that there is *a solution*—again in the singular—to be discovered and applied universally in all urban communities. If we accept the thesis that as institutions vary in their actualization so do the events occurring in terms of them, we can neither conceive of an urban crisis nor of *the* solution to the crisis. Instead, we must conceive of urban *crises* as they occur in variable contexts and seek a *range of solutions*, each, hopefully, appropriate to a specific case. Social planning for the cities of our epoch—as we shall see—is a process that, if it is to be effective, must bypass glib generalizations and slogans and be grounded in a refinement of urban analysis, the need for which is not so well understood as it ought to be.

Chapter 3
How the Urban Economy Functions

THE NORMATIVE BASE OF THE URBAN ECONOMY

Like the urban polity, the urban economy in America is both normatively and structurally dependent. The values and norms that govern the economies of cities are derivatives of those values and norms that characterize the national economy of the United States. And just as no urban polity is completely self-contained and self-determined, no urban economy is self-sufficient. No city produces all that its inhabitants must consume, and consequently the economy of any city exists in a network of exchange with counterpart units throughout the nation and, indeed, with counterpart units scattered throughout the world.

As problematic as our analysis of the urban polity was, understanding the urban economy promises even more difficulties. For while the ideal, or normative, content of the American urban polity is fairly stable and thus easily characterized, the ideal, or normative content of the economy (national or urban) is in a state of transition and, consequently, it is difficult to describe. Whereas a random sample of respondents would no doubt agree overwhelmingly with the expectations for political behavior and organization as we have described them, a similar presentation for the economy would evoke a distribution of responses much less indicative of such a consensus. There are *competing value rhetorics* vis-à-vis the national economy and, consequently, the economy of cities.

On one hand there is the rhetoric of the *free enterprise market economy*. This complex of value statements about the processes and organization of production and distribution of goods and services has traditionally been regarded as quasi-sacred. Up until the "Great Depression" of the 1930s, to challenge the wisdom of free enterprise values was to commit heresy and to bring down upon oneself the kind of public vilification that in more superstitious times was reserved for those who dared to renounce their allegiance to God. Indeed, for the more conservatively oriented—even today—"free enterprise" evokes a reverence not unlike that which we usually associate with religious conviction. The free enterprise rhetoric itself holds the following to be desirable in the functioning of the economy.

1. *The production and distribution of goods and services ought to be governed by a free market mechanism.* The availability of specific goods and services ought to be a function of the *demand* for them and the willingness and ability of independent producers and distributors to *supply* them in accordance with the level of demand. The price of any specific good or service is thus a function of the interplay of supply factors and demand factors. When demand outstrips supply, the price of the goods or service will go up. When supply exceeds demand, according to this view, the price of the goods or service in question will go down. In the long run this process, it is believed, will result in prices that are fair and equitable.

2. *The greatest good for the population at large can best be achieved when the motivation for productive economic activity is the desire for individual rewards that distinguishes their possessor from those who are without them. The root process for the economy ought to be competition that is intensely individualistic.* In this conception individual competitiveness results in increases in efficiency, technological advances, and overall stimulation of imagination by driving out the less efficient, the less imaginative, and the less technologically sophisticated. This results in reductions in the costs of production and distribution as well as an improvement in the quality of goods and services so that the net result is a greater supply at a superior level of quality, whose price is within the reach of larger numbers of potential purchasers.

3. *The economy that works best is the economy that is least subject to noneconomic intrusions.* An economy that is self-governing, operating in terms of the supply-demand ratio and individual competion comes closest to perfection when judged in terms of the society's need for the economic support of its constituents. When the economy is interfered with, when it is controlled by the polity—or any other institution for that matter—it becomes sluggish and does not perform its function for society as well.

4. *The free enterprise economy ought to be the premier institution of society.* In most cases economic values ought to supercede all other values, and there is no greater success for a man than the success won

in the economy. Conversely, those who fail economically are likely to be morally untrustworthy and prone to failure in other areas of life as well.[1]

As a result of great traumas in an economy legitimated by such a value rhetoric—most particularly the Great Depression of the 30s—some have become disenchanted with "free enterprise" as the best mode of organizing the production and distribution of goods and services in American society. The new value rhetoric these critics have embraced may be called "welfare economics" (or "the New Economics"). The rhetoric of welfare economics contains explicit criticisms of free enterprise values. Briefly the values that are characteristic of it may be enumerated as follows.

1. *The production and distribution of goods and services ought to be consciously planned.* Welfare economics holds that the production and distribution of goods and services ought to be governed by planned determinations of needs in the society. Such a determination supersedes the operation of the largely undirected forces of the market.

2. *The function of economic planning should be to guarantee economic security for every individual in the society.* Welfare economics downgrades competition and individual self-aggrandizement as effective engines for adequate production and distribution of goods and services. In this view, uncontrolled competition does not result in greater efficiency and inventiveness from which the public at large benefits; competition is viewed as wasteful to the point where the society's resources are poorly distributed when this is the process underlying the functioning of the economy.

3. *The economy should be the handmaiden of the polity.* To the extent that the polity represents the power to mobilize a society's resources in the service of the common good, the economy should be inextricably linked to the polity. This, of course, implies a democratic polity. Concomitantly, economic values should not dominate in the society because the economy is really an institution of means serving the ends of the commonwealth as expressed in the polity.[2]

1 R. Joseph Monsen, "The American Business View," *Daedalus, XCVIII* (Winter 1969), 159–173. For an ideological statement of the free enterprise position, see Clarence B. Randall, *A Creed for Free Enterprise,* Atlantic, Brown, Boston, 1952.

2 For an intelligent discussion of the American economy undertaken in terms of welfare economics or the new economics, see John Kenneth Galbraith, *The Affluent Society,* Houghton Mifflin, New York, 1958, especially chapters 1, 8, 18, 22, and 25.

The "free enterprise" and "welfare economics" value rhetorics are clearly antithetical. One celebrates the economy as the source of our well-being so long as it is left alone; the other places the economy in an important but ultimately subordinate position encouraging as it does external control. Thus, whereas we could describe the ideal, or normative dimension of the urban polity in terms of a coherent and universally accepted set of beliefs, we are unable to do so for the urban economy. All we can say is that both value rhetorics will probably be present in any given community. In some communities where traditional businessmen are clearly the opinion leaders, the "free enterprise" rhetoric is most likely to be predominant while in others, such as the large metropolitan areas of the northeast, there has developed over the past few decades an emphasis upon "welfare economics" in response to complex problems of production and, in particular, of distribution. In still other communities it is difficult to determine which value rhetoric is dominant; both "free enterprise" and "welfare economics" seem to be important, each to different segments of the community.

In spite of significant differences in economic value rhetorics that characterize the national economy and the urban economy, there is a modicum of consensus over the *operational norms* of the national and urban economies. The *operational norms* are the rules that govern everyday action in the economy. Theoretically, they ought to be justified by the values in one rhetoric or the other. However, it is a curious characteristic of the American economy that the operational, or pragmatic norms seem only tenuously related to the values of either "free enterprise" or "welfare economics." The relationship between operational norms and values is so tenuous that adherents of either can be comfortable with the complex of operational norms. It is interesting to note that the major part of economic scholarship in the United States does not focus upon the competing value rhetorics, but when it deals, as it often does, with the "ideal" aspects of the economy, its focus is the *operational norms*. These norms are regarded as the legitimate guides to economic behavior and organization throughout American society and, therefore, by definition within all American cities. They may be stated as follows.

THE NORMS OF PROCESS 1. *Distribution of goods and services depends upon the use of a generalized medium of exchange—money.* Money is in fact a symbolic representation of goods and services available in the economy. The greater the monetary accumulation of an individual, the more extensive is his claim to goods and services within the economy. In its representational characteristics money allows for easy generalized consumption on the part of actors whose role in the economy is specialized. Without the commitment to money as a symbolic medium of exchange, the process of distribution would be so complex as to prove unworkable. The writer of books in need of bread finds the baker uninterested in his books. He would either have to find a baker who is interested in his books and who would thus be willing to exchange his bread for them or he would have to seek out someone who is interested in his books who at the same time has goods the baker desires to exchange for his bread. Such a barter system is impossible to conceive of when economic roles are highly specialized.

The cash link allows for such specialization because money, either in cash or in credit, symbolizes all the available goods and services in the economy. Money in the hands of the individual symbolizes the goods and services he needs at a given time—providing, of course, that he possesses amounts of this medium equal to the value of the goods and services he desires.

2. *Agreements governing the production and distribution of goods and services are made in contractual form, the factors entering into the nature of such covenants being those that are demonstrably relevant to their economic purposes.* All forms of exchange involve preagreements between consumers and producers or between consumers and exchange middlemen (wholesalers and retailers), governing the terms and conditions under which the exchange will take place. Such preagreements are concluded before the actual exchange of goods or services takes place. The validity of the exchange or the satisfaction one or more of the participants in the exchange takes in the endeavor is measured according to the degree to which the actual exchange approximates the terms and conditions governing the process as set out in the preagreement or contract.

Contracts governing exchange may be roughly classified into two groups: *generalized covenants* and *specific covenants. Generalized covenants* occur in the form of unstated assumptions made with reference to a wide range of exchanges. Generalized covenants are most frequently operative when the transaction in question is relatively simple or routine involving goods and services that are in common use and are relatively inexpensive. Generalized covenants, for example, cover the range of purchases one might wish to make in a supermarket. When the purchase of an item is made, both the consumer and the distributor (who may also be the producer) act in terms of an unstated but nevertheless enforceable covenant. The consumer agrees to pay a fair price to the distributor upon receipt of the goods in question. The distributor in turn guarantees the quality of the product being purchased as well as the fact that the product has not been misrepresented. Each participant is thus liable for his half of the preagreement. In this case no specific and explicit covenant is entered into; there is no negotiation with legal consultation preceding the exchange itself. The only observable social action is the exchange process. Nevertheless, an agreement does exist prior to the exchange, indeed, if it did not, the purchase of a chocolate bar would have to be preceded by just such explicit negotiation with regard to the consumer's and distributor's rights and prerogatives vis-à-vis chocolate bars.

Specific covenants are usually entered into when the nature of the exchange is complex, involving goods and services that are expensive and not exchanged routinely. In such instances the consumer and the distributor make an explicit agreement, usually in writing, governing their mutual responsibilities in the actual transaction. Such a covenant is, for example, likely to occur prior to the exchange of large amounts of capital goods.

3. *Economic order is underwritten by agencies of the polity.* The American economy does not function independently of the polity. Even most of those who hold "free enterprise" most dearly recognize the necessity of presumably impartial agencies to guarantee order in economic functioning. This guarantee is made by agencies of the polity. At minimum there are the courts who are the final arbiters of contractual disagreements. There are also regulatory agencies on all levels of the polity whose task it is to maximize fairness in exchange proceedings. The involvement of the courts can be described as a generalized *trusteeship* of economic process. The involvement of the regulatory agencies—the Interstate Commerce Commission, the State Public Utility Commissions, down to the local licensing departments—involve consistent, more-or-less direct *stewardship* of a *specified* area of economic activity. Behind all regulatory endeavors is the recognition that economic process often involves transactions between parties of unequal strength and as a result there needs to be some protection for the weaker units lest they be driven out by the stronger, or at the very least be taken unfair advantage of.

THE NORMS OF ORGANIZATION 1. *The primary production and distribution units are collectivities whose first purpose in existing is to function in the economy.* Although organizations representing other institutions do become involved in the economy, those that function in the areas of production and distribution (as opposed to a consumer involvement alone) are organizations that are economic before they are anything else (with some important exceptions such as the federal government which does produce and distribute certain services in areas of health, education, recreation, for example). Indeed, if it were not so, one would hesitate to consume the product being offered. Would you purchase an automobile manufactured in a monastery and distributed by the local church? The incongruity is obvious.

2. *Self-interest in the economy over the long run finds expression and protection in organized groups of individuals with similar economic purposes.* The economy consists of actors whose economic interests vary. Captains of industry, laboring men, professionals, and shopkeepers have all their characteristic connections with economic process. The interest of each is to maximize his rewards in the economy. Such maximization, although individually motivated, tends to be pursued collectively.

Quite often, maximization of one interest can only occur at a loss to another. (This can be understood as an *intergroup* and *intragroup* condition. The interests of one union local may run counter to another, or the interests of the captains may run counter to those of the union.) There then ensues a struggle or conflict that may not always be strictly economic in nature. In some cases, as in a strike, when government agencies do not feel compelled to intervene, the conflict may be considered purely economic. In others the maximization of economic interest necessitates an attempt to get legislative change or an attempt to prevent such a change. In still others, maximization depends upon getting responsible government functionaries to render decisions favorable to the group's economic interests. In cases such as these the conflict is as much political as it is economic—indeed, it may be more so.

3. *Consumer units may or may not be organizations primarily oriented to the economy.* Some consumer units, such as the automobile plant that purchases steel and rubber in order to manufacture its product and the retail grocer who purchases his inventory from a wholesaler so that he himself may be able to sell in response to over-the-counter demand, are obviously units that are primarily oriented to economic activity, that is, they are organizational manifestations of the economy as an institutional order. On the other hand there are consumer units whose primary orientation is toward another institutional order. Even though those units are important to the functioning of the economy, they do not exist for the purpose of economic func-

tioning. Examples of these are the family, educational organizations, governmental organizations, and religious organizations, all of which are large consumers of goods and services produced in the economy. It is largely through the consumer roles of such organizations that the economy is linked to other institutional orders.[3]

These norms, as we noted above, are not in the least controversial; they are operational statements adhered to more often than not without any conscious awareness of their existence. Their relationship to the competing value rhetorics of "free enterprise" and "welfare economics" is tenuous, if indeed there is any demonstrable relationship at all. They are, finally, *universal throughout the society;* they exist in those social systems that we consider to be urban as well as in those areas that fall beyond the pale of this label. *Thus it is that in terms of the normative dimension of the economy, there is a unity between urban and rural in American society.*

With the above discussion about the normative dimension in mind, let us now turn to an examination of the *actual* dimension in the American urban economy. In doing so we are confronted with a major information problem at the outset. By the testimony of a leading urban economist, only a few major economists have paid any sustained attention to this area of inquiry.[4] Thus we are proceeding with a handicap not of our own making, but one that leaves us relatively uninformed in certain areas. We will, however, try in the following pages to describe the actual workings (or processes) and organization of economies associated with those social systems that, in American society, are commonly regarded as cities.

ACTUAL PROCESS AND ORGANIZATION IN THE URBAN ECONOMY

PROCESS The economy of any urban community can, in its operation, be divided into two major sectors. First, there are those activities that are primarily oriented toward the *export* of goods and services to other communities and social entities that exist in a network of exchange with the city. Second, there are those activities going on within the boundaries of the community that are primarily oriented

3 Any of a number of basic economic texts can be consulted for more elaborate depictions of the norms of process and organization. Among them are Paul A. Samuelson, *Economics: An Introductory Analysis,* McGraw-Hill, New York, 1967, especially chapters 3, 4, 5, and 7; Robert Henry Haveman and Kenyon A. Knopf, *The Market System,* Wiley and Sons, New York, 1970, especially chapters 1, 2, 3, and 4.

4 Wilbur R. Thompson, *A Preface to Urban Economics,* The Johns Hopkins Press, Baltimore, 1963, p. 255.

toward production and/or distribution for consumption within the community. We may designate these two sectors by the markets they serve, *the export sector* and *the local sector*. In reality there is likely to be some overlap between the two sectors and there can be no question that the city's economic vitality or its problematic economic state is a function of the interplay of factors from both sectors. This will be clarified by a closer look at each sector.

The *export sector* depends for its vitality and growth upon conditions in other communities and segments of society. In general usage the *export sector* is seen as linking the economy of the local community with the economies of communities scattered throughout the society and even throughout the world. The export sector, as we have noted, consists of those activities of production and distribution that are primarily oriented on a regular basis toward markets beyond the boundaries of the community in which they exist. As examples the production of automobiles in the city of Detroit is primarily oriented toward markets beyond the borders of that city; the production of steel in Pittsburgh is primarily an activity oriented toward consumption beyond the borders of that city; the insurance industry of Hartford, Connecticut, produces a service primarily intended for consumption beyond the corporate limits of that city; the production of sonar equipment located in one small California community is obviously an economic activity attuned to an external market; and finally, many transportation services regularly performed in the city of Chicago would not exist at all were it not that such services, although performed in that city, are really being purchased by consumers who are located beyond its borders.

The export sector can be relatively homogeneous or, conversely, heterogeneous. It can consist of a single industry (homogeneity) such as exists in "the company town," the limiting case in which the only export is the product that is literally the community's reason for existence; or it can consist of a great number of industries, all producing for markets beyond the city in which they are located, as is the case in large metropolitan centers such as New York and Chicago. The more heterogeneous the export sector is, the more complex will be the exchange network that links the city with other economic units both within American society as well as beyond its borders.

What is probably most important about this distinction between the *homogeneous* and the *heterogeneous* export sector is the relative economic security provided the city possessing the latter as opposed to the former. A city whose export sector is dominated by a small number of industries runs the risk of having its economic vitality sapped because of a change in the market structure for the products that those industries produce. The fewer the products or services exported, the greater the risk of damage to the local economy if the demand for any of these products or services evaporates or even diminishes. One need only look at the demise of many "ghost towns" of the West, or many of the coal towns in West Virginia, Kentucky, and Pennsylvania to understand how devastating the loss of the single or dominant export can be to a community's economy. When the availability of new and cheaper fuels caused the demand for coal to diminish markedly, those communities in which it was the main or only export began to suffer economically. Not only did the mines close but the loss of paychecks for large segments of the labor force brought about considerable concomitant damage to local retailers and service people whose own economic destinies depended to a great extent upon the purchasing power of those directly employed in the mining operations.

While it is true that a similar shutdown or marked diminishing of a major industry in a city with a *heterogeneous* export sector can have serious implications for that city's economy, the export sector is not likely to be destroyed by a failure in any one industry. As long as the other industries in the export sector continue to function relatively well, the community's economic viability will not be endangered. At least some of those displaced by the failure will be absorbed by the still functioning industries. Moreover, because such communities are more likely to have diversified resources—human, educational, and cultural—than are the communities with homogeneous export sectors, they are also more likely to attract new industry. Thus the slack in the economy caused by failure in an export industry is likely to be taken up sooner in a city with a heterogeneous export sector because of its attractiveness to replacement for the failed industry.

The *local sector* of a given city's economy consists of all those economic activities that are primarily oriented to locally based consumption. These are inclusive of production activities that are primarily intended to meet a demand in the local market (that is, a local dairy or bakery); distribution activities in local wholesaling and retailing; and the performance of services such as intracity transportation, local legal services, medical services, educational services, entertainment, etc.

Local enterprise can be subcategorized according to the nature of its relationship to the export sector. First, there are those enterprises that exist in a *direct exchange relationship* with one or more enterprises in the export sector. An industrial laundry service that serves the big factories in the community, or a local trucking firm that leases its trucks to one or more exporting firms are examples of such enterprises. The economic well-being of such businesses is thus a direct function of the economic well-being of the export industries it services. Significant cutbacks in these export industries have immediate negative implications for such local businesses in loss of sales and, ultimately, in loss of wages. Should the export firms with which they are directly linked go out of business, the chances are very good that these businesses themselves will soon cease to function. Far more numerous are those enterprises serving local markets that may include export industries but are not directly dominated by them. These local enterprises, ranging from the corner drugstore to the publicly or privately owned transportation companies, are complementary to the industries of the export sector, but more often than not, they do not have to depend for their well-being upon direct exchange relationships with them.

When we say that a business in the local sector exists in a complementary relationship with the export sector, we mean that although there is often no direct or contractual link that ties the destiny of such business to the functioning of one or a number of enterprises in the export sector, there exists a condition of mutuality that, in a general way, makes the success of such enterprises ultimately contingent upon the economic health of the export sector and, conversely, to a certain extent makes the efficient economic functioning of local sector business a condition for the successful operation of export industries. For example, we have already noted the case of the coal mining town in which the mines shut down. When this happens the immediate unemployment stemming from a massive shutdown in the export sector will bring about a scarcity of cash in the community, a consequent cut in local consumer spending, and ultimately the closing out of retail business like groceries that, in turn, means further unemployment within the community.

Let us consider another case: a small New England city is in serious economic difficulty because some of the major textile firms having mills (export) in the community have shut down and have proceeded to move their operations to communities in North Carolina. Some of the other mills remain functioning and the few other export industries are still operating. The city has suffered a serious cutback in its export sector. As a result, there has been an abrupt rise in the number of unemployed within the community. Unemployment and the consequent dropoff in local purchasing power threatens the local sector with an enforced cutback. For the time being the city's economy is limping along. However, the real danger is appearing on the horizon.

If the cutback in the local sector is prolonged, if local transportation ceases to function efficiently, if the reduction in clients and patients able to pay their way drives independent professionals from the community, and if the school system, because of a shrinking tax base, falls behind systems in other communities, *then the remaining export industries may themselves begin to consider migrating to communities where the local sector looks more favorable.* Such migration would have the consequence of even greater loss in local purchasing power and the remaining local sector enterprises would be cut back even further. The net result for our hypothetical city would be a moribund economy.

Some economists have come to regard the export sector as the *basic* sector or component in the economy of any city.[5] This means that the economic destiny of any city is essentially a function of the character of the export sector. Growth in this sector, they believe, means growth in the local sector, high incomes in the export sector mean high incomes in the local sector, and conversely, retrenchment in the export sector means retrenchment in the local sector and low income in the export sector has, as a consequence, low income in the local sector. As Wilbur Thompson has put it ". . . the local economy is seen as the lengthened shadow of its export industries."[6] Charles Tiebout, a foremost proponent of this point of view, has stated, "Export markets are . . . the *prime mover* [italics mine] of the local economy."[7]

On the other hand, some economists take a more cautious position with regard to the role of the export sector in determining the economic characteristics of a given community. Certainly an argument can be made to the effect that expansion or shrinkage in the export sector can, in some instances, be seen as a function of the character of the local sector. When inefficiency and poor management result in a poorly run and understaffed local transport system or when, for example, the local retail outlets offer little variety in the goods they have for sale, the result may be that the influx of new export industries will be discouraged. Or, as we have seen in our discussion of the hypothetical New England mill city, when the local sector shrinks—for whatever reason—to a point where it is incapable of giving ade-

5 Charles M. Tiebout, *The Community Economic Base Study,* A Research Memorandum prepared for the Area Development Committee, Committee for Economic Development, September 1962, p. 99. Also see Thompson's *A Preface to Urban Economics.*

6 Thompson, p. 2.

7 Tiebout, p. 4.

quate indirect support to industries that are functioning well in the export sector, there exists the threat of outmigration of these industries.[8]

We need not trouble ourselves about the issues raised by these alternative points of view on the relationship between the *export* and *local* sectors of the city's economy. In lieu of definitive evidence supporting one position as opposed to the other, all we need do is recognize that the economic status of any city is a function of the interplay of factors characteristic of both sectors. It is true that export industries bring money into the local economy and to the extent that this is effectively accomplished they provide the cash or exchange basis for economic growth.[9] But their ability to do so effectively is, in part, a function of local sector conditions. Whatever the external market demand for the products and services of the export sector, the industries in that sector cannot thrive when the local sector is inadequate in its support.

From a purely economic perspective, assigning primacy to the export sector probably makes the most sense. Without the influx of money which depends primarily upon export it is doubtful that the local sector would thrive very well. However, we ought to recognize that while such an inflow is a necessary condition for expansion in the local sector, it is not a sufficient condition. Such an influx will have little impact in a city where there is (1) little motivation to expand in the local sector, (2) little innovative imagination or, conversely, a great emphasis upon tradition, and (3) where the labor force—beyond those already employed in the export sector—is largely unskilled or overspecialized in their skills so that they are ill-prepared for change. Thus, in some measure, the condition for economic expansion is noneconomic, said in another way, it is cultural and social.

In sum, the economy of a city—at least from the perspective of productive enterprise—is analogous to the economy of a nation-state, albeit on a smaller scale.[10] It consists of a complementary network of export and local sector enterprises. And while it would seem that the health of the economy as a whole depends more basically upon the healthy functioning of the export sector, there is good reason not to

8 For an exposition of the position championing the local sector as the key to local economic growth and retrenchment, see Hans Blumenfeld, "The Economic Base of the Metropolis," *Journal of the American Institute of Planners* (Fall 1955), pp. 114–132.

9 John Syrjamaki, *The Sociology of Cities,* Random House, New York, 1964, p. 137.

10 See Thompson, for a similar statement, p. 27, cited in footnote 4.

ignore the local sector's contribution to the overall state of the economy.

Our discussion of urban economic processes is not yet complete. We have not, up to this point, dealt with the city's need to import a large number of goods and, in some cases, a significant number of services. While it is characteristic of cities that the total production of certain goods and services within their boundaries cannot be consumed locally, it is also true that, in terms of the *range* of goods and services necessary for human sustenance and comfort (or, indeed, for export production), no city produces all that its constituents will need to consume. Thus, all cities must import, a fact of economic life which unequivocally stamps the city as a *dependent community*.[11] Of course some cities are more dependent upon imports than others. All cities must import the major portion of their food supply. But the more diversified and elaborate the local sector, the greater the likelihood that locally produced goods and services will constitute a higher proportion of the goods and services available for consumption within the city.

The entire matter of urban imports is very complex. For example, while some goods and services may be local from raw components to productive synthesis, others may represent a locally based productive synthesis of imported components in whole or in part. A moderately sized dressmaking establishment serving the local community produces clothing that when purchased, does not itself fall in the import classification. However, in all likelihood the materials used in the production of these clothes will had to have been imported. Indeed, it is difficult to think of any product that is purely local, that involves no imports at all. The more diversified, elaborate, and mature the local economy, however, the greater in number will be the locally based steps in the productive process for a higher proportion of products available for local consumption. At one end of the continuum there are those communities that must import almost everything consumed locally. Intermediate are those communities in which the local productive synthesis is relatively superficial involving only production of consumer goods but for a relatively wide range of products. Finally, there are those urban communities whose economies are capable of productive synthesis in depth over a wide range of consumer goods and services.

11 For a discussion of "dependent" and "independent" community types, see Amos H. Hawley, *Human Ecology: A Theory of Community Structure*, Ronald Press, New York, 1950.

The character of a community's import relationships with other communities and economic units is of some significance. While, as we noted above, the economic well-being of a community depends in large measure upon the diversity and multiplicity of its export relations, from the import perspective it may be argued that the well-being of the community's economy is better served when its import relations are relatively homogeneous and limited. If imports equal dependence, then the greater the range of imports, the greater the economic dependence of the community. If dependence implies the absence of control over processes in other communities and economic units, then the greater the range of imports, the more vulnerable is the importing community. The chances of uncontrollable events disturbing the local economy are greater according to the range of import or dependent relations within which a given community is enmeshed.

Theoretically, the urban economy that minimizes its dependency is the economy that is in the best position to insure its continued viability. Thus, it may be argued that as far as the probabilities of economic stability are concerned, the fewer the imports the better. Conversely, the probabilities of economic stability in the community are improved by a greater range of exports. In both cases the condition described maximizes the degrees of freedom available in the local economy: the first because the more local consumption can be met by local production, the greater will be the control exercised by local economic agents over their own destinies; the second because the diversification of export hedges against serious retrenchment of demand in that sector, thus giving local economic agents some room to maneuver when a market for one or even for a number of exports (depending upon the extent of diversification) shrinks or, indeed, collapses. *From the point of view of economic soundness, therefore, the predicament of the cities resembles the predicament of nation-states: ideally, a city, like a nation, prospers when it can maximize diverse exports and minimize the range of imports necessary to its basic sustenance.*

ORGANIZATIONAL ASPECTS OF THE URBAN ECONOMY Organizationally speaking, no treatment of the urban economy can avoid the fact that it shows great complexity. The economies of urban areas consist, in varying proportions, of the following organizational units: (1) *organizations primarily oriented toward economic activity,* that is, those organizations that would not exist except for their economic functions, and (2) *organizations that are primarily oriented toward noneconomic activity but that have considerable impact upon the economy nevertheless,* that is, those organizations whose *raison d'etre* is to be found in another institutional order—the polity, the educational system, and the family—but that also function in the economy.

Organizations that are primarily economic can be subcategorized according to *function, scale,* and *structure.* Every economic enterprise must in some measure be involved in the consumption of goods and services. However, no primarily economic enterprise can be involved in consumption to the exclusion of production and/or distribution of goods and services.[12] Thus, every primarily economic enterprise links consumption with either production or distribution functions, or with some combination of both. While it is true, for example, that the local shoe manufacturing firm purchases goods in the form of raw materials such as leather and rubber, and while it is true that it purchases services such as those provided by industrial laundries, the manufacturing firm is foremost an economic enterprise since it produces tangible goods (shoes) and distributes those goods through its marketing department. While a drug wholesale firm regularly purchases (or consumes) the services of an accountant, it is an economic enterprise to the extent that it markets (or distributes) a range of merchandise with retail druggists.

Community enterprises can range in size from the owner-operated grocery store to the behemoth export-oriented production units employing hundreds and, in some cases, thousands of local people. It goes without saying, of course, that scale is an important indicator (albeit not the only one) of the enterprise's contribution to the economic well-being of the community. The greater the number of employees, the more significant is the enterprise's fortune—good or ill—for the economic life of the community. The closing of Jones' hardware store will undoubtedly be mourned by a number of faithful customers and the 10 employees who have lost their jobs, but the closing of an automotive plant employing 1000 workers can have serious dislocating effects in the local economy, particularly if it happens to be one of a small number of large-scale employers.

Economic enterprises in any given community are characterized by a range of structural characteristics. The larger enterprises tend to be organized bureaucratically. Such enterprises have a structure consisting of specialized departments coordinated in a hierarchical system of control and responsibility. Theoretically, each specialized department has a delimited sphere of competence that cumulates with the competencies of other departments in the optimization of the enter-

12 This is true by definition—an organization primarily oriented to the economy must be oriented to the production and/or distribution of goods and services.

prise's economic functions. Coordinating this cumulation of specialized functions falls to high-level managers whose responsibility it is to see that the economic purposes of the enterprises are consistently well-served by their sub-units.[13]

Let us take as an example the A & H Textile firm located in a middle sized North Carolina city. The prime economic output of A & H Textiles is a line of finely woven fabrics that it sells to apparel manufacturers located throughout the United States. In order to produce its fabrics, A & H has a number of specialized departments. There is, first of all, the manufacturing division itself in which personnel operate and maintain the great looms that weave the fabrics, The marketing department seeks and receives the orders and the design department creates and produces designs. There is, of course, a purchasing department that is in turn subdivided into a fibers division that has responsibility for purchasing the raw materials, natural and synthetic, necessary for the production of the finished textiles, and a capital goods division that has the responsibility of purchasing the machinery necessary for an efficient productive process. A & H also has a shipping department whose responsibility it is to make sure that customers throughout the country receive their orders on time and undamaged, a personnel department whose responsibility it is to see to it that the other departments are adequately staffed, an accounting department to insure the fiscal integrity of the firm, and a legal department that negotiates the firm's sales and purchase contracts while at the same time overseeing its labor relations.

Each of these departments has a chief, usually with the title of Vice President, who delegates supervisory responsibility to other officers and who reports to the enterprise's executive committee (consisting of all vice presidents and presided over by the president of A & H). The executive committee makes the operating decisions for the firm and is responsible, through the president, to A & H's board of directors, whose function it is to set the company's economic objectives. Thus, the board of directors defines the objectives, and the executive board makes the operational and coordinating decisions in terms of these objectives and directs each department to pursue its particular competency in terms of these operational decisions. The head of each department then plans his particular operation and delegates responsibility for its actualization to his subordinates.

At the other end of the continuum are those enterprises whose

13 For a discussion of economic bureaucracy see Wilbert E. Moore, *Industrial Relations and the Social Order,* revised ed., The Macmillan Co., New York, 1951, pp. 71–97.

organization involves no such elaborate structuring and cumulation of diverse functions. For example, there is the firm of Abruzzi and Associates, cabinet makers. The firm consists of Mr. Abruzzi and five other cabinet makers. Mr. Abruzzi takes the orders, keeps the accounts, and purchases wood and tools, while he and his employees together build fine cabinets and other furniture and deliver them personally to their customers in a small van. In such a business there is a minimal division of labor and *generalized competence* replaces the *intense specialization* of the economic bureaucracy.

The economy of any given urban community is likely to have an enterprise profile inclusive of a range of structures falling between the polar cases noted above. In general, the larger the firm and the more complex the operations involved in its economic function (that is, the nature of what it produces and/or distributes and the market which it serves), the more bureaucratic will be its structure. As a rule of thumb, one that has exceptions, as in the case of the company town, the larger the urban community, the greater the presence of bureaucratized enterprises in its economy.

Up to this point we have been concerned with economic enterprises or those organizations that deal directly in the production and/or distribution of goods and services. In any community, however, there are other economic organizations that, although they are not enterprises in the sense that the term has been used here, are nevertheless functionally significant. Organizations like labor unions, professional groups such as the local bar association, and business groups such as the Chamber of Commerce can have considerable impact upon the economic life of the local community. These are *economic interest organizations* that represent people diversely located in the local economy. They represent differential economic claims—the workingman's, and the manager's, for example—that cut across enterprise boundaries.

Unions, for example, can affect the local economy by increasing the purchasing power of large segments of the population when they bargain with employers for higher wages. On the other hand, it is certainly true that a prolonged strike in a high employment industry may have serious consequences for the local economy. Such a strike can have the same effect as the closing of a large firm (or several large firms). It seriously reduces the availability of money to be spent in the local economy and, consequently, can lead to a weakening of the economic position of enterprises that, to a certain extent, depend for their well-being on the spending power of those who are on strike.

Moreover, should the strike occur in an industry that provides vital direct support for other industries, major diverse segments in the economy can be ground to a virtual halt. If the Teamsters call a strike against the truckers in a community, then industries as diverse as dairy and steel fabricating may be negatively affected simultaneously.[14]

Business groups like the local Chamber of Commerce can likewise affect the character of the city's economy. Earlier in this chapter we discussed the importance of a vital local sector for the maintenance and indeed the growth of the high-income-producing export sector. We noted that limitations of business imagination and efficiency in the supportive local sector could adversely affect the functioning of industries in the export sector and discourage the location within the community of new export industries. On the other hand, a well-managed, imaginative local sector would likely help to keep already existing export industries within the community and encourage new industries of this *genre* to locate within the community. To the extent that the local Chamber of Commerce is concerned with the functioning of the local sector, it becomes a key organization in determining the overall character of the city's economy.

If the Chamber is tradition bound and inflexible, it will not operate to create a climate receptive to export industry growth. Indeed, coupling these characteristics with the Chamber's likely ability to affect political decision making in local government, it is probable that it can block the entrance of export industries by supporting highly restrictive zoning procedures, as one example. On the other hand, if the Chamber is a progressive organization of businessmen who adequately perceive the positive and complementary relationship between a strong export sector and the local sector, it will operate aggressively along many fronts—economically, politically, educationally and culturally—to encourage the growth of high employment and high income export industries within the community. It will encourage diversity in retailing, efficient and economical transport services, flexible zoning policies, tax support for quality public education, and philanthropic support of cultural and recreational facilities.

Appropriate to our earlier discussion of the dependency of urban economies is the notice we must take of the organizational dynamics, which are characteristic of many of the larger economic enterprises

14 Strikes and their consequences are not solely the responsibility of labor unions, for employer policy may create conditions against which the unions find it necessary to strike.

and interest representatives. Many large enterprises are *trans-urban* in that they are not located within a single community but have operating units in a number of urban communities. In such cases the management of any given unit does not have final decision-making authority but must defer to a centralized upper management, often located at a great distance, that governs the enterprise in terms of its status in the national economy. When such a situation exists, decisions are likely to be made in terms of maximizing the well-being of the enterprise as a whole, irrespective of the impact such decisions might have on the operations of any given unit. Consequently, such decisions are often made without regard for the impact they might have on the local economies of the communities in which such operating units are located.

It may happen, in the extreme, that the corporate managers will decide to close down a unit in a given community because they have concluded that its operations are too costly and can better be accomplished in some other location. Or, again in the extreme, upper level management may decide to cease producing the line of merchandise manufactured by a given local unit. In consequence of this the unit may be closed without regard to the impact of the closing on the economy of the city in which the unit is located. More frequently, the local economy will be affected by less drastic centralized decisions such as those that cut back or increase production in a given unit, according to an assessment by the upper level management of the firm's market position in the national economy. The point of these illustrations is that in trans-urban enterprises managerial decision-making is attuned to national economic conditions instead of to the local economic needs in those communities in which their operating units are located. To the extent that such a situation predominates in any given community, that community is without control of its economic destiny.

The trans-urban nature of many large-scale enterprises has another consequence that may seem minor at first but that can have serious consequences for the economies of the communities in which operating units are located. When a firm has dispersed operations, occupational mobility for managerial personnel is likely to be coupled with physical mobility. Aspiring young managers are likely to move from one assignment to the next and from one city to the next in their climb up the corporate ladder. As a result, there is a relatively high degree of transience among managers of local units while the labor force of those same units is likely to be relatively stable, consisting of individuals who, if not natives of the area, are nevertheless "locals" in their life-style orientation. The transient managers have the higher level decision makers in their firms as their economic reference group. They are more likely to act with an eye toward the expectations and interests of those to whom they are organizationally responsible, and toward those who have the power to advance or retard their career mobility rather than to the needs and interests of any particular local group. Thus, while they manage locally important enterprises, they manage them in a manner that is only *secondarily* sensitive to the needs and conditions of the local economy.

This circumstance increases the potential for conflict in the local economy. In the first place, the distrust of labor for management may be heightened because local labor may feel that the transient managers are even more unsympathetic to their claims than would be the case if the managers were relatively permanent. Second, the relations between local businessmen who have a permanent stake in the community, and the transient managers who do not, have a higher potential for strain than would otherwise be the case. The simple fact of the matter is that although they are all businessmen and may even belong to the same clubs—the Rotary, Kiwanis, for example—they are responsible to different constituencies; their loyalties are disparate.

Care should be taken not to give the impression that a state of conflict always exists between transients and locals. Large trans-urban enterprises do regard harmonious community relations as important for the well-being of their operations in a given community. For this reason they often strongly encourage their local managers to collaborate with local people, businessmen and others, in helping to make the community a "good place" for business. These efforts notwithstanding, the transient managers must meet company expectations above all others, even when these conflict with the requisites for local well-being. Given his position, the transient manager cannot have the same stake in the community as the local businessman.[15]

Interest organizations, like enterprises, may be of sufficient scale so that they are trans-urban in their organization. When a given city has a large trans-urban component in its profile of interest-organizations, its control over its economic life is reduced in inverse proportion to the size of that component. Perhaps the most economically significant of the trans-urban interest organizations are the labor unions. Union organization is a complex phenomenon and it is beyond our purpose

15 For a discussion of management's role in community affairs, see Wilbert E. Moore, *The Conduct of the Corporation,* Random House, New York, 1962; also see Moore, *Industrial Relations,* pp. 296–322, cited in footnote 13.

to explore it in great detail.[16] However, we should point out that unions *do* vary in the extent to which *locals* (community-based units) have autonomy within the structure of the national organization or federation.

Theoretically all locals and their subunits, the shops, are empowered to act to rectify the grievances that their members may have against their employers. To the extent that the union, both nationally and locally, is meeting its commitment to its members, the local will act on grievances by means of negotiation when possible or by instituting work slow downs or even strikes when necessary. In some cases the local may be empowered to take action on its own, but in other cases grievance action has to be cleared through the national office of the union. The "wildcat" (or unauthorized) strike, a tactic familiar to observers of the labor scene, often occurs when the local involved does not have autonomy and cannot get a grievance action sanctioned by the union's national officers.

In the area of collective bargaining for new labor contracts, there is also some variation. In industries such as construction in which the labor demand is determined in large by conditions in a given community or area, local affiliates of national unions have considerable autonomy in the bargaining procedure. As a result of this, electricians in New York City, for example, have a much more favorable contract than, let us say, their counterparts in Champaign, Illinois. On the other hand, unions that represent workers in such trans-urban or nationally organized industries as steel or automotive production bargain on an across-the-board basis. The locals may have the power of ratification, and there are undoubtedly provisions written into national contracts that seek to make adjustments possible where community conditions warrant them; but the fact remains that the contract is centrally negotiated and nationally applicable. For good or for ill, all steel workers, whatever their location and company, are parties to the same collective bargaining agreement. The degree of centralization and uniformity is so great in that particular industry (as well as in others like automotives, chemicals, and rubber) that the bargaining is not restricted to a single firm but often goes on between the union and representatives of those firms that together are the major employers in the industry. The resultant collective bargaining agreement is applicable on an industry-wide basis and an authorized strike, should it occur as a tactic in pursuit of such an agreement, would similarly be industry-wide.

16 For a detailed analysis of union organization, see Moore, *Industrial Relations and the Social Order,* cited in footnote 13.

In light of the above, we can conclude the following with regard to the local community trans-urban "quotient" vis-à-vis unions. Local autonomy would seem to be greatest where the union represents workers in enterprises where the economic condition is primarily determined by conditions in the local community. Unions functioning, for the most part, in *local sector industries* can be expected to have considerable autonomy. Local autonomy would seem to be less characteristic of those unions that represent workers in industries that are themselves organized on a trans-urban or national basis. Since by far most of these are classified in the *export sector* of a given city's economy, we may argue that it is in that sector where we find the least responsiveness of organized labor to local conditions. Thus, while a large and growing export sector may be conceived of as making a major contribution to the economic vitality of a given city, we must also recognize that the growth of industry in this sector concomitantly decreases local control over labor conditions as well as management prerogatives. Consequently, growth in the export sector signals proportional loss of local control over economic decision making.[17]

There are other interest organizations which have trans-urban structures and that are, to a greater or lesser degree only partially sensitive to local conditions that their national policies affect. Organizations like the National Association of Manufacturers and the American Medical Association, both of which make national pronouncements of intent and policy that ultimately have local economic implications, are examples of such interest organizations. All of the foregoing discussion serves to underscore the earlier noted *dependence* of urban economies. The absence of local control over the local community's economy makes cities in which this condition is extensive somewhat like those underdeveloped nations—for example, many of those in Latin America —that, due to large components of foreign investment, have little control over their economic destinies.[18]

There are, as we have noted above, primarily noneconomic organi-

17 This is true even in those cities that house the national headquarters of export sector firms and/or their bargaining correspondents, the unions. The location of the economic decision makers may indirectly affect their efforts—they may project to other localities their experiences in these communities—but they ostensibly bargain in terms of national conditions, and the communities that house them receive no overt special dispensation because they do so.

18 For a treatment of the consequences of trans-urban economic organization see W. Lloyd Warner and J. O. Low, *The Social System of the Modern Factory—The Strike: A Social Analysis,* Yale University Press, New Haven, 1947, pp. 108–133; see also Roland L. Warren, *The Community in America,* Rand McNally and Co., New York, 1963, p. 301.

zations that in their operation have important effects on the city's economy. Among the most important of these are governmental organizations (local and, in some cases, state and federal) educational organizations and families. Let us briefly examine the economic implications of the structure and functioning of these organizations in turn.

Economically speaking, government organizations are producers of services for the local populace. Local government, for example, may be responsible for providing a range of services from dog-catching through police and fire protection to mass transportation and public welfare. In order to provide such services, local government must in turn be provided with revenues. In part, such revenues are derived from taxes and licensing fees that the city government is empowered to collect. However, such revenues are hardly ever, if at all, enough to underwrite the provision of local services, consequently, cities must depend upon grants of financial aid from the state and federal governments and bond issues to make up the difference between the revenues they need and the revenues they are able to collect by means of taxation and fees.

Because government does provide such services it is often a large-scale employer in the community. Although many positions are appointive, thus often making incumbency a matter of political fortune (that is, a matter of "knowing the right people," working faithfully for "the party," or otherwise contributing to the victory of a candidate for public office), in most cities of any size the large majority of government positions are covered by civil service regulations and are thus filled competitively according to merit (or at least according to merit as evaluated by civil service examinations). In most cities all policemen and firemen are under civil service, as are welfare personnel, also under civil service in many places are sanitation workers, transportation workers, public works functionaries, lower level staff in the city planning office, parks and recreation employees, building inspectors, public housing employees, and public health employees.

The civil service domination of public employment has some important implications for the local community's economy. The principles of civil service organization are, first and foremost, *bureaucratic*. Civil service operations assume a hierarchical form of coordination and control over the activities of specialists who are in their jobs by virtue of the fact that they have demonstrated a specialized competence to accomplish the tasks specifically assigned to their job classifications. This is true for personnel at all levels in a given department. Civil service bureaucracies, however, have one further feature that is only infrequently if at all present in nongovernmental or private bureaucracies. After a trial period, an individual who has performed his assigned tasks satisfactorily has to be granted *tenure* in his position. He thus becomes a permanent employee who can only be removed from his position on specified grounds of malfeasance and then only after this malfeasance has been proven in a hearing the results of which the employee may appeal.[19] Thus it is that public bureaucracies are highly stable organizations and it is this stability that is functionally important for the local economy.

This functionality has two sides. On the plus side, it would seem that civil service stability based as it is upon the presumed competence of incumbents insures the community of continuous provision of adequate services in those areas in which the government bureaucracies operate. This would seem to insure the citizenry of a reasonable service return for their tax dollar. Government service is one component of the *local sector* of the community's economy. To the extent that such service is continuous and adequate, it contributes to the economic attractiveness of the community, thereby encouraging growth in high income potential *export sector*. The greater the number of services provided by government, the more stable the quality, and the more attractive will the local sector be to prospective export industries. Beyond this, the stability of civil service employment creates a work force in the community that has a consistent income. Business may be bad, layoffs may occur, but the government goes on and most of its employees continue to draw their salaries.[20]

In this light it may also be noted that relative to private industry, serious labor-management disputes that often result in strikes and lost income are less frequent in public bureaucracies. This is true in spite of the fact that in recent years strikes by public employees have become frequent. While civil service employees often belong to unions, strikes by such unions have been consistently ruled illegal. Indeed, in some states there are specific prohibitions against strikes by any public employees, urban or otherwise. Thus, extensive public employment in a community may contribute to its economic health by contributing to the stabilization of its employment and income profile.

19 The tenure rules of civil service were instituted to protect public employees from the vicissitudes of politics. Without the tenure rule, a new city administration could replace government personnel almost at will.

20 It is interesting to note that many parents who experienced the trauma of the Great Depression used to encourage their children to go into civil service because of the economic security it was thought to provide. Teaching was usually included under this rubric.

On the negative side, the stability of public bureaucracies can often become rigid, and the services they provide can in such circumstances deteriorate in quality. Robert K. Merton has noted that bureaucrats tend to relegate the ends they are ostensibly pursuing to a level secondary to the maintenance of the prerogatives and perquisites of their positions. When this occurs, they develop strategies calculated to subvert their prescribed functions in a manner that serves their own interests.[21] In a government bureaucracy with its tenure protections, such an occurrence becomes very difficult to remedy. Except in cases of gross malfeasance, the tenure rules that protect the employee from undue external pressure also make him relatively inaccessible to those who have a just grievance with regard to his performance. Thus, when bureaucratic ritual sets in, the civil service rules are themselves an impediment to necessary reform. If this should become widespread in the community's governmental bureaucracies, the citizenry will be deprived of the kind of service it expects for its taxes. And to the extent that these bureaucracies contribute to the quality or lack of quality in the *local sector* of the community's economy, such deterioration of public services can seriously undermine the overall viability of the economy by lessening the attractiveness of the local sector to export industries.

The public education system of a city might justifiably be included under the governmental rubric. It is being considered separately here because (1) in most communities educational administration and control is relatively independent, and (2) education has a distinct functional relationship to the economy.

Educational systems in urban communities are public bureaucracies. They are hierarchically structured organizations operating with tenure rules presumably based upon the demonstrable competence of incumbents.[22] As such, they possess the stable quality that we have previously noted with regard to civil service organization in the polity. The educational system of any given community operates in the local economy. The school system is a large-scale consumer of local goods and services. And because it is unlikely to "go out of business," the system provides the community with a predictable market. Estimates

21 Robert K. Merton, *Social Theory and Social Structure,* revised ed. The Free Press, Glencoe, Ill., 1957, chapter 2, particularly pp. 199–201.

22 In large cities the bureaucracy is so extensive as to boggle the imagination. For a study of how such a large scale bureaucracy can itself become a distinct impediment to the approximation of its professed goals, see David Rogers, *110 Livingston Street: Politics and Bureaucracy in New York City,* Random House, New York, 1968.

of population growth and, consequently, of the school-age population for a given community can serve as predictors of future demands for a range of goods and services covering such things as building construction, school transportation apparatus and service, school-based food consumption, and a heterogeneous set of school supplies too numerous to describe here.

Beyond its long-range market-providing function, it should be noted that the school system is also a long-term employer of considerable scale. In large metropolitan cities such as New York, Chicago, Los Angeles and Philadelphia, the school systems employ a work force numbering in the tens of thousands, the majority of whom are professional personnel. Although smaller cities employ fewer persons than do larger communities, it is nevertheless true that school systems of smaller cities may be among the largest single employers in those communities.[23]

Perhaps the most significant economic operation of the local school system can be seen in terms of the service it supplies the community. The schools contribute directly to the viability of the economy by providing a consistent flow of reasonably educated persons into the manpower pool. Thus the school system, if it is doing an adequate job, provides the community's economic enterprises with a large bloc (although not its entire manpower pool, for account must be taken of in-migration) of employables. As the nature of business enterprise becomes more complex involving ever greater levels of technological sophistication (such as the introduction of business machines, new communication devices, and computerized production processes), the manpower role of the schools in the local economy becomes even more pronounced. Whereas in the past basic literacy was the primary requirement for employability (thus making it possible for those with incomplete secondary school educations to enter the community's basic manpower pool), the present technological sophistication in the economy has elevated the entry level requirements thus necessitating a greater educational input to maintain an adequately prepared manpower pool.

It should be noted, moreover, that the schools serve as a first level selection mechanism for the community's enterprises. Although few school men would readily admit to it, the schools differentiate the

23 This is a fact that is often overlooked by those who complain of the soaring costs of education. Together with goods and services consumption the large payrolls of city school systems function to turn back to the community large amounts of the tax funds collected for educational purposes.

community's potential labor pool by providing different and unequal educational experiences to students who are perceived as possessing unequal intellectual abilities. For example, in New York City it has been common practice in the schools to assign secondary level students to one of three basic programs: (1) the academic, that theoretically prepares the student for college attendance, (2) the vocational, that theoretically endows students with marketable skills that will enable them to enter the labor market immediately after high school graduation, and (3) the general, which is a catch-all for the poorest students who don't seem to fit either of the other established programs. The net result of this and of curricula like this in other cities, is to provide local enterprises with a heterogeneous pool of workers who enter and function in the economy at different levels.

The schools play an important role in shaping the economic destiny of a community. A city enjoying the reputation of possessing a "good" school system—one that runs smoothly and is "up to date" or "progressive"—is usually in a better position to attract high-income and high-employment industries (particularly in the export sector) than is a community that is saddled with a reputation to the contrary. The presence of a "good" school system is usually interpreted by high level management (those who make locational decisions) to mean that there will be an adequately educated labor supply in the community and that the schools will be sufficiently attractive so that in-migrating personnel, particularly transient supervisory personnel, will not be averse to moving their families into the community in question. A city with a "bad" school system must show some promise of improving that system if it is going to attract new industry or, indeed, if it is going to keep the industry it already possesses. The school system is a component of the *local sector* in the community's economy, and to the extent that it performs poorly in the provision of its service, it lessens the attractiveness of that sector for prospective and already existing enterprises in the *export sector*.[24]

The economic functions of the family are widely recognized and while they are not specific to urban communities, they can be considered in terms of their implications in such contexts. One *caveat*, however, should be offered: It is difficult to speak of *the* urban family

24 Improvement of schools usually depends upon the availability of additional revenues. If increased educational expenditures are resisted it will be difficult, if not impossible, to improve the schools. Another impediment to improvement may be the very stability of the school bureaucracy noted earlier. Even with increased revenues, entrenched personnel may resist the need for *change* because they see change as a threat to their interests.

and *its* functions as it is to speak of *the* American family and *its* functions.[25] Those who do so are guilty of gross oversimplification that frequently results in the confusion of whatever family-related issue they are addressing.

The family type usually identified as typical in American society and its cities may be described as follows. The major organizational unit of this type is the nuclear family consisting of husband and wife and their minor children. The nuclear family is part of a bilateral kinship system in which descent is determined in terms of both mother's *and* father's lineal ancestors; and interaction with kin, though limited in nature, can occur equally between members of the nuclear family and the kindred of either side (mother's and father's relatives). In general, the residence of any given nuclear family is separated from the residences of any kindred; or, in other words, the *rule of residence* is neolocal. Finally the phenomenological or, indeed, common sense *raison d'etre* of this family type is the mutual interpersonal satisfaction that is derived by individuals through their interactions in the nuclear unit.

In general, this family type is considered positively adapted to the urban-industrial social environment. Functionally speaking, it is perceived as articulating with the economy in what might be termed a *double interchange relationship.* The family motivates and otherwise encourages its members (husband/father in particular) to participate in the economy, receiving in compensation wages (first interchange). The family's income in cash or its equivalent is then exchanged in the economy for the goods and services necessary to its maintenance and tastes (second interchange).[26]

An adequate depiction of the relationship between family and economy in American cities (or indeed in American society) should not, however, accept such a formulation at face value. For while there is some general validity to it, the actual variations in urban family types imply concomitant variations in their economic functioning. In the first place, family types characteristic of the cities vary according to objective socioeconomic class and ethnic identities. The patri-centered (father centered) upper class family with its heightened kinship consciousness (concern for relatives beyond the nuclear unit)

25 A more complete treatment of the urban family institution will follow in the next chapter.

26 Norman W. Bell and Ezra F. Vogel, "Toward a Framework for Functional Analysis of Family Behavior," *A Modern Introduction to the Family,* revised ed., ed. Norman W. Bell & Ezra F. Vogel, The Free Press, New York, 1968, pp. 1–36.

is significantly different from the more or less equalitarian limited kinship family of the vast American middle class, and both differ still from the matricentered (mother centered) family of the lower class. While it may be true that ethnicity is less significant than it once was in establishing social identity,[27] those who keep alive the consciousness of their ethnicity (usually older people) approximate in their family and kin contacts qualities that mark them as different. And there is at least one "ethnic" identity that carries with it a high probability of significant family variation: the Black family, particularly the lower class Black family, which is intensely matricentered and matriarchal.[28]

Variations in the economic functioning of these family types can be noted as follows: upper class families, for example, are often involved as *organizational units* in the economy. They are frequently sole controllers of large business enterprises with various members of the extended kin grouping holding offices in the enterprises they control. The Du Ponts and the Rockefellers are prominent examples of upper class families who play important organizational roles in the national economy, and in most cities some families can be found taking the same kind of organizational role (albeit on a smaller scale) in the local economy. In such a circumstance, family decision-making can have considerable direct impact upon the local economy. When a family is itself the basis for economic organization, it is not simply a matter of motivating economic activity that makes it important, but the fact economic decisions of consequence for nonfamily members are made in a family context and are to some extent, therefore, subject to noneconomic influences. Given the importance of *"family"* among the upper class, decisions may be made that maximize family economic gains at the expense of community interests. To the extent that family loyalties come before community concerns, there is the potential for economic decision-making that is detrimental to the community. Just as the economic interests of the Rockefellers and the Du Ponts are not at one with the well-being of the national economy, neither are the interests of the Jones or Smith families at one with the economic well-being of the local community in which their interests are actualized.[29]

27 See Will Herberg, *Protestant, Catholic and Jew,* Anchor Books, Garden City, N.Y., 1960.

28 The classic descriptions of this family type may be found in E. Franklin Frazier, *The Negro Family in the United States,* revised ed., MacMillan, New York, 1957.

29 This problem is elucidated in Ferdinand Lundberg, *America's Sixty Families,* Vanguard, New York, 1937. Although this book was published in 1937, there is no reason to believe that its analysis is dated.

The typical or modal family type described at the beginning of this section is most characteristic of the American middle[30] in the economy. Except in those cases where a family owns a relatively small business, such families do not serve as organizational units in the economy. The economic significance of these families in any community is a function of the interpersonal norms which characterize them. The high *affect* component of the nuclear family, in which the well-being of its members is a prime concern, is a major spur to economic effort particularly on the part of the head of the family. A man works not for himself but for his loved ones who depend upon him. While the presence of a wife and children does not insure the maintenance of economic effort (there are some who default economically in spite of their family affect and presumed responsibility), the working man is less likely to default in his economic efforts if he recognizes that such default will harm those whom he holds dearly. On the positive side, it is the high affect component that moves a man to work especially hard to provide the goods and services to which he feels his loved ones are entitled. *One must provide for his family.* The married man is the more dependable. In many businesses the family status of a prospective employee may be important in determining whether or not he gets the job, even though family status is not a formal criterion for acceptability. It is the affect (or feeling) component that underlies the operation of the double interchange with the economy that is most clearly observed among the typical nuclear families of the American middle. Familial concern becomes translated into economic motive which in turn underlies gainful employment and patterns of consumption.

The lower class matricentered family type presents itself to the local economy in yet another posture. In such families the male head of household plays a less than central role in the organization of activities (inclusive of those that are economic in nature). In a disproportionate number of cases, there is no male head of household present. Because of the functional lacunae (or gap) created by the relative insignificance of the adult male, families of this type are often linked to the economy in what might be termed a *truncated interchange*. In its purest form the family motivates no labor in the economy and thus cannot be said to be engaging in the interchange that exchanges labor for income. In such cases, family income is received most frequently

30 The term *class* is purposefully *omitted* because of the difficulties of distinguishing between the "middle" and "working" classes in American society. The *middle* is taken here to mean all those usually identified as middle or working class.

in the form of a regular grant from the public sector (or polity), as from the Aid to Dependent Children program of public welfare. This limited income—rigorously prescribed as to amount by law—is then exchanged for goods and services in a manner approximating the *second* interchange between family and economy. What is involved in this is a family mediated flow of funds from the public sector (or polity) to other sectors of the local economy.

In other instances the *affect* component, that in the typical or modal family (of the American middle) binds the male head of household to his "loved ones," is sufficiently weakened so that it is relatively unimportant as a motivating factor for economic activity. A man in such circumstances is more likely to work for his own gain than is otherwise the case, and his expenditure of income is more likely to reflect his own consumer needs than would be the case if his affective link with a nuclear family was strong. Without such strong affective bonds he is likely to be less reliable as a productive worker and the consumption function of the family unit—*as a unit*—is likely to be limited.

Ethnicity can have a number of economic implications as mediated through the family. Without belaboring the point of familial variation, we should note that the consumer behavior of families of different ethnic backgrounds may vary. It is, for example, not uncommon to find products aimed at a particular ethnic family market in those communities where ethnicity maintains its vitality. There are, moreover, family work traditions that characterize different ethnic groups. In such instances the family directs the flow of labor from one generation to the next into certain occupational spheres as in New York, for example, where Italian-Americans continue to be overrepresented in the construction trades. In the case of lower-class Negroes, the high degree of the matricenteredness and matrifocality characteristic of their families results in an overrepresentation of the *truncated interchange* among them.

One major facet of familial variation likely to have important implications for the economy is the *family life cycle*. The concept of life cycle is an analogy drawn from the stages of growth and deterioration in an organism and applied to perceived careers of family units. In general, life cycle formulations as applied to the family attempt to specify differences in organization and function of the nuclear unit that are concomitant with the newly-married conjugal pair, the child bearing and rearing unit, and the so-called "empty nest" phase of the family career. For the most part, these formulations have been used heuristically (illustratively) and have counted for little in the way of research.[31] However if we posit a cycle or series of stages in the life of a family unit, then, it would follow that these stages should have some implications for the economy. Certainly we can expect consumption patterns to vary according to the makeup of the family unit. Childless newlyweds are likely to consume goods and services in a different combination and in different quantities than those marrieds who have a full complement of children, and both types, in turn, are likely to vary in their consumption habits from the family that is in the "empty nest" stage. Moreover, the quality of labor motivation and labor force participation is likely to vary according to the stage of family life. In the typical or modal family, for example, the probability of the wife's participation in the labor force is greater before the onset of the childbearing and rearing stage. And sometime during the "empty nest" stage the male head of household will probably retire, thus ceasing to participate in the labor force on a regular basis. In any case, although relatively unexplored, there is reason to believe that the life cycle of a family unit, whatever its type (class or ethnic variation), will have as its concomitant changes in the economic behavior of its constituents.

The matter of variable impact upon the local economy of different family types at different stages of the life cycle is not merely academic. If, as we have indicated, variable family types have varying relationships with the economy, then, in some measure, the economic character of any community can be considered a function of the distribution of family types within that community. In short, the particular mix of family types at different stages of the life cycle in the community is predictive of the overall character of such things as labor force characteristics, domestic consumption patterns, public welfare expenditures, and, where upper-class families are involved, of some of the qualities of economic organization in the community.

Let us briefly summarize what has been said about the impact of essentially noneconomic organizations or collectivities upon the economies of local communities. Units representative of the polity, the educational system, and the family all have considerable functional

31 However, one interesting research treatment that links life cycle to economic behavior can be found in John B. Lansing and Leslie Kish, "Family Life Cycle as an Independent Variable," *American Sociological Review, XXII* (October 1957), 512–519. For a treatment of consumer behavior that is more or less tied in with a life cycle conception, see David Reisman and Howard Roseborough, "Careers and Consumer Behavior," *Consumer Behavior,* ed. Lincoln H. Clark, New York University Press, New York, 1955, pp. 1–18.

implications for the local economy. The polity, providing services and large-scale stable employment, contributes to the attractiveness or unattractiveness of the economy's *local sector*. The school system, also a relatively large-scale employer, functions as a manpower producer and screening mechanism. To the extent that the schools of a given community are perceived as being "good" the attractiveness of that community to relocating industries is enhanced. Finally the profile of family types in a given community determines in part the nature of consumption patterns in that community, the characteristics of its labor force, and, in some cases, the character of at least a segment of local economic organization and decision making.

RECAPITULATION OF CHAPTER 3

The urban economy is normatively and structurally dependent. The economies of American cities are governed by operational norms that are general to American society, and the competing value rhetorics—"free enterprise" versus "welfare economics"—of the national economy are also characteristic of urban economic controversy. No urban economy is self-sufficient since no city can produce all that is consumed by its inhabitants and no urban economy produces goods and services for strictly local consumption. Consequently, the economy of any urban community must in some way be linked in exchange relationships with economic units external to it and over which economic functionaries can have little or no control.

The economy of any urban community consists of essentially two subdivisions, the *export sector,* consisting of those activities primarily oriented toward the export of goods and services to other communities and social entities, and the *local sector,* consisting of those activities primarily oriented toward production and distribution within the community. While there is some debate among economists as to the relative importance of each of these two sectors for the growth and viability of a city's economy in the absence of convincing evidence to the contrary, we have argued that neither of the two sectors appears to be preeminent. While it is true that export activities bring new money into the community's economy thus promoting economic well-being (and growth), it is also true that without adequate support from locally oriented activities the industries in the export sector cannot thrive.

Urban communities vary according to the extensiveness of their export activities as well as the diversity of the goods and services that they export. Diversity or heterogeneity of exports is desirable economic condition because the greater the diversity the less vulnerable is the community's economy to the negative effects of a reduction in demand for any given export.

Attention must also be given to the fact that the city's economy has its dependency increased in direct proportion to the extent that it must import goods and services for local consumption. Municipal economies vary according to the extensiveness of their import needs. The more mature and elaborate the local economy, the greater its ability to produce for local consumption, and the greater the degree of economic autonomy.

The economic stability of an urban community—like that of a nation-state—is directly related to the degrees of freedom present in its exchange relationships with other economic units. The degrees of freedom are maximized according to (1) the extent of diversification in the export sector and (2) the extent to which import need is minimized.

The economy of any city is likely to be organizationally complex. The organizational context of the economy will vary from one community to the next in its particular mix of the following components.

1. Those organizations that would not exist except for their economic functions.

2. Those organizations that represent other institutional orders, such as the polity and the family, but that also function in the economy.

The organizations themselves may be distinguished according to their scale and their particular structure ranging from large-scale bureaucracies which function according to the principle of cumulation of specialized competence, to owner-operated enterprises in which the generalized competence of individuals is the organizing principle.

The extent to which a community's economy can be influenced by events and forces external to it can (in large measure) be determined by the character of the organizations that constitute it. Local control of the community's economy is diminished according to the extent to which economic organizations within the community are divisions or subsidiaries of trans-urban enterprises or interest organizations. The more extensive the trans-urban component (those units which are part of large-scale enterprises and interest organizations with units in other urban communities) the more dependent will the local economy be upon decisions which are made without reference to the specific needs and conditions of the given community.

Urban communities vary in the degree to which organizations representing the polity function in the economy. In larger cities, bureaucratized government agencies—more often than not governed by civil service rules and procedures—provide a wide range of services that may be counted as part of the *local sector* of the economy. As such, public bureaucracy may be a large-scale employer within the city and to the extent that the civil service tenure procedures are operating appropriately (they frequently do not do so), these organizations can guarantee competent services, such as transportation, sanitation, and police and fire protection in the local sector. On the other hand, large-scale public service organizations increase the dependency of the local economy because their operating revenues must be supplemented by state and federal aid.

The public schools must also be considered as having important economic functions in the urban community. The schools are, in large measure, responsible for the quality of trained manpower available to economic enterprises within the community. Cities with "good" schools tend to be more attractive to expanding industry than are those whose schools are reputed to be weak. Beyond this the schools are often stable, large-scale employers and they are themselves large-scale consumers of local goods and services.

There is, finally, no question but that the family makeup of a particular urban community will have an impact on the character of its economy. Upper-class families not only function as consumption units in the economy but are often involved as organizational units as well when they control the functioning of economic enterprises. The family of the American middle plays a crucial role in that the affectional expectations that are characteristic of it motivate productive economic effort and consumer behavior. The matricentered lower-class family, on the other hand, does not provide the same motivational base for employment and consumption on behalf of dependents. Ethnicity can affect family work traditions and consumption habits. Families at different stages of the *life-cycle* are likely to have different consumption patterns and are likely to be represented in the economy by differentials in the employment of their members. To the extent that our discussion of differential impact has been accurate, it follows that the distribution of different family types in a given community must in some manner characterize its economy. Variations in such a distribution from one community to the next must, of consequence, be accompanied by corresponding differences in the economies of these communities.

In this chapter an attempt has been made to introduce the reader to the intricacies of economic process and organization in American urban communities. The economy of cities, like the polity of cities, is a *primary* institution in that it is one of the institutional orders that is likely to have a profound and farreaching effect upon the destiny of the community as a social system. While it is not possible to claim that a city is simply a reflection of its economy, there can be no doubt that together with the polity, the economy is a major determinant of community character. The vitality of a city's economy does not necessarily mean the city will be a good community for its inhabitants. But should the economy fail, one can be sure that the city will *not* be a good community. Indeed it may become all but uninhabitable.

Chapter 4
The Secondary Institutions: the Family and the Education System (No. 1 The Family)

INTRODUCTION In this chapter and the next, we shall explore the role of the family and the education system in American urban communities. Relative to the polity and the economy, the family and the education systems, like religion, are *secondary institutions* in American cities. To say that such important institutions as these are secondary may strike the reader as curious if not inaccurate. How is it possible to hold that the family, often considered by sociologists to be the basis for society, is secondary to any other institutional order, or to argue that in a technologically advanced society where 12 years of schooling is a minimum requirement for a modicum of economic success, the education system is less important relative to other institutions?

The family and the education systems are of course *secondary* only in the sense that (1) in any given community they are more likely to be influenced by the polity and the economy than they are to influence these institutions[1] and (2) in consequence of the proposition just stated, the family and the education systems are less likely than the polity and the economy to have an immediate impact in shaping the destiny of the community. Thus, in spite of their undeniable importance as social institutions, they are secondary in American cities in that they are not the "pace-setting" and goal-directing institutions in the community.

The social organization of the city is not an extension of family and kinship as it is in the nonindustrial communities of Africa and the East. And while it may be true that nepotism exists in the polity and the

1 We *must not,* however, overlook the fact that the family and the education system *can* have an impact upon the polity and the economy.

economy, it is also true that nepotism in those institutions (or the entrance of family kin norms) is generally regarded as a form of highly censurable deviance.

In many respects the public education system of any American community can be conceived of as a subsystem of its polity. While the schools are managed by professional educators, teachers and administrators are responsible to a lay board usually elected or else appointed by officials who are elected by the community's citizenry. Because of this circumstance, educational issues often become political issues in the community. Matters of curriculum, of personnel selection and promotion, of budget control and of student placement (that is, racial balance in the schools) are likely at one time or another to become political issues, hotly debated throughout the community at large and resolved not on educational merit, but as a matter of the relative power possessed by the contending groups. The only reason for considering the education system of any community as separate from the polity is that its ideal or normative prescriptions do indeed characterize the system as a distinct institution. On the operational level, however, it is difficult to conceive of the education system as anything but an extension of the formal polity or local government.

Before proceeding with our consideration of family and education in American urban communities, we will note the reasons for including special analyses of them in this volume and, parenthetically, the reasons for not according similar systematic treatment to another secondary institution, the religious system.

Almost everyone likes to be a sociologist where the family is concerned. It is probably true that no other institution in this society receives as much finger-wagging attention as does the family. The butcher, the baker, the school principal, the clergyman, the physician, the social worker, the farmer, the mayors of our cities great and small —are all sociologists regarding the family and what they perceive to be as its demise. In their popular sociology they often reduce all the vastly complex problems of modern America to a single protoproblem —*the problem of the family*. They tell us the family is not what it used to be. Once the lines of authority and respect were clear; now they are so blurred that husband, wife, parents and children do not know what is expected of them. Once the family had an economic purpose and function; now it has none. Is it any wonder, exclaim these social analysts, that the disintegration of the family is the cause of so many social problems? Marriage counselors and child psychologists are in great demand and the divorce rate is climbing. Juvenile delinquency is the result of family breakdown. Student unrest can be charged to parents who have abdicated their disciplinary responsibilities. Mental illness is the obvious result of family uncertainty and the ambiguities of domestic role playing. Generalized alienation and anomie are the results of the family's failure to communicate the purity of America's purpose and the blessings of life in a free society.

Of course, amateur sociologists committed to such *familial determinism* would have no truck with our earlier contention that the family is a secondary institution in urban communities. And, disregarding for the moment the gross exaggerations and inaccuracies characteristic of this popular sociologizing, there is something to be learned from this. The extent as well as the intensity of this "people's sociology of the family" indicates that whatever the *actual* functional importance of that institution in American society, it is *believed* to be functionally irreplaceable. When we bemoan the "breakdown" of the family and its supposed implications for the quality of our lives—we testify to the fact of a *family myth* that permeates throughout American culture. Whatever else may be true of the family in this society the belief in its functional necessity is an inviolable *cultural fact*. Except for the relatively few avant garde sexual revolutionaries and social experimentalists who profess to see the emancipation of the human spirit in the weakening of the family, Americans of all persuasions do agree on the desirability of a sound family system for their well-being.

So great is our concern for the family, so poignant is our nostalgia both private and public for its ideal manifestation, that in every community we support, with little or no public debate, caretaker agencies staffed by social workers, psychologists, and home economists, for example, whose mandate it is to support and rehabilitate those families having serious problems. So concerned are we that on virtually every level of government funds are allocated to support action programs as well as research, the intent of which is the "preservation and enrichment" of family life.

It is because the cultural importance (as opposed to the institutional–functional importance) of the family is unquestioned in American life that we must take pains to analyze its place in urban communities. The family in the context of the community presents us with an intriguing sociological problem. On one hand the family seems to be secondary to the polity and the economy—at least in a functional and/or organizational sense; on the other hand there is a great cultural investment in the idealization of the family. We are confronted by what may be termed a *sociocultural imbalance,* in which the cultural significance of an institution far outstrips its functional significance.

If there is considerable popular sociologizing about the family in American society, there is also widespread popular concern about education this society. The industrialization of the American economy with its manifold increment in technological complexity has revolutionized education in this society. This revolution, yet unfinished has so changed the American education system[2] from its condition prior to the onset of industrialization that the difference may be recognized as qualitative rather than quantitative. It is not simply that today there are more people getting more education—although that is certainly true—but *what, how,* and *why* they learn has changed markedly as well.

Prior to the great leap into industrialization during the decade of the 1870s, education for the masses was simply a matter of learning to read, write, and cipher enough to keep from being cheated, and education for the elite was a classically based preparation for the ministry, law, or the academy. Mass education today covers preparation in everything from the study of Swahili to the highly technical operations involved in data processing, from the study of economics to the study of literature, and from specific vocational training to generalized preparation in the liberal arts. The education of the elites (those who pursue postgraduate degrees) is so variegated and specialized that just to list the areas of study would require an extensive investigative effort. The preindustrial teacher was the proverbial "schoolmarm" (her male counterpart, the bookish young man who taught because he had neither talent or initiative for anything else) whose credentials usually consisted of a secondary school education with perhaps an additional two years of normal school training. The contemporary teacher is a highly trained—if not well-educated—professional in possession of advanced university degrees. Unlike their predecessor, today's teachers do not ply their profession in little school houses—called upon to cover the entire curriculum for several grades—but in great educational plants where, using a range of "hardware" from standard audio-visual aids to closed circuit television, they teach the disciplines in which theoretically, they have a special competence.

Finally, if the typical student of the past went to schools to gain rudimentary skills for participation in an essentially undeveloped, technologically simple economy, today's typical student goes to school to become certified as possessing much *more* than these rudiments. Today, mere possession of rudimentary skills does not qualify an individual for sustained economic participation. These can be learned in eight years of schooling or less, yet those with less than 12 years of schooling, or those without a high school diploma, find themselves unemployable in any but the most menial and least remunerative jobs. Moreover, even a high school diploma is increasingly less than

2 The term "American education system" refers to the overall educational enterprise and not simply to the public schools.

adequate as a license to enter the economy on a more than menial level. This is reflected in the fact that nearly 50 percent of today's high school graduates elect to continue their education by attending some form of postsecondary institution.

In our preindustrial past, when the economy was still immature, unformed, and incompletely institutionalized, a man of little learning but great imagination and vigor could make his fortune and gain the accolades of his fellows by "building a better mouse-trap" or, as was the case with the Robber Barons, by exploiting those who were less imaginative and less vigorous. In the language of the sociologist, vertical mobility could be achieved on a minimum of formal training so long as one possessed the swashbuckle and daring of the entrepreneurial personality. In the industrial present the untrained dreamer has little chance of making it big, no matter how assiduously he applies himself. Success in our well-institutionalized technologically complex economy usually depends upon demonstrated ability to manage complexity. Managing complexity usually depends upon prolonged training—or formal education. Success and social prestige more than ever before depend therefore upon educational attainment. Thus, it may be said that in contemporary America the major accessway to social mobility is the educational system. If in the past people studied to merely get along today they study to make it—to end up above their starting point.

Because education is so intimately bound up with social mobility, and consequently with the whole question of personal destiny, it is the subject of great controversy often developing into marked conflict. In any community, and particularly in those communities that are urban, parents who are concerned that their children achieve a status higher than their own (and they are legion) must also be concerned with the kind of education these children receive. Once the schools were taken for granted; today they are the object of close scrutiny. If the schools are to be instrumental in their children's future success, the parents will insist that they be "good" schools.[3]

3 Although it is difficult to ascertain just what a "good" school is—or what it does that differentiates it from a school that is not good—there does seem to be a popular consensus about goodness that may be summarized as follows: "good" schools are those which (1) prepare children *thoroughly* in the rudiments of literary and mathematical manipulation; (2) provide students with a sufficient academic training so that they will not be at a competitive disadvantage when they attend institutions of higher learning; (3) inculcate an appreciation of and loyalty to the American success system; (4) contain the latest in educational hardware: (5) provide opportunity for extracurricular activities which are consonant with the values of the American success system; and (6) segregate "slow learners" and "troublemakers" from "those who want to learn" so that the "better children" will not be held back.

Out of this concern for "good" schools emerges educational controversy. In some instances the controversy is related to the economics of education. On one side there are parents who seek more public funds for the schools in order to keep them "up to date." On the other side are those people, often without offspring or with grown children, who feel that their tax burden in maintaining the schools is already too great. Consequently, they resist mightily attempts to raise more public funds for educational purposes.

Then there are those parents and their sympathizers who believe that their children have been systematically excluded from "good" schools. These are usually black or other minority group parents who have lately been vehement in their complaints about segregated ghetto schools. As evidence, they often point to aged and overcrowded school buildings, to text books that should have been discarded years ago, to the assignment of poorly prepared teachers to the schools in question, and to the resulting failure in the education of a very great number of children. The black parent who sees his children denied access to the "good" schools also sees them being denied social mobility, and like any normatively conventional American parent, he is quite ready to struggle for his children's future. In many urban communities this struggle takes the form of a movement to desegregate the ghetto schools, but an increasingly large number of blacks and other urban minorities are committing themselves to a course that endorses local community control over the schools in place of city-wide desegregation.

Both the desegregation strategy and the local control strategy have met with concerted opposition. City-wide desegregation has been opposed by many whites, by some whose reasons cannot be described as anything but manifestations of bigotry, and by others who fear that the influx of poorly prepared children will lower the quality of instruction in their schools, thus depriving their own children of an education in "good" schools. The community control strategy has been opposed by teachers' groups who see in it a threat to their professional prerogatives in the areas of instruction and curriculum development.

In any case, because the education system has become indispensable to "success" and social mobility, it has become the focus of widespread concern in almost every urban community in American society. Thus, in spite of its secondary nature in such communities relative to the polity and the economy the education system can have a long-range effect on the character of any given community, and therefore an understanding of contemporary urbanism demands that we pay special analytic attention to it.

To some it may seem nothing short of arbitrary to exclude the *religious system* from special analytic treatment as an urban institution. Certainly, it must seem to such critics, the religious system as a secondary urban institution can make the same claims to the need for thorough analysis as does the family and the education system. There may be some justification for this view. Nevertheless the position taken here is that while the religious system has some cultural significance in the cities, it has very little impact—cultural or functional—upon the urban community. In this secular age it is difficult to view the religious system as having very much to do with the present day character and future development of any community which we would call urban. Undeniably, religious organizations function as the setting for a great amount of voluntary association activities. Moreover, religious organizations have significantly involved themselves in political and economic issues such as civil rights and poverty. For the most part, however, voluntary association activities have little to do with religion as such. The church bowling team is, after all, a bowling team; the choir is an aggregation that performs sacred music, and may indeed attract those who simply like to sing, those who in other circumstances might join another kind of choral group; the ladies' auxiliary bazaar has little to do with religious values, although it may contribute to meeting the cost of building a new rectory for the minister; the men's group may be more involved in planning social and charitable activities than it is in the evocation of a peculiarly religious point of view. Church involvement in public issues is less religious than it is political. Church organizations involved in civil rights struggles, for example, do not seem to employ tactics that are unequivocally inspired by their creed. They may employ religious symbolism to legitimate their cause or otherwise draw attention to it, but the actual behavior beyond the symbolism is a function of a political definition of the situation.[4]

Public issues that are themselves religious in nature are almost nonexistent in American cities of the present. There is an occasional flap over the prerogatives of religious organizations (such as the tax-

4 The actions of the Southern Christian Leadership Council, originally led by the late Dr. Martin Luther King Jr., are oriented toward the secular politics of protest. Of course, the SCLC has made effective use of religious symbolism and the black man's church culture in their efforts. Most localized protest groups organized in the context of the religious system are even less informed by religious values. For example, there is little difference between the efforts of the "Judeo-Christian Laymen for Racial Justice" and the local "Committee of Citizens for Racial Harmony." These two groups protest injustice and petition for reforms. The Citizens Committee in the name of the just community and the Laymen in the name of Judeo-Christian ethics are each doing the same thing.

exempt status of the holdings of such organizations), or over a critique of public morals by a man of the cloth, but religious organizations generally keep their proselytizing within prescribed limits and thus a conflict over creed and the activities inspired by it hardly if ever becomes a community issue.

There are those who are concerned with the fate of religion in this society. But aside from an essentially older group who cling to traditional beliefs together with the professional clergy who strive for a "spiritual reawakening" in American life, they are relatively few in number. It is safe to say that religion has ceased to be a cultural issue for most contemporary Americans. We ritualistically proclaim our faith in one of the "big three"—Protestantism, Catholicism and Judaism—but most of us go about our lives with little thought to the strength or weakness of our belief. Religion is here to stay, but in a remarkably limited capacity. We use it to mark our joys and bereavements, to reaffirm the solidarity of family ties, but we are little governed by its values and teachings. The religious system as an urban institution is therefore not included in our analysis.

With these prefatory remarks let us now proceed to an analysis of the urban family and the urban educational system.

THE FAMILY

The ideal depiction of the urban family is, in reality, the ideal of the family in American society. Therefore, it must be emphasized at the outset that we are not discussing the urban family as special institutional type but rather the American family system as it is manifested in *urban communities*.

The idealized normative content of family/kinship as found in urban settings may be described as follows.

1. The major operational unit of the system is expected to be the *nuclear* family that consists of a conjugal pair (husband and wife) and their progeny.
2. The rule of residence most generally endorsed is that of *neolocality* that prescribes a separate residence for each nuclear family.
3. The kinship norms governing descent are *bilateral*. An individual considers himself equally descended in the paternal and maternal line and equally a member of the kinship groups of both his father and mother.

4. The *kinship group* of an individual consists of a relatively loose network of relatives. The intensity and functional significance of interpersonal relationships between members of the kin group (aside from those existing within the nuclear family) is determined volitionally by those who are party to the relationships. Beyond the immediate nuclear family, there are few institutionalized prescriptions governing the character of kin relations.

5. The nuclear family is characterized by highly *personalized affective ties*. Relationships within the nuclear family are expected to be *primary* in that they should involve a high order of mutual self-investment on the part of family members. No matter how limited or segmented relationships are in other institutional orders, within the family the rule is commitment of the whole self.

6. The family—in particular the nuclear family—is expected and indeed required by law to (1) provide nurturance and material sustenance for its dependents, (2) govern the behaviors of its dependents, and particularly its children, and (3) be a major agent of socialization (together with the schools) for its young.

It cannot be emphasized too strongly that the characteristics just noted are *normative* idealizations. The *actual* behaviors in terms of these normative expectations are variable. The resultant family patterns characteristic of the cities may be visualized as an array around the ideal. Let us explore the character of variation in the actual patterns of behavior.

THE NUCLEAR FAMILY No one would deny the centrality of the nuclear unit to the functioning of the urban kinship system. There is, however, evidence which indicates that it is not the *sole* functioning unit. Contrary to the notions of Louis Wirth, city life has not meant the atrophy of extended family relations.[5] Contrary also to Talcott Parsons' formulation, urban industrialism does not appear to demand the total isolation of individual nuclear units.[6] A number of studies executed in American cities since World War II have indicated that *extended* families of one type or another are still characteristic of urban settings. The findings of these studies may be summarized as follows.

5 Louis Wirth, "Urbanism as a Way of Life," *The American Journal of Sociology, XLIV* (1938), reprinted in *Cities & Society: The Revised Reader in Urban Sociology,* ed. Paul Hatt and Albert J. Reiss, Jr., The Free Press, Glencoe, Ill., 1957, pp. 46–63.

6 Talcott Parsons, "The Social Structure of the Family," *The Family: Its Function and Destiny,* ed. Ruth N. Anshen, Harper and Brothers, New York, 1949, pp. 241–274.

Urban dwellers characteristically maintain a range of meaningful kin relationships beyond those in their own nuclear families of procreation.[7] At the very least each individual is a member of two nuclear families, *the family of procreation* and *the family of orientation* (the family into which the individual was born) thus linking these units into an extended network. Usually the minimum number of nuclear units in the extended network is *three*—the family of procreation, the husband's family of orientation, and the wife's family of orientation. In many cases the kin network is extended laterally as well, including the nuclear families of procreation of the individual's siblings as well as those relations of his spouse. The exact shape of the extended network is difficult to ascertain since the studies which deal with extensions of relationship beyond the nuclear family have methodological difficulties which make them somewhat less than definitive. Nevertheless the evidence of extension is plentiful.

The functional character of the extended kin network seems to involve (a) intergenerational financial assistance, most typically a flow from the nuclear family of parents to the newly established nuclear family of procreation; (b) interfamilial (nuclear) cooperation in times of crisis (e.g. serious illness); and (c) regularized socializing and visiting among kin particularly among those who have relatively easy physical access to one another. Based upon admittedly limited evidence there seems to be some variation in functional character according to socioeconomic differences. It seems to be true, for example, that middle-class kin networks maintain their viability more easily in the face of geographical separation than do lower class extended networks. The economics of accessibility may be a more formidable barrier to maintaining the network among the lower class than among the middle class. As noted in the previous chapter, upper class families quite often in an extended form provide the organizational contexts for economic enterprise. This is less likely to be the case among extended networks in other social strata.[8]

7 The nuclear *family of procreation* is the family to which an individual belongs by virtue of his or her marriage.

8 A number of reports may be cited in support of the conclusions noted here. Bert N. Adams, *Kinship in an Urban Setting,* Markham Publishing Co., Chicago, 1968; Eugene Litwak, "Geographic Mobility and Extended Family Cohesion," *American Sociological Review,* XXV (June 1960), 385–394; Marvin B. Sussman and Lee Burchinal, "Kin Family Network: Unheralded Structure in Current Conceptualization of Family Functioning," *Marriage and Family Living, XXIV* (August 1962), 231–240; Lee N. Robins

NEOLOCALITY AND BILATERAL KINSHIP Relative to other family/kinship systems the American system (the urban system) *is* neolocal in its residence pattern. In the traditional Chinese system, for example, a residential unit among the well-to-do was characteristically made up of a man and his wife and their unmarried children together with the nuclear families of procreation created by their married sons. The *joint* family of traditional India is another case in which multiple families in the male line often shared the same residence. In the United States, for the most part, neolocal expectations for residence are met and the nuclear family created at marriage takes up residence independently of the nuclear families of the parental generation. However, the implications of neolocality are not so clearly played out as one might expect.

Theoretically the location of residence should have the implication, at least in part, of determining with whom, among the kindred, the married couple and their offspring will interact.[9] Thus in unilineal societies (societies where descent is determined in terms of father's kin or mother's kin, but *never* both) there is an association between descent rules and residency rules. In a patrilineal society (descent through father's kin) the rule of residence will most likely be patrilocal (new nuclear families take up residence with parents of the groom). In a matrilineal society (descent through mother's kin) the rule of residence will most likely be matrilocal (new nuclear families take up residence with parents of the bride). The presence of these rules insures a preponderance of interaction with members of the kin group that gives the nuclear family in question its kinship identity. In a bilateral society such as ours, it would seem fitting that neolocality be the residence rule because neither patrilineage (father's kin) nor matrilineage (mother's kin) can have sole claim upon the nuclear family.

A number of sociologists, most prominently Talcott Parsons, have suggested that the nuclear family in urban-industrial societies tends to be structurally isolated from its kindred.[10] Moreover, they argue that

and Miroda Tomanec, "Closeness to Blood Relatives Outside the Immediate Family," *Marriage and Family Living, XXIV* (November 1962), 340–346; Marvin B. Sussman, "The Isolated Nuclear Family: Fact and Fiction," *Social Problems, VI* (1959), 333–340; William J. Goode, *World Revolution and Family Patterns,* The Free Press, Glencoe, Ill., 1963.

9 William J. Goode, *The Family* (Englewood Cliffs, N.J.): Prentice-Hall, Inc., 1964), p. 46.

10 Parsons, cited in footnote 6.

such isolation is consonant with the demands of physical and social mobility that is characteristic of urban industrial society. In the preceding section we noted evidence which suggests the contrary, that extended kin relations *do* exist in urban settings and that such relations can have *functional* as opposed to merely *symbolic* characteristics. Neolocal or physically independent residence of the typical nuclear family is generally taken as an indicator of functional isolation of the nuclear unit from its kindred. It would seem, however, that in the context of the demonstrated presence of extended kin relations, such an apprehension of the functional significance of neolocality is overstated.

In all probability this exaggeration is the result of an oversimplified conception of family organization and life styles in urban society. Sociologists who hold to the isolationist position tend to see family organization and style as being largely determined by the breadwinner's relationship to the economy, independent of any kinship affiliation. There are other students of the family who have introduced a corrective on this position. While agreeing that in many, if not most, cases, the relationship to the economy is of great significance in determining the character of family organization and style, they argue that this is not universally so and that there are other volitional and cultural factors which can determine such characteristics. To the extent that this is so it may very well be that neolocality or physical independence does not of necessity indicate isolation of the nuclear family from its kindred. Let us explore this matter in some detail.

Neolocality does seem to be associated with what Bernard Farber has termed the *efficiency strategy* of family organization.[11] The efficiency strategy refers to a condition in which the organization of family life is adjusted to the needs and exigencies of maintaining or significant aspect of family organization—is a consequence of the breadwinner's attempt to maximize his opportunities in the vocational improving the community position of nuclear family members. Because community position is largely a function of the occupational activities of the family's major breadwinner the organization of family life is extensively dependent upon the character of his relationship to the economy. Accordingly the choice of residential location—a most structure of the economy. Put quite simply, he will go where the best job or economic opportunity is located and take his family with him. For example, it is fairly typical for the family of a corporation execu-

11 Bernard Farber, *Family: Organization and Interaction,* Chandler Publishing Company, San Francisco, 1964, pp. 269–271.

tive to relocate several times in different cities as the breadwinner moves up the occupational ladder. Without the expectation of neolocality in the urban family/kinship system, it is indeed true that the efficiency strategy so depicted would be nearly impossible to put into effect. A strict adherence to patrilocal or matrilocal expectations for residence would reduce significantly the ability of the breadwinner to respond to expanding opportunities in the job market. He would, in effect, be able to respond only to those opportunities which were within commuting distance of his patrilocal or matrilocal residence. Consequently, the possibilities for improvement, or indeed maintenance, of the family members' community position would similarly be much more limited than they are under the condition of unrestricted geographic mobility, which is one of the consequences of the neolocal rule of residence.

The emphasis upon the consonance or goodness of fit between the economically based necessity for physical mobility and the neolocal rule of residence does not in itself demonstrate a necessary relationship between actual neolocality and the isolation of the nuclear family. Given the sophistication of modern communications technology, interpersonal access between physically separated kin can be maintained with a minimum of cost and effort. In societies where the communications technology is insufficient to the task of overcoming spatial or distance barriers to interaction, patrilocality (or matrilocality as the case may be) insures interpersonal accessibility of large segments of the kindred in a given location. As this is not the case in urban society, it is conceivable that economically based physical separation—or neolocality—need not imply functional isolation of the nuclear family from its kindred. Physical separation and isolation can only be equated when a volitional element—in this case the *efficiency strategy*—is a component in the situation. It is the *choice* to sustain and augment the community position of the nuclear family irrespective of kindred claims that endows physical separation with the social characteristic of isolation. As we shall see, contrary choices are possible and when they occur physical separation cannot be equated with isolation.

Farber suggests another strategy that can characterize family life and that exists to some extent in contemporary urban America. To some degree there are those families whose organization and behavioral qualities seem to be governed by a *welfare strategy*. The welfare strategy encompasses a commitment that emphasizes the mutual assistance and emotional support of family members above all else. Family members are thus less sensitive to the needs and exigencies of improving or maintaining community position than they are to the intra- and interpersonal needs for the well-being of one another.[12] Families organized in terms of the welfare strategy will be neolocal in their choice of residence—but this is likely to be neolocality that is more nominal than functional. When the welfare strategy is considered in conjunction with the already noted predisposition for many urbanites to maintain extended family relationships, and when we also consider the fact that modern technology makes intimate interpersonal communication instantaneously possible—even when those with whom we are interacting are not physically present—then we must conclude that nominal neolocality can, in our urban society, be functionally similar to either patrilocality or matrilocality. In the absence of electronic augmentation of accessibility, patrilocal (or matrilocal) residence insures a *unitary family location* that provides the basis for sustaining mutual assistance and support. Under modern conditions of communication the same kindred mutuality can be accomplished without a unitary family location. Thus for those who pursue the welfare strategy in their family behaviors the functional mutuality of the kindred can be effected without resort to either patrilocation or matrilocation.

In such instances, neolocality as a rule of residence is not accompanied by the functional implication of isolated nuclear families. Where the welfare strategy is being pursued, neolocality would not seem to imply a social meaning recognizably distinct from that which is associated with patrilocal or matrilocal patterns of residence. Nominal or apparent neolocality in the urban context may simply be masking the specific functional implications of patrilocality or matrilocality. Where the welfare strategy is in effect, some nuclear families are oriented in their mutual assistance and support activities to a kin network primarily consisting of the father's relatives (the equivalent of patrilocality), while others are oriented toward a network primarily consisting of the mother's relatives (the matrilocal equivalent). In actuality—given the bilateral nature of the American kinship system, most families whose activities occur primarily in terms of the norms of the welfare strategy can be located on a continuum the polar points of which are exclusive orientation toward paternal as opposed to maternal relatives on one end, and exclusive orientation to maternal as

12 Well-being and community position concerns are not necessarily mutually exclusive. They are, however, popularly construed as such. One often hears, "I'd rather my husband be healthy and happy than have him ruin his health working to make us rich."

For a discussion of the welfare strategy, see Farber, pp. 266–269, cited in footnote 11.

opposed to paternal relatives at the other. Given bilaterality in the kinship system, relatively few families are likely to be located at either extreme. Most will fall somewhere in between being *primarily,* rather than exclusively, oriented to kindred on one side of the nuclear family as opposed to the other, although the likelihood seems to be greater for any given nuclear family to be more oriented to the maternal relatives than to the paternal relatives in their kin network.[13]

There is a third organizational strategy that Farber brings to our attention: the *conservative strategy.* When the conservative strategy is being pursued, family members essentially commit themselves to the maintenance of a specific family tradition—a heritage, an estate both material and symbolic—or the lineage (kin group) from which the nuclear family derives its kinship identity. Because kinship identity and maintenance of lineage are of limited social importance in urban America—those families that organize their affairs in terms of the conservative strategy constitute a small minority of the total population of families. Nevertheless, there are segments of the urban population among which it would seem that the conservative strategy is frequently undertaken and is functionally significant. Among the Protestant upper class, it appears to be operative as well as among those urban ethnics who, against great odds, struggle to keep their present and their future in touch with their past. It seems fair to say that the conservative strategy in family organization is operative among those groups that, for one reason or another, view the family as intimately bound to a cultural tradition or status advantage that is threatened by the events and trends inherent in the character of modern urban society.

Although most families pursuing the conservative strategy are neolocal in that the nuclear units maintain physically independent residences, it is also true that such a residence pattern does not imply the isolation of the nuclear unit. The essence of the conservative strategy is a commitment to family tradition or estate that to some extent supersedes needs and desires the locus of which is the nuclear unit. Again, as in the case of those families committed to the welfare strategy, the technology of modern communications makes possible the necessary access to kin without actual patrilocal or matrilocal residence. Thus the functional quality of neolocal residence, that is, the isolation and freedom of the nuclear family, is once again absent in spite of super-

13 See Paul J. Reiss, "The Extended Kinship Systems in the American Middle Class," Dissertation, Harvard University, 1960. Also see Sheldon Stryker, "The Adjustment of Married Offspring to their Parents," *American Sociological Review, XX* (1955), 149–154.

ficial appearances to the contrary. Because of the relative unimportance of the conservative strategy in urban America, these comments will suffice for our purposes without further elaboration.[14]

In summary the following should be noted with regard to the neolocality of urban American families: relative to other family kinship systems the American urban system evidences as characteristic a pattern of neolocal residence. However, the social meaning of this widespread neolocality is not, as is typically assumed, overall functional isolation of the nuclear family from extended kindred. In many instances, where the *efficiency strategy* of family organization is in effect, neolocality can be equated with functional isolation. In others, notably where the *welfare* or *conservative* strategies are in effect, the sophistication of modern communications technology undermines the impact of physical separation thus enabling the nuclear family to maintain functional relationships with its kindred in accordance with the norms or requirements of either of these two strategies.

Relative to other societies, particularly those which are nonindustrial and/or agrarian, the urban American system of descent recognition and kinship is unquestionably *bilateral*. The traditional Japanese, for example, traced their descent unilineally in the patriline (in terms of the father's side of the family). Not only did this practice establish the individual's kinship identity but also his legal rights to property and other material inheritance. Typically, it is true that urban Americans consider themselves equally descended in both the patriline (father's side) and the matriline (mother's side). Moreover, this customary recognition of descent in the matriline and the patriline is codified and has legal standing in the courts. As such there are no distinctions in law with regard to the "side of the family" when it comes to pressing a claim for material inheritance based upon kin relatedness.

These facts notwithstanding, there is nevertheless *variation* in the meaning of bilaterality in urban kinship. There is evidence that indicates a tendency for nuclear families to be more oriented to the mother's side (matriline), as opposed to the father's side (patriline), in the establishment of a kin network. Typically, it appears that this can be accounted for by the fact that women are more likely than men to concern themselves with maintaining the kinship ties of the nuclear family, and that in doing this they are likely to be more sensitive to the maternal side of the kindred than the paternal side.[15]

14 For Farber's discussion of the conservative strategy see Farber, pp. 271–275, cited in footnote 11.

15 Farber, p. 154, cited in footnote 11.

Aside from this apparently overall (if covert) tendency toward matricentered—if not matrilineal—kinship there are kinship characteristics associated with certain urban groups that do not conform to the norms of bilaterality. Among lower class blacks, for example, the high proportion of broken families and illegitimacy intensifies the matricenteredness of many kin networks. In many cases there is no formal recognition of paternity, while in many others the recognition of paternity on the part of the father does not link the mother and the child to his kindred in any functionally meaningful manner.[16] Among groups maintaining ethnic identities we find patterns that deviate from the expectations of bilaterality. For example, traditional Jews, who rarely, if ever, live outside urban areas, display a mixed tendency toward kin emphases. On one hand, there appears to be a marked predisposition to emphasize affective sentiments and relationships with maternally related kin. On the other hand, instrumental, primarily economic ties seem to be located within patricentered kin networks.[17] In any case, bilaterality cannot be understood as describing the behavioral qualities that are characteristic of kin relations among members of this urban group.

In sum, bilaterality is real enough in American urban settings but within the general bilateral tendency found in American cities there are likely to be kin emphases that diverge, particularly in the direction of matricenteredness.

THE FAMILY AS A PRIMARY GROUP There is, undoubtedly, some variation in the extent to which individuals are able to personalize their relationships within the context of the nuclear family. The ideal of personal investment in the family, to be sure, is often an elusive goal and judging from the high divorce, desertion, and annulment rate in our urban society—about 20–25 percent of first marriages end in divorce, desertion, or annulment—and the oft-noted generational estrangement (or "GAP"), there are many for whom the ideal is probably never approximated in reality. Unfortunately, no systematic accounting of the variations in primary group realization exists in the sociological literature on the American (and therefore urban) family. Thus we are unable to specify with any certainty what pattern of variation exists—if, indeed, a pattern does exist. There are some hints

16 Daniel Patrick Moynihan, "Employment Income and the Ordeal of the Negro Family," *Daedalus, XCIV* (Fall 1965), 745–770.

17 See Candace L. Rogers and Hope J. Leichter, "Laterality and Conflict in Kinship Ties," *Readings on the Family and Society,* ed. William J. Goode, Prentice-Hall, Inc., Englewood Cliffs, N.J., 1964, pp. 213–218.

in the literature that are worth noting, but aside from these there are no good indicators of how the urban family system may be characterized with regard to personalization or primary-group realization: it is really terra incognita.

We *do* have evidence that indicates that among lower class groups sexual segregation seems to be the rule. Among such people the most intense or personalized interaction appears to occur in the same-sex groups, both within the family and in the larger community. On a sustained basis women are more likely to have their closest relationships with other women, while men are then likely to have their closest relationships with other men.[18] We may reasonably extrapolate from such a finding a conclusion (however tentative) that holds that as far as cross-sex relationships (particularly between husbands and wives) within the lower class nuclear family are concerned, the ideal of primary personalization falls far short of realization. Other evidence seems to indicate that marital satisfaction is more probable in higher as opposed to lower status groups.[19] Higher status families tend to evidence a greater degree of husband-wife companionship. And since companionship can be taken as an indicator of interpersonal intimacy and satisfaction with one's mate, we can conclude that in so far as the conjugal relationship is concerned higher status families are more likely to approximate the ideal of primary group personalization than are lower status families.

Moreover, it may be argued that the key to the character of interaction within the nuclear family as a whole is the quality of relationship obtaining between husband and wife. If the husband-wife relationship is characterized by warmth and interpersonal commitment, so too will be the relationships between this couple as parents and their children. If, to the contrary, the husband-wife relationship is bereft of these qualities the parent-child relationships will probably

18 See for example David L. Harvey, "An Ethnography of a White Working Class Community," *Community, Kinship and Competence,* Bernard Farber, David Harvey and Michael Lewis, Research and Development Program on Pre-School Disadvantaged Children, III (May 1969), Department of Health, Education, and Welfare, Washington, D.C., pp. 68–77.

19 See for example Robert O. Blood Jr., "Impact of Urbanization on American Family Structure and Functioning," *Sociology and Social Research, XLIX* (1964), 5–16; William J. Goode, "Family Disorganization," *Contemporary Social Problems,* eds. Robert K. Merton and Robert Nisbet, Harcourt, Brace and World, Inc., New York, 1961, pp. 390–458. For a graphic account of personalization problems in the lower class black family, see Elliot Liebow, *Tally's Corner,* Little Brown and Co., New York, 1967, pp. 103–136, particularly.

be somewhat troubled.[20] Assuming the validity of such an argument, we may suggest that since higher status families have been found to be characterized by greater interpersonal satisfaction between husband and wife (as compared to lower status families), it is also probably true that in such families there tends to be greater intimacy and personalization between parents and children. Thus we can conclude (again tentatively) that higher status families overall are more likely to approximate the ideal of primary group personalization and commitment than are lower status families.

By definition, family instability means the absence of primary-group personalization. When the conjugal relationship is broken by divorce, separation, or desertion, there is an end to whatever interpersonal intimacy existed between husband and wife. Furthermore since divorce, separation, or desertion do not happen, as it were, on the spur of the moment, their occurrence signifies a troubled relationship between spouses over some period of time. Again on the assumption that a troubled conjugal relationship is a good predictor of generalized interpersonal difficulty within the nuclear family, the occurrence of divorce, separation, or desertion can be taken to mean that primary group personalization within the nuclear family as a whole probably had not been realized for some time. Divorce rates, separation rates, and desertion rates are all higher in the lower socioeconomic strata (as opposed to the more advantaged strata) and thus we may conclude that marital instability is more characteristic of lower status groups than of higher status groups. To the extent that marital instability is an indicator of the failure to realize primary-group personalization within the nuclear family, these rates suggest that lower socioeconomic groups are less likely to be characterized by primary group personalization within their nuclear families than are groups whose social location is more fortunate.[21]

20 Psychiatrists and psychologists have repeatedly made this kind of observation based upon clinical experience. Of course, this represents a conclusion based on a biased sample. It is quite possible that they do not see patients in whose families this pattern does not pertain.

21 Our conclusion here must be quite tentative because troubled interpersonal relationships do not always eventuate in the abrogation of the conjugal bond. It is quite conceivable that upper strata families do not realize primary group personalization even when a formal break of the conjugal bond does not occur. Thus divorce rates, for example, may underrepresent the extent to which there is failure to realize primary group personalization in upper strata families. If this is so then the apparent variation between upper and lower socioeconomic groups may be spurious. However, since we do have other evidence which suggests greater realization of primary

It is important to reiterate that the above conclusions are highly tentative, and that they are based upon extrapolations from very limited research. If, however, the pattern we have begun to ascertain —that is, that primary group personalization within the nuclear family is more likely to be realized among the higher as opposed to the lower socioeconomic strata—can be substantiated by systematic inquiry, such a finding would be of some significance. Let us *assume* that the pattern does exist, and with this assumption in mind let us reflect upon its implications for our understanding of urban communities in the contemporary United States.

Primary group personalization is a very potent social force when it occurs. The intense investment of the self in a relationship or in a number of relationships means that the other people in these relationships become the most significant "others" for the individual. These are the people whose esteem he most cherishes and whose well-being he is most committed to maintaining. On a sustained basis, no other people are as likely to affect his behavior. His actions are invariably taken with their needs and desires in mind. More than anything else, he strives to make his behavior palatable to them.

Beyond the significant other function, primary group personalization also creates a "safe harbor" for the individual who has been able to effect relationships thus characterized. Life in modern society is hectic and competitive. Most of the relationships we engage in involve but little of our selves. Our contacts with others are all too purposeful. We interact with students to teach them a subject matter. They interact with us to learn (we hope) or to receive a grade. We smile and exchange pleasantries with the sales clerk at the supermarket but our friendliness is superficial, an accommodation to the real theme of our interaction—the necessary exchange of money for goods. We work with another person not for who he is, not for himself but because he is necessary to some purpose quite extrinsic to his person. His collaboration with us is similarly motivated. And with nothing but minimal regard for their well-being we engage others in a competition so that we may gain some social or economic advantage. Day in and day out we are thus involved in contacts that are segmented, extrinsic to ourselves, and sometimes threatening to our interests. We express

personalization in the upper strata—that is, greater marital satisfaction, a greater companionship component, and the fact of characteristic sexual segregation among lower status groups, it is probable that the variations in the rates of formal abrogation does accurately signify a corresponding variation in the extent to which primary group personalization is realized.

ourselves very little in these relationships and we recognize that others behave to us in a similar manner, caring not at all about who we are or about what will likely become of us.

Only in those special relationships, our primary relationships—that are relatively few in number and in large measure family based—do we really express ourselves beyond the most superficial levels, only in such relationships does the self count for much. As such, they constitute the safe harbor, the place where we can "be ourselves," where who we are "comes out," and where interpersonal reserve and defensiveness so necessary in so much of our day-to-day interaction has no place.

The nuclear family, of course, is not the only primary group affiliation we are likely to experience in society. There are peer group relationships that involve intense personalization and friendships that take on this quality. But in our modern, mobile, urban society the nuclear family still provides the best opportunity for effecting primary group personalization on a sustained basis. Peer groups tend to split up in time and intense friendships, although maintained through correspondence, are subject to the vicissitudes of geography and social mobility. The nuclear family based upon cohabitation and blood ties is thus most likely to provide the most stable setting for personalization.

If primary group personalization provides the individual with his most basic set of significant "others" and the safe harbor in which he may "let it all hang out," and if the nuclear family is the most significant setting in which primary group personalization occurs, then assuming that such personalization is differently distributed within nuclear families at different socioeconomic levels, the two functions of personalization are also differentially distributed at these levels. If the probabilities for primary group personalization within the nuclear family are greater at the higher socioeconomic levels than they are at the lower levels, the probabilities of an individual being involved in a network of intensely significant others (on a sustained basis) and having a safe harbor for his expression of self will also be greater at the higher levels as compared to the lower ones. To the extent that this is so the following is also true.

> Individuals in lower socioeconomic groups tend to arrive at decisions about their behavior with minimal regard for their effects upon a network of familial intimates. They are likely to be relatively insensitive to claims and restraints emanating from such a network because they do not, in fact, regard the "others" in the network as particularly significant. Overall, they tend to

weigh courses of action in personal terms. If a particular behavior is perceived as serving their interests, it will be embarked upon irrespective of its possible impact upon others.

Individuals in higher socioeconomic groups tend to be sensitive to the restraints and claims placed upon their behaviors by familial intimates. Personal interest is likely to be defined in terms of the needs and claims of the significant others in the individual's nuclear family and, therefore, decisions about any particular course of action are likely to be made with full consideration being given to the impact of the prospective behavior upon these significant others.

The major conclusion to be drawn from what has just been noted is that lower stratum individuals are less subject to interpersonal social control as compared to higher stratum individuals. And if such a conclusion is warranted it has significance, as in this kind of situation. While it may be that *as a rule* men work to provide for their families, to give them the things that they need or want, to make life "better" or "easier" for them, the fact that there are differentials in the extent to which men are sensitive to the needs and claims of their dependents implies that there will be corresponding differentials in the degree to which they are motivated to provide for them. The work motivation of lower stratum men is likely to be less subject to primary group claims than will the corresponding motivation of more advantaged men. The lower-class man may decide to quit a job because he does not like it, without too much concern about the impact of his decision upon his dependents.[22] An upper-middle-class man, on the other hand, will probably weigh carefully the implications of such a course for his family before he decides to go ahead. He is more likely than his lower class contemporary to remain in a personally unsatisfactory job if only because his concern about depriving his dependents (who are his most significant "others") of the sustenance to which they have become accustomed is probably greater.

Differentials in the intensity of interpersonal social control are likely to be manifest in other ways as well. When it comes to possible confrontation with public authority—whether we mean participating in

22 Obviously primary group personalization is not the only factor which affects the character of work motivation. For lower status men the kind of work available may in fact be quite discouraging. Nevertheless the absence of personalization does influence people to respond to their work situations in terms of their individual predispositions. For an excellent analysis of the work motivation of lower-class black men, see Liebow, pp. 29–71, cited in footnote 19.

political movements that are beyond the pale of conventional acceptability or engaging in behaviors that are deviant and perhaps illegal if judged by conventional standards, interpersonal social control will more likely be manifest for upper-stratum individuals as compared to lower stratum individuals. On the day he leaves for college, the upper-middle-class mother tells her son to avoid trouble (meaning do not "get busted" for smoking pot or for "trashing" the R.O.T.C. building), for it would break her heart and ruin his father's health. He may in fact "light up a joint" or even smash some windows but before he does so he is likely to think about mom and dad and their wishes for him. If he should confront public authority, he must first work through the affective controls that his personalized relationship with his parents has imposed.[23] Often enough he is unable to disregard the claims or strictures of familial significant others and so—no matter how tempting the unconventional behavior—he demurs from participation. The lower-class mother tells her son to stop being truant from school and to stop hanging around the local candy store where the numbers runners congregate because he ought to make something of himself and should he get into trouble . . . well, doesn't she have enough trouble as it is? He hears her but he continues to be truant and to hang around the wicked candy store. Because of lack of primary group personalization within his family, his mother's claims simply do not register with enough intensity to control his behavior.[24]

It is not that upper-middle-class young men and women never stray from the conventional, and never disregard parental wishes, nor is it that lower class children always disregard their parent's desires. It is clear that in BOTH cases children both respect and ignore parental claims upon them. But if we accept as valid that personalization within the nuclear family is more characteristic of the higher as opposed to the lower strata, then we must conclude that the frequency of such disregard is higher among the lower class than among the upper middle class because the differentials in primary group personalization make it easier for lower class children, as compared in this case to upper-middle-class children, to go their own way.

Other examples may be cited to support this point. The lawyer who

23 For indirect evidence of this see Kenneth Keniston, *Young Radicals,* Harcourt, Brace and World, New York, 1968, pp. 60–70. Keniston notes that the young middle class radicals he studied at the very least did not have to overcome strong parental disapproval of their actions. If such disapproval did exist it is likely that the path toward radicalism would have been much more difficult to traverse.

24 For example, see Lee Rainwater, "Crucible of Identity: The Negro Lower Class Family," *Daedalus, XCV* (Winter 1966), 172–216, 196 in particular.

sees the justice in an unpopular cause within his community refrains from lending his skills to its adherents because his wife and children implore him not to subject them to the displeasure of their friends and neighbors. He would do it, he maintains, if it was his decision alone, but it is not; he just cannot ignore the wishes of his family. The young black woman wants to join a militant protest group. Her parents implore her not to do it. They speak of the dangers that threaten the militants and remind her that most people in their community really do not support them. They would rather have her go to college and learn to fight racial injustice from within the system. She joins the militants, however, because she feels it is her decision and that it is her struggle, and family wishes will just have to be sacrificed to the cause. Some lawyers do indeed defend unpopular causes in spite of family pressures and some blacks refrain from joining militant groups because of family pressures. Nevertheless, if we accept the differentials in personalization within the nuclear family at different strata, it is probable that these differentials mean that individuals will be more or less controlled by family claims according to where they are located in the social structure.

It is, of course, very easy to fall into the trap of identifying the social control emanating from the more intensive primary group personalization in the families of the higher socioeconomic strata as positive while bemoaning its relative absence stemming from less intensive personalization in the nuclear families of the lower strata. In our "pop" or "people's" sociology of the family, we see many of the social troubles afflicting us as the products of family breakdown, and such breakdown translates easily into the absence of intensive personalization. In point of fact, however, the social control emanating from intensive personalization within the nuclear family can be either *positive* or *negative* depending upon the issue in question. If such control prevents men and women from acting on their beliefs, from being true to their principles, is it positive or negative? Your response, negative or positive, may depend upon your support or rejection of the principle at issue. If you support the principle, the familial-based social control preventing others from taking action in its behalf is certainly negative. If you oppose the principle, the fact that individuals are subject to such inhibiting controls is positive.

Personally, I am grateful for the intense personalization that prevents potential neo-Nazis from acting on their beliefs, while I bemoan the fact that such personalization within the family prevents many people from actively supporting more aggressive equal opportunity programs. When our concern is the far right, the more family-based control the better; when we discuss many of the principles (but not all) of the left, such control seems to me to represent the curse of privatization wherein injustice is ignored for the sake of one's intimates. When the absence of such controls contributes to the self-destructiveness of narcotics addiction, it can only be the source of grief and concern. When, however, it frees the dispossessed to take up the arduous struggle for social justice it may be a blessing. The point is that the presence or absence of social control resulting from intensive primary group personalization within the nuclear family is a morally or normatively neutral phenomenon except as we define it good or bad in terms of our own values.

A second implication of the differential distribution of primary group personalization within the nuclear family is as follows.

> For people in the lower socioeconomic strata, it is probable that there are fewer "natural" mental hygiene resources as compared to those available to people in the higher socioeconomic strata. If primary group personalization within the nuclear family is significantly less frequent among the lower strata, then people so located are less likely than their more advantaged contemporaries to have access to supportive social settings in which they can give full expression to their feelings and draw sustenance for the development of a positive sense of self.[25]

The major extrapolation drawn from the circumstance just described would be that lower-stratum individuals as compared to higher stratum individuals are more likely to be less in touch with themselves or, put another way, they are less likely to have a positive sense of self. A couple of examples may help to give concrete meaning to this generalization. Juan, a 17-year-old high school dropout, works as a delivery boy in New York's garment center. He has worked very hard in the year that he has been on the job in the hope of being promoted to shipping clerk. His hard work has been to no avail, for someone else has received the promotion and the raise in pay he had hoped for. He comes home from work and tells his family of his disappointment—but no one really seems to understand his feelings. No one in his family really recognizes his disappointment and his frustration and

25 For accounts that indicate that this is so among lower stratum families, see Liebow, cited in footnote 19, chapters 4 and 5; also see Michael Lewis, "Problems of Competence Development Among Ghetto Residents in a Middle Size City," in Farber, Harvey and Lewis, cited in footnote 18, pp. 195–202. For an account focusing upon "middle class" families, see Kenneth Keniston, *The Uncommitted,* Dell Publishing Co., New York, 1965, pp. 277–281.

anger at having been passed over. No one reads his need for sympathy or for encouragement toward a renewed sense of his personal importance. He is left harboring a negative sense of self.

On the other hand, Bruce, a 17-year-old high school senior has just received some bad news: he was not accepted at the college of his choice. Everyone in his family rallies around. His older sister, who attends the state university, tells him that State (where he will be going) is just the place for him anyway. It has a great program in bio-medical engineering and since that is what he has planned as his major, she has no doubts that he will thrive there. His father says that an alumnus of the school, from which the rejection was received, informed him that the school just decided not to take many kids from "this region" as they preferred a better geographic distribution. This father is telling his son that he did not fail, that he was not rejected as a person, that the policy of the school was to blame and not any characteristic weakness on the boy's part. Bruce's mother reminds him that he made the honor roll for three of his four years in high school, that he was the junior class president and a letter man in track. No—he is not at fault for being rejected. Bruce is still disappointed, but his sense of self is not damaged. His family has labored successfully to make him feel that in spite of the rejection he has suffered he is still first rate, and that in their eyes he is still esteemed because the rejection really had nothing to do with him as a person.

Surely there are instances in lower class families when interpersonal support is forthcoming. And just as surely there are instances in higher class families when it is absent. However, if the nuclear family is the major source of support and affective sustenance, and if the ability to generate this support is likely to be greater among higher as opposed to lower-stratum families, then in all probability lower-stratum individuals will suffer more grievously, and will have more frequently damaged sense of selves as the result of the turn of events characteristic of everyday life.

All this may be interesting enough from the perspective of the sociology of the family—but what has it to do with understanding urban America? Assuming that the differential in primary group personalization and its consequences exists, how shall this inform our understanding of life in the cities? Again we can only speculate.

Urban communities in American society vary in what may be termed the *demography of stratification*. The large central cities (for example, New York, Philadelphia, Chicago, Detroit, Pittsburgh, Los Angeles, Boston, and Newark) increasingly house a disproportionate number of the nation's poor and socially dispossessed. The suburbs, on the other hand, increasingly harbor those among us who are more advantaged—the vast range of middle Americans. To the extent that such variations in the demography of stratification exist, different communities will also vary in the probable extent to which primary group personalization in the nuclear family will occur within them. The community housing a disproportionate number of the poor and the socially dispossessed will also be disproportionately characterized by families within which there is relatively little primary group personalization. The community that is largely constituted of the more advantaged (relatively speaking) will also be disproportionately characterized by families within which there is more intensive primary group personalization.

If we assume that the presence or absence of such personalization has important consequences,—that is, variations in the extent to which work motivation is family based, to which family based social control and consequent normative conventionality exist, and to which individuals receive emotional support in their daily confrontations with the world beyond the family—then communities that house a disproportionate number of people on or near the bottom of the stratification hierarchy will have a greater potential for individual as opposed to family based work motivation within their populations. They will have a greater potential than would otherwise be the case for overt confrontations with normatively conventional authority, and they will have a greater potential than would otherwise be the case for personal alienation and emotional difficulty within the populace. Alternatively, a community that disproportionately consists of those who are more advantaged within the stratification hierarchy will have a greater potential than would otherwise be the case for family based work motivation within its population, for overt conformity with the local conventional wisdom, and for personal integration and emotional well-being within the populace.

Surely we would *not* want to lapse into *a family determinism* where it is argued that the character of the community is a function or the "lengthy shadow" of family life. We know that urban communities are much too complex for such a monistic explanation of their character. Nevertheless, assuming the consequences of the presence or absence of primary-group personalization within the family, and recognizing that because of differentials in the demography of stratification from one community to the next, these communities are likely to vary in the extent to which such personalization and its consequences are present or absent, it is probably accurate to say that some very important qualities of community life can be understood, at least in part, in terms of the character of interaction within the nuclear family. Communities with a relatively high degree of individual work motivation (low primary-group personalization within the nuclear family) are probably characterized by a higher degree of job turnover and work force instability than are communities in which there is a relatively high degree of family based work motivation (high primary group personalization within the nuclear family). Communities with relatively high degree of overt rejection of normative conventionality (low personalization—less intense affective control) are, it would seem, more prone to public conflict and problems such as delinquency and crime than are communities with a relatively low degree of overt rejection of conventional wisdom (high personalization—more intense affective control). Communities characterized by a relatively high incidence of personal alienation and emotional difficulty among their populations (low personalization and familial emotional support) are likely to be more prone to public tension, volatility, and threat producing situations than are communities characterized by a relatively low incidence of personal alienation and emotional difficulty among their populations (high personalization and familial emotional support).[26]

What emerges from these observations is a differential profile. Communities in which the demography of stratification is skewed toward the lower strata are likely to have a more-or-less pronounced potential for work force instability, public conflict, overt flouting of conventional authority, tension, and a persistent sense of personal threat. Communities in which the demography of stratification is skewed toward the more advantaged strata are likely to have a more-or-less pronounced potential for work force stability, general public peace, overt conventionality, and a persistent sense of personal well-being. In the first instance the characteristics described are the implications of a predicted overrepresentation of primary-group personalization within the nuclear family, in the second the characteristics are the implications of a predicted underrepresentation of such personalization.

Two points of caution must be noted before we leave the matter of primary group personalization within the nuclear family. First, all that has been said here stands on the assumption that differentials in such personalization actually do exist. The reader should not lose sight of

26 Public tension, volatility, and threat producing situations increase the salience of the public conflicts and social problems that are a product of overt rejection of normative conventionality.

the fact that such an assumption may *not* be warranted, standing as it does on very incomplete empirical findings. Second, since urban communities are highly complex social entities, characteristics other than the extent of primary group personalization within the nuclear family are likely to have an effect on the presence or absence of such phenomena as work force instability, community conflict, public tension and sense of personal threat. Certainly one would be foolish to analyze work force instability without reference to the character of the local economy. The character of the local polity must likewise be taken into account when we are considering community conflict and tension, as must also be the extent of social and demographic heterogeneity within the community. If the assumption of differential nuclear family personalization is valid, it must be understood as describing a characteristic that *contributes to but is not the sole cause of* the phenomena we have concerned ourselves with in this section. If it is valid it would be a mistake to ignore its implications—but it would also be a mistake to give undue weight to its causal impact.

NURTURANCE AND SOCIALIZATION WITHIN THE NUCLEAR FAMILY

Both nurturance and socialization are familial processes that contribute to individual growth and maturation. When we speak of *nurturance* we are referring to those activities that provide material sustenance—including food, clothing, shelter and medical care—necessary for the physical development of the individual from his earliest moments of life through adulthood when he is presumably capable of providing for himself. When we speak of *socialization* we are referring to those actions and experiences that culminate in the individual's ability to participate as an adult in the society of which he is a member and in which he must work out his personal destiny. The two processes can be considered independently of one another, but since they both are related to individual growth and maturation it makes sense to consider them jointly at this juncture. Moreover, it may be argued that a modicum of nurturance is a precondition for successful socialization. If an individual's physical needs for sustenance are inadequately met, then it is unlikely that he will be able to learn and develop the competence necessary for independent participation in society. If his energy is sapped by poor diet and consequent infirm health, he will be little able to learn and internalize the things he must if he is to come to full social maturity.

Before beginning our explorations of the way nurturance and socialization are varied in different family contexts within urban communities, some comments about the acquisition of skills and knowledge seem appropriate with regard to socialization as a process in modern urban society.

In order to function as an adult in modern urban society, an individual must have mastered a number of complex skills and developed an extensive pool of knowledge that he or she can draw upon in a wide variety of situations. No adult—no matter what his or her social location is—can function independently if he or she cannot read and write. So many transactions in modern life depend upon the written and not the spoken word that an illiterate individual is at a great disadvantage and virtually needs a guardian to look out for his interests. Without reading ability one cannot travel except with help, without reading few jobs are available, and without reading even grocery shopping can be a problem.

In order to function, one must also have mastered the basic rudiments of quantitative reasoning. An individual who has no concept of the relationship between quantity and cost, for example, is constantly in danger of being cheated, of paying too much, and of working too hard and too long for a fixed rate.

Beyond such cognitive skills as these an adult must be capable of a modicum of interpersonal competence. An independent adult must not only possess the ability to gauge the emotions and intentions of others in order to respond appropriately in routine situations but, given the rapidity with which new experiences and new situations impinge upon modern men and women, an independent adult must also be adaptive and possess the ability to assimilate new interpersonal cues.

Besides possessing these general skills the independent adult must have internalized the norms of the world of work. To remain generally independent, one has to remain economically independent. At the very minimum, one has to understand and subscribe to the expectations of the world of work to remain economically independent. Moreover, the more skilled the individual the more likely is he or she to be able to maximize economic advantage and consequently the potential for continued independence.

Finally, the more knowledge the individual possesses as to the complexities of the social worlds of urban life, the better able will that individual be to protect his interest and maximize his options for independent action: the person who receives a bill for something he never purchased but who does not know how to proceed in getting the creditor to correct the error is at an obvious disadvantage. Knowledge of certain facets of the law allows the individual to insure himself against others who might wish to take unfair advantage in the course of the many transactions to which he is a party. An informed individual is better able to choose among political alternatives and is less likely to be manipulated by those in power. The individual who knows how to go about accruing relatively objective information on the quality of goods and services he is about to purchase is less likely to purchase goods and services of an inferior quality.

In sum, then, in order to function with even a modicum of success as an adult in modern, urban society, the individual must learn a great deal about a variety of activities, conditions, and situations. Put another way, the individual must be *socialized* to cope with a variety of complex demands that are characteristic of life in urban society.

The wide range of skills and knowledge necessary for independent functioning makes it virtually impossible for the family in modern society to be the sole socializing agent for the developing child. Even when parents are themselves well-socialized and capable of operating with relative independence in society, they are not likely to possess all the teaching skills necessary to impart the competence they themselves possess to their children. (It is one thing to be literate yourself and quite another to teach your children to read and write.) Moreover, the length of time necessary for the preparation of youngsters for independent social maturity is so great—given the wide range of skills and knowledge to be learned—that few parents are able to make the required temporal investment in order to take full responsibility for the social development of their children. To do so would require parents to do little else, and for most this is an impossibility.

Thus when we speak of the nuclear family as having responsibility for the socialization of the young we do not mean that all socialization occurs within the context of the family. We do, however, mean the following.

> The nuclear family is the first socializing context in which the developing child finds himself. His first knowledge of, and orientation toward, the world beyond himself is therefore acquired as a result of his contacts with significant others within the nuclear family.
>
> The individual's first knowledge of and orientation toward the world beyond himself is likely to have a profound influence upon his ability to learn and develop in other socializing contexts (such as in the schools and neighborhood). When the individual goes into these contexts, he does not proceed *tabula rasa,* but rather interperts his experience in terms of what he has learned within the family context. The family is considered the key to his success or failure to learn in these other contexts. If the knowledge and

orientations he has accrued within the family context are consonant with the experiences in these other contexts, he will probably have little difficulty learning or internalizing the information, skills and cues imparted therein. If, however, the knowledge and orientations accrued within the family are not consonant with those in the other contexts he will have some difficulty in learning and internalizing that which is imparted in such contexts.

The nuclear family is primarily responsible for the development of sex-role styles and competence on the part of maturing children. Through the processes of interaction, observation, and identification with the same sex parent the child internalizes the role style and interpersonal competence appropriate to his or her gender. The female child becomes a woman largely in the image of her mother. The male child becomes a man largely in the image of his father. If the parental models of sex role performance are consonant with general normative expectations in the society at large, and if the child successfully identifies with the appropriate parent, he or she will develop a sex-role orientation which is socially unproblematic. If, on the contrary, the parental models are not consonant with general normative expectations, or if the child fails to identify with the appropriate parent even when the model is consonant, the child will probably develop a sex-role orientation that is socially problematic for its lack of agreement with conventional expectations.[27]

Let us now turn our attention to the matter of how the ideal expectations for nurturance and socialization are realized within families typically found in American urban communities. There is considerable *variation* in the extent to which urban families adequately nurture their young. There are, of course, those families of more than moderate means in which the matter of material sustenance requires little more than routine attention—just enough managerial concern, as it were—to insure an equitable and serviceable distribution of goods and services of which there is a surfeit. In the widest range of families—those that constitute the modal middle American group—sustenance usually requires more than minimal attention. While, as a rule, the family is able to command material resources sufficient to the needs of its members, and in particular to the needs of its dependent children, there are likely to be scarcities from time to time. The relationship of

27 For a systematic treatment of the family as a socializing context see Talcott Parsons and Robert F. Bales, *Family: Socialization and Interaction Process,* The Free Press, Glencoe, Ill., 1955, chapter 2.

such families to the economy is one in which relatively small-scale economic fluctuations are likely to affect their power to consume the goods and services necessary for the nurturing function. Whereas a recession is unlikely to have an impact on the nurturing function in families of more than moderate means, it is quite likely to have an impact in families who do not possess much in the way of monetary reserves.

For such a family, a recession or an economic slowdown may mean a change in diet since the family money available for purchase of foodstuffs may shrink, if only temporarily. For such a family, an economic slowdown may mean that there will be less money available for the purchase of new clothes. It may mean "doing without" goods and services that family members have come to expect as normal in their lives.

Because relatively minor economic fluctuations can have such an impact, maintaining the nurturing function at a consistently satisfactory level requires a kind of attentiveness and resourcefulness on the part of the adult members of the family that is largely unnecessary in families of greater means. It may mean that the mother has to learn how to shop carefully, always on the lookout for sales. It may mean that she has to practice those household arts of sewing and cooking with such skill that she can make old clothes look like new, and cheaper foods so palatable and healthful that no one objects to such fare. It may even mean that she must take a job in order to supplement the family income. Maintaining a satisfactory level of nurturance may mean that the father has to work at more than one job, and that he must perform household chores and repairs instead of hiring others to maintain his property. (Many a do-it-yourselfer has been born of economic necessity.)

In sum, mother and father in the nuclear family of moderate or average means must devote a significant amount of time and energy to the planning and execution of nurturing activities. Attention to nurturance is a significant aspect of the family life-style. But in spite of the difficulties arising out of economic slowdown that such families often confront, they are distinguished by the fact that the parents are indeed able to compensate and adapt in such a manner that, for the most part, the level of nurturance remains fairly stable and generally satisfactory. It would take a major economic disaster—a national depression, the closing of local business for example—to significantly disrupt nurturant activities within such families as these.

There are, finally, the families of the poor or the welfare poor in which nurturance is a perennial problem. The level of nurturance in such families is so low that it has serious negative implications for the physical and social development of the children who grow up within them. These are the families who are ill-housed in overcrowded slum apartments, in quarters that are poorly ventilated in the summer and inadequately heated in the winter, have long since become the habitats of rats and vermin, and in apartments that lack even minimally acceptable sanitary facilities. These are the families in which a balanced diet is a rarity, in which health care is consistently below standard, and in which the provision of adequate clothing is an exception to the rule.

The negative implications of the low level of nurturance for the development of children within these families can be illustrated as follows: nurturance problems for children in such families actually begin before they are born. A pregnant woman whose diet is lacking in proper nutrition cannot adequately nourish the fetus she is carrying. Inadequate nourishment of the fetus often hinders brain development and increases the probability that the baby will be born prematurely, a condition that imposes physiological trauma upon the child at the earliest moments of his life. A child born in such circumstances is likely to have physical problems that are in need of immediate remediation if he is to have a fair chance to develop normally. He is not, however, likely to have these problems attended to in the necessary measure because his family is unlikely to have easy access to medical services. Moreover, the same nutritional deficiencies that originally caused his prenatal problems are likely to further complicate his condition. Because his diet is nutritionally insufficient, the physical handicaps with which he was born are likely to be exacerbated, and he is likely to develop other difficulties as well. The net result of this chain of substandard nurturing is a child who is sickly, listless and dull in appearance, a child who gives the appearance of being unable to learn, a child who is likely to be labeled retarded and who therefore will most probably fail to mature to full physical and social competence.[28] Whatever his potential, it will be imprisoned in a body betrayed by the circumstance of birth and the inadequacy of the context in which it is sustained and in which it must develop. Among the urban poor there are many "might-have-beens" lost to themselves and all of us because of substandard levels of the process of nurturing.

To say that the nurturing levels are substandard or inadequate in the families of the poor is not to hold them responsible for this condi-

28 For a discussion of nutritional problems and medical problems among the nation's poor, see *Poverty Amid Plenty: The American Paradox.* The President's Commission on Income Maintenance Programs, Final Report (November 12, 1969), U.S. Government Printing Office.

tion. It is all too easy to forget (and many do forget) that, for the most part, the circumstances that result in inadequate nurturance within these families are not of their own making. The nurturing process is not likely to be a problem in families of more than moderate means because the economic well-being of their situation virtually assures that the needs of family members will be met irrespective of what anybody does. Nurturing is a focus of concern among families of moderate or average means because minor economic fluctuations affect accessibility to necessary goods and services. However, the economic situation of these families is such that a modicum of attention on the part of the adults can assure the maintenance of a satisfactory level of nurturance.

Nurturance is a persistent problem for the poor precisely because they are poor, because they exist in the midst of permanent economic disaster. No matter how adept a homemaker the poverty-stricken mother is, she is not likely to overcome all the obstacles to nurturing adequately. And since the competence of such women varies (as does the competence of more advantaged women), it is likely that only those families in which the women are extraordinarily competent even come close to approximating an adequate level of nurturance. Among the wealthy, nurturance is maintained almost universally, for the economically determined margin of allowable incompetence is so great that it is hardly a factor. Among those of average means the margin of allowable incompetence is narrower but not so narrow as to pose a real problem. Among the poor, there simply is no margin of allowable incompetence and it is extremely likely that even exceptional competence cannot insure an adequate and stable level of nurturance.

There is evidence that indicates that there is variation in the manner in which socialization occurs within differentially located nuclear families. However, most of this material focuses upon characteristics of parental child rearing (that is, what the parents do vis à vis their children) without systematic exploration of the socialization outcomes of these varying practices. It is often assumed that different parental practices will result in different types of development, but the assumption rarely receives an adequate empirical test. Moreover, the studies that have generated this evidence of variation have usually been executed in such a manner as to limit our confidence in the generality of their results. Therefore, care must be taken not to place too much faith in the existing evidence of differential socialization. The following should be read with this proviso in mind.

On the basis of some of these studies the following differences seem to pertain when the dimension of variation is social class or strata. In middle class families (the studies usually neglect upper-class families) parents seem to engage in early child-rearing practices that presumably result in the development of personal orderlines, conscientiousness, self control, the need to achieve, and a drive to be successful in conventional terms. Lower class parents, on the other hand, appear to engage in child-rearing behaviors that are less likely to produce such outcomes.[29] To the extent that such findings have general validity, it is probably true that middle-class children are more likely than lower-class children to be oriented to the cues, information, and skills proffered within other socializing contexts—and in particular within the context of the school. If the reported differential is accurate, children in middle-class families are more likely than their lower stratum counterparts to have familial experiences that are consonant with values and expectations that are dominant in the school setting. They are therefore more likely to be successful in school and, as a consequence, they are more likely to develop the kind of competence that is highly valued in the society at large.

As far as the development of appropriate sex-role orientations is concerned, very little is known about social-class variation. We do seem to know that among the lower strata, matricenteredness predominates within the nuclear family, most prominently in the matrifocal lower-class black family. Where father is functionally irrelevant to the family unit or where he is not present at all (both situations are characteristic of extreme matricenteredness or matrifocality), it may indeed be difficult for the boys in the family to develop conventional masculine styles, but the evidence on this is meager indeed.[30]

As the argument goes, father absence deprives the youngster of an

29 See the following: Allison Davis and Robert J. Havighurst, "Social Class and Color Differences in Child-Rearing," *American Sociological Review, II* (December 1946), 698-710; Melvin L. Kohn, "Social Class and Parental Values," *American Journal of Sociology, LXIV* (January 1959), 337–351; Melvin L. Kohn, "Social Class and the Exercise of Parental Authority," *American Sociological Review,* XXIV (June 1959), 352–366; Melvin L. Kohn and Eleanor E. Carroll, "Social Class and the Allocation of Parental Responsibilities," *Sociometry,* XXIII (December 1960), 372–392; Bernard C. Rosen, "Race, Ethnicity and the Achievement Syndrome," *American Sociological Review, XXIV* (February 1959), 47–60; Bernard C. Rosen, "Family Structure and Achievement Motivation," *American Sociological Review, XXVI* (August 1961), 574–585.

30 See for example Abram Kardiner and Lionel Ovesey, *The Mark of Oppression: A Psychosocial Study of the American Negro,* W. W. Norton and Co., New York, 1951, see also George R. Bach, "Father Fantasies and Father-Typing in Father-Separated Children," *Child Development, XVII* (May–June 1946), 68–80; Michael Lewis, "Competence and the American Racial Dichotomy: A Study in the Dynamics of Victimization," unpublished dissertation, Princeton University, 1967.

appropriate same-sex role model with which he can identify. When the father is present but is functionally irrelevant because he is unable to provide for his family, or because he does not engage in competent fathering, the youngster either identifies with a model of masculinity that deviates markedly from conventional expectations or he does not identify at all, in which case the situation is more or less equivalent to father absence. In any case, extreme matricenteredness or matrifocality is likely to impede the boy's development of conventionally appropriate masculinity. Since such a condition is more likely to prevail among the lower strata as compared to the middle and upper strata it is probably correct to argue that the development of conventional masculinity is more problematic at the lower socioeconomic levels. The development of conventionally appropriate femininity may also be affected by the differential incidence of extreme matricenteredness or matrifocality. But here again systematic evidence is meager. The functional default of the men in such families imposes undue burdens upon the women. Quite often they must support the family, reducing the time they have available for mothering. Or in a situation where the burdens and joys of parenthood go unshared the mother may find it too great a strain and take on the visage of the loveless domestic tyrant.[31]

In either case it may be difficult indeed for a young girl to develop a conventional orientation toward femininity. A woman who has little time for mothering plays a difficult role to identify with no matter what other conventionally feminine qualities she may possess. A "loveless tyrant" makes such identification highly problematic and therefore the mother does not function as an adequate same-sex role model for her daughter. If this default on the part of the mother is characteristic of extreme matricenteredness, and if extreme matricenteredness is more probable among the lower as opposed to the more advantaged strata, then we should conclude that the development of conventional femininity is more problematic for lower class girls than it is for girls in the middle and upper classes.

Finally, there is the problem of the nurturing basis for socialization. Earlier in this section we noted that the quality of nurturance can have an effect on the growing child's ability to learn. Inadequate nurturance creates a high potential for retarded physical and intellectual development. Since to nurture inadequately is most characteristic of lower-stratum families, it is safe to conclude that this factor differentially disadvantages lower-stratum children (it simply works against them)

31 See Lewis, cited in footnote 30; also see Kardiner and Ovesey, cited in footnote 30.

in the arduous process of becoming adult men and women in urban America.

In sum, it would appear that there is a dichotomy operating with regard to the familial role in the process of socialization. On one side there are those families of the more advantaged strata—roughly the middle or solid "blue collar" classes and above—in which physical and social development is *normally* problematic. In such families the potential for a favorable predisposition to conventional social expectations is relatively high. While there are obvious problems that both parents and children must confront in the socialization process, these problems are not as a rule so overwhelming as to seriously impede the development of the child according to such expectations. On the other side, there are those families of the clearly disadvantaged lower strata—the very poor blacks or whites, those who may be identified as belonging to the welfare class—in which physical and social development is *abnormally* problematic. In such families the potential for a favorable predisposition to conventional social expectations is relatively low and the problems confronted by both parents and children are so great that the socialization process is quite often unsuccessful—at least in a conventional sense.[32]

The implications of differential nurturance and socialization for the character of community life derive once again from the *demography of stratification.* If the large central cities house a disproportionate number of the poor and the socially dispossessed they will also be characterized by a disproportionate number of families in which nurturance and conventional socialization is a problem. Given the physical implications of nurturance problems, such communities will be faced with health problems among the very people who do not have easy access to adequate health care. Unless public means of providing better nurturance levels within these families are developed (the present welfare approach is inadequate), and unless such communities possess effective public health services (this is presently a problem even with such programs as Medicaid and Medicare), the physical and mental vitality of a significant population segment within these communities will be inadequate to the tasks of full economic and social participation. In conjunction with other differentially distributed

32 Other possible differentials vis à vis socialization have not been considered here. We might have examined the impact of ethnic differences on the familial role in child development. It is probable, however, that ethnicity is not a significant dimension with regard to socialization in American society, and therefore it would probably not be worthwhile examining the impact of such differences in great detail. See Will Herberg, *Protestant, Catholic and Jew,* revised ed., Anchor Books, New York, 1960, for a discussion in support of this position.

characteristics (such as primary group personalization), this may well account for such phenomena as high turnover rates on jobs and high vocational absenteeism.

In communities such as the large central cities, where conventional socialization is likely to be a problem because of the characteristics of families among the disadvantaged strata, the result, again in conjunction with the existence of other characteristics such as the relative absence of interpersonal social control, is likely to be a widespread manifestation of personal deviance. Moreover, the inability of a large number of families to contribute effectively to the process of conventional socialization implies that there will be a significant number of individuals who grow up unprepared to cope effectively with the exigencies and expectations of the conventional culture in that community.

The widespread manifestation of personal deviance and the inability to cope implies the necessity of public services that are not necessary in communities where such a situation does not exist (or in communities where the demography of stratification results in an underrepresentation of families in which conventional socialization is relatively unproblematic). Given the potency of conventional standards of behavior, widespread personal deviance generates a demand for police controls and ancillary services such as youth workers and social agencies. The widespread manifestation of an inability to cope with the exigencies and expectations of the conventional culture generates the need for social services intended to be supportive of those who are characterized by such incompetence. To the extent that these are public services they add to the tax burden within the community. Thus problems of socialization are not simply private problems of specific individuals in specific families. Because certain communities are likely to have an overrepresentation of families in which these problems exist they are also likely to be the repositories of an overrepresentation of problematic behavior (in conventional terms) and as a result they will devote a significant proportion of public monies to the control and alleviation of the implications of such behavior.

THE FAMILY IN URBAN AMERICA: A CONCLUSION

Our survey of the family in urban America has been hampered by the lack of definitive empirical investigation that is characteristic of this field of sociological work. Several patterns of actual variation around ideal expectations do, however, suggest themselves. To begin with, while the nuclear family is obviously the crucial organizational unit in the family system, it is not the only such unit. There is evidence that extended families do in fact function in urban areas. The neolocal rule of residence, while operative, does not necessarily imply the functional isolation of nuclear families from other elements of the kinship system. Depending upon the character of the organizational strategy of a given nuclear family, neolocality may or may not imply such isolation. Relative to other kinship systems the American urban system is bilateral in terms of descent. However, this fact does not rule out unilineal emphases as they develop among identifiable segments of the urban population. Primary group personalization appears to be manifested differentially with a higher probability of occurrence among relatively advantaged social strata. And finally, the effectiveness of nuclear families in meeting nurturance and conventional socialization needs also appears to vary—the nuclear family having a higher probability of effectiveness among the more advantaged strata.

Of these variant patterns, those relating to primary group personalization, nurturance, and conventional socialization seem to have important implications for the character of social life in discrete communities. In the large central cities where lower strata families are congregated the relative absence of primary group personalization, of effective nurturance, and of conventional socialization implies an increasing probability of such characteristics in the population as work-force instability, personal deviance, and the inability to cope effectively with the expectations and exigencies of the conventional public culture. In communities where lower strata families are underrepresented, such characteristics are less likely to be manifest.

Irrespective of the specifics of variation and their probable implications for the character of community life the most important lesson that our excursion into the sociology of the urban family can render is the fact that actors (individuals in community systems) are not free agents in their response to community conditions and the demands of the primary institutions, the polity, and the economy. The character of an individual's family life—of the private sphere of his existence—can have a very potent influence upon his actions. Viewed collectively, this means that the urban community cannot be properly analyzed or understood merely in terms of its pacesetting or primary institutions. If the effect of the family and its varied manifestations on community processes and conditions is now very incompletely understood, this is to be regretted. It would certainly seem that our understanding of American urban life can only suffer until the issues we have only begun to touch upon in this section are definitively researched.

Chapter 5
The Secondary Institutions: the Family and the Education System (No. 2 The Education System)

EXPECTATION AND OUTPUT IN URBAN SCHOOL SYSTEMS

Among laymen as among public school educators, there is widespread consensus with regard to some of the intended outputs of the educational system. This consensus can be described as a series of *three* normative themes that may be stated as follows.

1. The community's public schools have as their first and foremost objective the preparation of youngsters for future usefulness and responsibility as citizens.

2. In particular the public schools should provide youngsters with an opportunity to develop sufficient literacy and knowledgeability so that they will be able to be productive participants in the world of work.

3. The public schools should at once be both progressive and conservative. Because the economy makes increasing demands for technologically sophisticated personnel the schools should be progressive or "up-to-date" in curricula and teaching methods intended to prepare individuals for the changing character of vocational opportunity. At the same time, however, in areas of learning unrelated to technological change, the schools should strive to inculcate among students an appreciation for and a commitment to the values inherent in the conventional wisdom characteristic of the communities that they serve. Conversely, the schools should not nurture alienation from the existing values of the community and society. The rebelliousness of youth should be channeled into "constructive activities." In sum the schools

should reflect the community and the society in which they exist: progressive in their response to dynamic technology, and conservative in their defense of continuity between past, present, and future with regard to those values and norms that govern the social relations of men and women in almost all other spheres of behavior.

It matters very little whether you are black, white, rural, small urban or large urban in residence, these themes are typically, if not universally, those that claim one's affirmation. Beyond these, however, there are conceptions of educational output about which there is little or no consensus, conceptions that are endorsed by some and rejected by others, conceptions of educational functions that, because of their dissential qualities, become the foci of intracommunity conflict at one time or another. These may be enumerated and discussed as follows.

1. The schools should educate youngsters in the means by which they, when adults, will be able to make effective and productive use of their leisure time. This theme may be considered as one variant on the "whole man" conception of educational function. Among those who hold this view, education is not simply training for responsible citizenship and economic independence. It is instead a preparation for self-realization and awareness, preparation that will allow the individual to develop to the fullest his potential for self-expression and creative endeavor.

Those who champion education for leisure argue that the increasing technicalization of the economy will have as its concomitant shorter work weeks and earlier retirement. Correlatively, they argue, medical advances will continue to extend life expectancy. As a consequence, there will be an increase in uncommitted time and in leisure. Without preparation for the use of leisure, there will be an increment in boredom and dissolution. Life itself, instead of becoming easier and more rewarding, will become burdensome in direct relation to the possession of "free time." Thus, they argue, it is necessary for the schools to undertake the preparation of individuals in areas of self-expression that will allow them to fill their leisure hours with activities of personal value and enhancement. Generally, proponents of this position identify art, music, drama, and literature in particular as those areas of endeavor in which enriched school programs would be of lasting benefit.

2. The schools should undertake to sensitize students to psycho-

logical and social self-awareness. This theme is another variant of the "whole man" conception of educational function. Those who endorse such a view argue that human beings are not simply organisms dominated by a highly developed cerebral capacity for cognitive and intellectual function. They are highly complex personalities moved and motivated by frequently obscured desires and needs that have as their wellsprings the erotic, the thirst for power, and the wish for status and prestige. This being so, they argue, education is incomplete if it simply attends to the cognitive intellectual functions.

Insensitivity to the sources of the "human condition" as they reside in others as well as oneself can only render the individual incompetent to deal sympathetically and intelligently with his fellow men. The consequences of such incapacity are perceived as grave indeed. The individual must suffer unhappiness that in his ignorance of self and others he finds inexplicable. Moreover, the absence of sympathy and intelligence in human relations is perceived as the underlying cause for the manifold problems and distresses of contemporary society. Education that sensitizes individuals to themselves and their "condition" can thus contribute to the improvement of the individual's lot and to the society in which he must act out his destiny. Thus it is that the proponents of this position support and actively champion efforts to introduce and expand school curricula offerings in such areas as sex education and personal adjustment. Beyond this, they are the bulwark of support for increased personal counseling and other non-classroom mental health efforts within the context of the school.

3. The school should sponsor efforts to foster intergroup (particularly interracial) understanding and amity. Those who argue in behalf of this position perceive the school as an agency of attitude change in addition to its standard cognitive functions. Since contemporary American society, particularly its urban component, is faced with increased intergroup tensions and interracial estrangement, proponents of the attitude-change function support both curricula and organizational reforms that theoretically will improve intergroup "understanding" and thereby (again theoretically) intergroup amity. Such programs range from assemblies focusing upon the fallacies of prejudice to cross-bussing that, among other things, is intended to increase the contact between black and white students. Thus it is hoped, there will be created conditions of learning in which each group learns to appreciate the strengths and problems of the other.

4. The schools should exert special effort in order to compensate for the disadvantages visited upon children who have been victimized by poverty or racial stigma. Although this conception has generated its share of controversy, it is, in fact, an extension of one of the consensual themes noted above: that the schools should prepare children for responsible citizenship and in particular economic independence.

Proponents of this position argue that large numbers of children come to the schools with major handicaps to learning that are the results of conditions associated with poverty and discrimination. Unless special effort is made within the context of the school, the argument continues, those possessed of such handicaps will not have successful school careers. This lack of success indicated by excessive dropout rates and substandard achievement in reading and mathematical skills renders the unsuccessful incompetent to take advantage of any except the most menial and low paying of economic opportunities (and such opportunities are themselves shrinking). As a consequence they are unfairly relegated, as their parents were, to the bottom of society and the cycle of poverty and racial stigmatization is repeated. Thus, in the view of those advocating educational compensation, classes with new and special curricula must be offered and the best teachers need to be induced to instruct the disadvantaged so that those who so often have been society's victims will have the opportunity to develop the skills necessary for the mobility competition that characterizes urban America.

5. The schools should institute educational programs specially designed for physically handicapped, mentally retarded, and emotionally disturbed children. Those who take this position argue that if public education is to be truly universal in this society, provision must be made within the school system for those children whom fate has marked as different. Those endorsing this theme see the necessity for such things as modifying the environment of the schools for the physically infirm, providing teachers certified in Special Education for the mentally retarded and emotionally disturbed, as well as the adoption of professionally approved special curricula for mentally retarded and emotionally disturbed children.

The dissension that has so often enveloped these conceptions of educational functions is, in fact, a reflection of deep seated value conflict and interest collisions that are themselves among the major social facts of the American urban experience. To many urban dwellers whose personal incomes are limited and whose high taxes place an almost unconscionable strain upon what financial resources they do possess, education for leisure seems to be a costly, unnecessary, and even frivolous undertaking particularly when, as is often the case, these same individuals do not value highly the artistic sensibilities and literary sophistication that the advocates of such a program recommend as the appropriate foci for development. It is true, perhaps unfortunately so but true nevertheless, that consciousness of the problematic nature of leisure seems to escape the hardworking average man who is only too glad after a week of strenuous effort in pursuit of the elusive dollar (often all the more strenuous because of the tedious nature of the pursuit) to stretch out in front of the television set with a six pack of beer. A leisure time problem? From his perspective the only leisure time problem he has is not having enough leisure time. Even a 30-hour week can be exhausting when effort and reward do not seem justly correlated. Bach, Beethoven, Matisse, de Kooning, Kafka, Faulkner—he can do without them. He *has* done without them. There are popular heroes enough who, by means of the "miracle of television," routinely make their way into his very own living room—Unitas, Sayres, Mays, and West. If others want to spend their time in concert halls, museums, or theaters, let them. He will resist any attempt to raise more funds so that the schools that, after all, are public and should to some extent represent his feelings and interests, might develop programs for inculcating values and tastes that are unquestionably beyond his universe of experience.

To many people, sex-education courses and their associated counseling programs are anathema. Some see in their presence an invasion of privacy, a usurpation of parental prerogatives. Others have an even more basic complaint against such endeavors. In a period of increasing sexual visibility and apparent freedom, more conservative elements of the population, defenders of the sanctity of home and family, feel themselves surrounded by Philistines and pagans. From the conservative point of view, the slightest relaxation of vigilance might very well result in their being overrun and debauched by those whose intent is the destruction of all standards of sexual morality and by those who would turn their communities into brothels. The introduction of sex education (particularly secular sex education) in the schools represents to these people a major defeat for the forces of purity. Eternally vigilant, they struggle mightily against the introduction of anything that goes beyond the reproduction of frogs. They are joined in this struggle by those who see the entire mental health movement in our society as an alien strategy calculated to undermine morale and confidence in the American way of life. Those who possess (or are possessed by) such a world view resist any educational programs that they perceive as tactically important to the advancement of the "mental health conspiracy."

The conflict generated over intergroup amity programs in the schools is of course often simply an extension of primitive prejudice. There are many people who, feeling justified in their own pejorative views of others, see no rationale for or utility in such programs. Schools that spend the taxpayer's money for such foolishness are wasteful. To admit to a need for such programs in the schools is often to admit that one's antipathy toward others is prejudicial and therefore without justification. Since most Americans abhor the idea of prejudice even while they are themselves prejudiced, resistance to anything that might highlight personal inconsistency on this issue is likely to be forthcoming, if only as a defense of one's psychic integrity.

In some instances, resistance is based upon perceived self-interest that is not necessarily the result of hard-core prejudice. This surfaces around the question of cross-bussing children out of neighborhood schools in order to establish contact between black and white children. A frequent parental justification for resistance to such a program is as follows: "I bought a house in this neighborhood because the schools are really good here. They have a new well-lighted building and the teachers are first rate. Now they tell me that my kids are going to be bussed over into the ghetto where everybody knows the schools are not up to par. If those schools were satisfactory why would the parents over there want to get their kids out? I've paid a stiff price for a good school for my kids and I don't want that money to go down the drain. It is not black or white, I just want my kids in a good neighborhood school!" While it is true that such an argument may often mask prejudice, it is also true that bussing threatens the interests of those who perceive an educational loss to their children as a result of the program.

Compensatory education programs and those programs intended for the handicapped are less often the focus of community conflict among the debated conceptions of the functions of education. This is probably true because they do not tie into highly volatile issues within the community at large. To the extent that compensatory programs are lumped together with intergroup amity programs, they are no doubt resisted by those whose pejorative feeling about minorities is so strong that they cannot support what they perceive as unfair assistance to people they believe are unworthy of it. On the other hand, since compensatory programs do not characteristically involve the educational careers of their own children, those who resist the intergroup programs do not usually oppose them. In fact, parents often support them as an alternative to those intergroup programs that would involve the participation of their own children. What resistance there is to such efforts, together with resistance to Special Education programs, comes most frequently in the form of economic recalcitrance. To many people the presence of special programs within the schools means an unnecessary expenditure of public money.

These are the intended functions of the urban educational system, both consensual and dissential. The extent to which these intentions are matched by *actual* output is a matter of some conjecture and considerable discussion among both professional educators and laymen. The problem in all such attempts to draw conclusions about the character of actual educational function is the difficulty in finding easily measured empirical indicators of output about which there is some confidence of validity. It would take us too far afield from the purpose of this chapter to discuss this difficulty in detail. Nevertheless, it must be pointed out that any closure to the conjecture and debate with regard to the extent to which the schools of any communitty actually function in close approximation of the educational intentions that we have just discussed must itself await some agreement regarding adequacy of empirical indicators. In our own discussion of the actual approximation, we must therefore proceed with an awareness of the tentativeness of our conclusions.

Superficially, it would seem that, at least as far as the consensual functional intentions are concerned, urban school systems are almost universally successful in the extent to which these intentions are approximated in actual output. In spite of the dissidence and restiveness emanating from among the young—in spite of the protest and the growing contrariness of the youth culture—it is undeniably true that the schools turn out conventionally useful citizens whose training is adequate enough (and perhaps limited enough) to fit them into one or another of the vocational niches in the American economy. Even when we take into consideration those youngsters whom the schools seem to have failed—the ghetto dropouts and others who do not have enough staying power to become properly certified—it would be accurate to maintain that an overall accounting finds the schools meeting conventional expectations of educational function. Some community school systems are more "up-to-date" than others in providing a basis for technological mastery—but few if any urban systems are so lacking in this area that their graduates are forever debarred from some "responsible" participation in the contemporary urban economy. In smaller cities the degree of "up-to-dateness" seems to be a reflection of the socioeconomic character of the community in question. The more well-to-do the community and the higher the educational level of the citizenry, the more money is likely to be spent in the schools in the pursuit of what may be termed the best possible enabling training for future economic participation on the part of present day school children.[1] In the larger cities such as New York, Boston, Chicago, Philadelphia, for example, such a relationship is not so easily posited. In such urban places as these the relative adequacy of *"enabling training"* seems to be the result of specific educational history more than anything else. There are, for example, no apparent structural reasons in the present why New York City, its many educational problems notwithstanding, not only has a reasonably sound academic program in the secondary schools, but also has a series of specialized secondary school programs. These range from strictly vocational curricula such as those found at Printing Trades High School and Aviation Trades High School to those advanced college preparatory programs such as are housed in the Bronx High School of Science and Brooklyn Technical High School. Cities such as Boston and Chicago provide much less in the way of specialized secondary school training. As noted above the explanation for such variation must be located in the educational and indeed the cultural histories of the cities in question.

Conservatism in defense of the community's conventional wisdom is probably the ideal most completely approximated in the educational system. There may be regional and community variations in the intensity to which the schools value continuity, and in the larger, more heterogeneous cities with their normative complexity it may not always be easy to ascertain the specific boundaries of such "wisdom," but we would claim with little fear of contradiction that often the last

1 In the better school systems, this preparation is often indirectly linked with the economy's needs. In such systems preparation is likely to emphasize the academic skills necessary for college entrance. Since higher education in America tends itself to be vocationally oriented, those systems that "smooth the way" for college entrance and completion of an undergraduate course of study may be considered as making a high level if indirect contribution to the economy as well as the vocational destinies of their students.

things that public education will challenge are the pieties that constitute the community's *symbolic estate*.[2]

As far as the actualization of dissensual functional intentions is concerned, there are two basic questions which need attention. First, in what kinds of communities is it likely that any or all of them will become part of educational policy? Second, how successful are the schools in meeting in practice these intentions or expectations?

In nonmetropolitan or smaller cities the education for leisure and self-awareness themes are most likely to become policy when school affairs are dominated by an articulate laity of above-average education. It is not necessary that such people constitute a majority in the community, but it is necessary that they be of sufficient numbers so that they represent a recognizable bloc on the local political scene, or lacking this, that they occupy community positions of sufficient power so that their requests and proposals are not taken lightly (as in the case of trans-urban plant managers whose views on educational policy carry weight because "good" schools are necessary to keep high employment businesses in the local economy). Although high average income in the community in itself is not sufficient to insure the presence of these themes as policy in the school system, when combined with a dominant educated laity high income averages would seem to increase the probability of their presence. Most proponents of "educating the whole man" tend to possess more than the usual modicum of education. And when income levels are relatively high, there is likely to be less resistance on financial grounds to the inclusion of the so-called "frills" in the local educational package.

In large metropolitan cities, such as New York, Chicago, Los Angeles, for example, it is likely that there will be at least some education for leisure and self-awareness. The extent to which these functions are actualized in a given system depends on a number of factors such as the educational-cultural tradition of the city, the "progressiveness" of the entrenched professional staff in the school system, the overall economic condition of the city, and the degree to which the schools have fiscal autonomy relative to other agencies of the municipal government. In cities where working-class and lower-

2 Bernard Farber has used the term "symbolic estate" to refer to the traditions that are handed down without challenge from one generation to the next within families. It is used in a similar vein here, the reference being the community instead of the family. David Reisman has commented succinctly on the extent of normative conservation in education. See David Reisman, "Secondary Education and 'Counter Cyclical' Policy," *Constraint and Variety in American Education,* Doubleday Anchor Books, Garden City, 1958.

middle-class interests dominate the cultural scene, where the entrenched professionals tend to define their educational missions narrowly, where a sluggish economy creates or threatens to create hardships for many among the populace, or where school budgets are reviewed by politically sensitive bodies like the city council—the whole-man conception of educational output is likely to be minimized. Limitation on the actualization of this conception is likely to be directly correlated with the extensiveness of the conditions just noted. The more such factors are present, the greater will be the resistance to developing and extending programs in leisure self-awareness.

The extent to which school programs in these areas are effective when undertaken is impossible to evaluate at present. To begin with, operationalizing a "more meaningful use of leisure time" is a task laden with difficulties. Second, a time period must elapse between the educational experience and the achievement of the adult status to which the program is directed. By the time such status is achieved many of those who have been exposed to the program may no longer reside in the community where it was undertaken. This need not necessarily foreclose the possibility of evaluation but it certainly makes the cost of such an evaluation almost prohibitive. Similar difficulties obtain when education for self-awareness is considered. How does one operationalize "self-awareness"? If you could agree on an operational meaning for the term, could you locate a meaningful sample of adults who have been exposed to the program in a given community? Difficulties such as these can be overcome but only infrequently have researchers done so. Thus we are without a reliable evaluation of the output of "whole-man" programs in those communities which have undertaken them.

Outside the South, *minimal* programs intended to encourage intergroup amity have been adopted without significant controversy. In most communities the schools plan assemblies marking such occurrences as Brotherhood Week, for example. Such programs as these are generally accepted because they do not infringe upon anybody's entrenched interests and they *do not* seem to be effective. There is little cost in having brotherhood as a theme in the schools—particularly if it occurs only once every school year. No children have to be bussed, no expensive curricula materials have to be purchased and few teachers are required to depart from their regular routines. Moreover, Brotherhood Week is no more effectual than Christmas, Thanksgiving, and Independence Day in promoting intergroup harmony. Like these holidays the school observance of brotherhood is little more than a ritual in service to an abstract ideal—divorced from the political mechanics that could make it real. The most bigoted parent has little to fear from the Brotherhood Weeks and their like in the public schools. In fact, by endorsing them he can avoid coming to grips with his own prejudices.

The amity programs that do become real issues are those that involve significant organizational changes in the schools. There has, for example, been intensive opposition to cross-bussing programs. Programs such as these are adopted in proportion to the political resonance of the blacks and other nonwhite minorities within particular communities. Where these groups have some political impact upon the community at large, where they can make it at least somewhat costly for their interests to be ignored (and this has been particularly so in the larger metropolitan cities) there is likely to be some adoption of the more thorough going amity programs.[3]

Often the minority group advocates of these programs find their staunchest allies within the community among the better-educated, economically secure upper middle class and upper class while the greatest resistance to such programs comes from among the less-educated and economically insecure lower middle class and working class. For a variety of reasons, lower-middle and working-class individuals are likely to identify much of their contemporary ill-ease as the product of "minority-group pushiness"[4] and they are thus most likely to oppose any school program that they perceive as benefiting the nonwhite minorities at cost to themselves.[5]

The question of whether amity programs in the schools really work when they are introduced is largely without a systematic answer. As noted earlier, the minimal programs (Brotherhood assemblies and the like) do not have an impact beyond the symbolic gesture that in itself may paradoxically deny that there is a real problem to be solved.[6] If once or twice a year the community's schools endorse the desirability of understanding and mutual acceptance, an illusion of amity may be

3 It must be noted however that the bussing programs even in such cities have continued to draw intense opposition and, as in the case of New York City, have failed as a solution to the problem of racial imbalance in the schools. This appears to be so even when the federal courts have intervened in behalf of bussing.

4 See the following chapter.

5 Many lower-middle class and working-class people also suffer from status insecurity and are thus quite defensive in the face of the mobility thrust emanating from among those whom they perceive as their status inferiors.

6 For a trenchant analysis of the role symbols in public affairs see Murray Edelman, *The Symbolic Uses of Politics,* Urbana, University of Illinois Press, 1964.

created in the place of a nitty-gritty confrontation with the tensions of intergroup hostility. As for the maximal programs, what evidence there is of impact or its absence seems to be inconclusive. For example, to the extent that desegregation is intended to improve intergroup relations,[7] it has not proven to be an unchallenged success. Desegregated schools often contain segregated classrooms because black children are disproportionately assigned to the slower achievement tracks. The result of this practice is to limit the mutual accessibility of white and black children. Moreover, because the slower tracks are often recognized by school children to be those classes that contain the "dummies," the blacks, by being overrepresented in those tracks, are often stigmatized by their white schoolmates. Finally, when desegregation mixes racial groups that represent different socioeconomic classes, the stereotypes that each group has of the other may be reinforced rather than mitigated.[8]

These counterindications notwithstanding, there is not sufficient evidence to date that would rule out the possibility of positive effects of such programs. It may very well be, for example, that in the long run intergroup exposure will result in a greater openness on the part of the majority to the point of view and just petitions of the minority. This possibility cannot, of course, be evaluated in the immediate context of the school.

There is little that can be said about the propensity to adopt compensatory and special education programs that we have not already mentioned. The major objection to these programs comes from those who do not wish to sustain their cost. In general, these tend to be people of limited income, the lower-middle class and the working class. The opposition of these groups is likely to be most telling where the taxing powers of the schools are constrained by a mandatory recourse to public referenda whenever an increase in the basic rate is being proposed. However, such opposition has been circumvented, if not overcome, by the availability of funds for such programs on the state and federal levels. It is more difficult to arouse an electorate to oppose such programs when they are unlikely to see the relationship between their tax bill and support for the programs, as is the case when support comes at least in part from federal and state levels. The

7 This is but one of its intended functions. Far more basic is the intent to improve the quality of education received by blacks. We are not evaluating this latter function here.

8 See Thomas F. Pettigrew, "Complexity & Change in American Racial Patterns: A Social Psychological View," *Daedalus, XCIV* (Fall 1965), 974–1008.

taxpayer may dislike paying taxes to the federal and state governments but he does not see his money earmarked for education as he does when the local school board asks for a mandate to raise the basic tax rate.[9]

On the face of it, we would probably expect opposition to the compensatory education programs to be forthcoming from those who are hostile to efforts undertaken in behalf of nonwhite minorities, these tending to be among the white lower-middle and working-class groups. As it turns out, there is less opposition to compensatory programs on racial grounds than we expect if only because such programs are often offered as an alternative to desegregation in the schools. For those who are hostile to nonwhite aspirations for quality education and social mobility, compensatory programs often appear to be the lesser of two evils. Thus when pressed, school systems having a large and vocal lower-middle and working-class constituency often offer compensation rather than desegregation.

As far as the actual output of compensatory and special education programs is concerned, the following should be noted. Among professional educators there is considerable if inconclusive debate over the effectiveness of special education techniques and curricula.[10] There seems to be general agreement, however, about the fact that the education of the physically, mentally, and emotionally infirm would suffer without the presence of such programs. On the other hand, there are many who question the educational efficacy of any and all of the extant compensatory programs. It has been the experience of many black parents in urban communities that compensatory programs have not appreciably improved their children's potential for success in the public schools. This experience finds corroboration in evaluations that indicate, among other things, that apparent gains made by children enrolled in preschool compensatory programs such as Head Start do not generally hold up (no matter what the curriculum or what teaching

9 At this writing, *community* financing of public education is under challenge in the courts. It is being argued that because educational financing is left to individual communities the quality of education varies from community to community, thus depriving those children who reside in poorer communities of equal opportunity to the best in education. Should this argument be sustained the states will probably be required to take over direct support of public education from individual communities, and taxpayers will probably (although not necessarily) be less sensitive to the purposes for which educational funding is put to use.

10 This can be seen in the publications and proceedings of the *Council on Exceptional Children*.

techniques are used) once these children enter the regular elementary school system.[11]

In sum then, while Special Education and compensatory programs are perhaps the most easily adopted of all the dissential functional intentions, there is serious question as to the effectiveness of their outputs, particularly in the case of the overall impact of the compensatory programs.[12]

The educational functions examined thus far, both consensual and dissential, have in common the fact that all have been intended by at least some segment of the urban population; in each case the examined function was part of *somebody's* conscious conception of what urban schools *ought* to be accomplishing. We have now to examine the matter of the *unintended* or *not necessarily intended* ouputs of the urban education system, those outputs that are social fact but for which no professional educator will make a case and no constituency consciously supporting their existence can be found.

The primary unintended function of the educational system is the socioeconomic placement of individuals. Urban society depends upon an extensive division of labor for its continued viability. The technological sophistication of the urban economy demands of the labor force that it possess a distribution of competence covering a myriad of vocational placements. No other characteristic is so significant to the individual's social location—his prestige, power, and wealth—as is the particular competence he possesses and, consequently, the probable vocational placement that will be his. In contemporary urban America, it is the economy that makes the man, not the family or the polity.

Thus both from the perspective of system maintenance in the urban community as well as the individual's interest in his own well-being and destiny, the matter of socioeconomic placement is of the highest significance. Few people will admit to it, but the schools do function as a socioeconomic *distribution mechanism* for the communities in which they are located and, indeed, for the society as a whole. In the

11 See Westinghouse Learning Corporation, *The Impact of Head Start: An Evaluation of the Effects of Head Start on Children's Cognitive Development*, June 1969. See also Merle B. Karnes, *Research and Development Program on Preschool Disadvantaged Children*, U.S. Department of Health, Education and Welfare, Office of Education, Washington, D.C., May, 1969.

12 Daniel M. Weiler, "Urban Education," *Cities in Trouble: An Agenda for Urban Research*, ed. Anthony Pascal, Rand Corporation Memorandum RM 5603-RC, August, 1968, pp. 27–46.

eight to 12 years that most Americans spend in the public schools, they are periodically tested and channeled into what might be termed *differentiated entry* pools for the economy. Those who manage to acquit themselves with a modicum of distinction in the testing process are elected to the *academic pool.* They will not enter the economy immediately upon their completion of the secondary curriculum but will most likely continue on to some college where they will prepare themselves to enter the economy at vocational levels that demand the greatest sophistication and that promise the greatest possibility of career advancement for those who "make it"—wealth, power, prestige.

Those who do not succeed as well in the educational testing process but who manage to remain on the "normal" pace of progression through the primary and secondary schools are channeled into the *immediate entry pool.* Such individuals will characteristically enter the economy upon finishing the secondary curriculum (except when the obligation of military service intervenes or when they elect to continue their educations in junior or community college vocational programs), and will enter at vocational levels that require less general sophistication and that correspondingly place a ceiling on the possibilities for career advancement and the accrual of wealth, power, and prestige.

Some of those in the immediate entry pool have been the beneficiaries of specific technical training in the public schools. They are likely to pursue the vocations for which they have received training. Others in this pool have rather undifferentiated abilities having received a general secondary education with little if any specific preparation for a particular vocation. These individuals are thus likely to require on-the-job training in whatever vocation they choose, and because their training in the schools has not pointed them in any particular direction, they are more likely than their vocationally trained fellows to try several different jobs before settling on any given one. There are finally those who, for one reason or another, do not succeed at all in measuring up to the standards that underlie the educational evaluation procedures. These are the dropouts, or those who manage to finish school but who test out below minimum standards, those who are clearly retarded in mental development, and those who have been "problem children" and who are thus channeled into what may be called the *surplus pool.*[13] Those in the surplus pool are

13 This designation is derived from Bernard Farber's concept of *surplus population,* which he uses to refer to the mentally retarded. See Bernard Farber, *Mental Retardation: Its Social Context and Social Consequences,* Houghton Mifflin, Boston, 1968.

likely to spend their productive years in jobs with very low levels of remuneration when they work at all, and more than any other segment of the population, they are likely to be unemployed. They are in fact unnecessary to the main thrust of the economy; they are unprepared to participate fully in it. They are surplus in that their severely limited skills and accreditation makes them perennially available and employable in the most transient and undesirable jobs.

The schools differentiate among the students in their charge as they ready them for their special niches in the opportunity structure of the economy. In doing so the schools not only generate functionally appropriate labor supply for the economy but also are largely responsible for determining the personal destiny and quality of life of every individual who passes through them. The schools are thus a major stratification mechanism in modern urban America.

The schools in American communities do not differentiate among students merely on the basis of relative academic ability. Upper-middle-class children from homes where "education" is presumed to be of utmost importance find the "deck stacked in their favor" when it comes to the probabilities of academic success; conversely, children with working class or lower class backgrounds where "school" is presumed to be less important find more than their share of in-school obstacles to academic success. Academic standards seem biased in the direction of skills more highly valued in upper-middle-class homes than in lower-middle-working or lower-class homes. Thus even under such a circumstance as straight academic evaluation the socio-economic placement game would not be a fair one.

In fact, however, the game is less fair still—because the evaluation process does not occur on academic grounds alone. Teachers and administrators tend to react more favorably to children from the "better homes" than to children whose parents' life styles do not excite similar admiration. Thus advantaged children appear to be brighter to the teachers whether or not this is in fact so. They often "do well" in school because they are expected to, while on the contrary other children *do* less well because the teachers do not expect much of them.[14]

14 Evidence for these assertions may be found in Robert Rosenthal and Lenore Jacobson, *Pygmalion in the Classroom: Teacher Expectation and Pupils' Intellectual Development,* Holt, Rinehart and Winston, Inc., New York, 1968; R. A. Cloward and J. A. Jones, "Social Class: Educational Attitudes and Participation," *Education in Depressed Areas,* ed. A. H. Passow, Bureau of Publications, Teachers College, Columbia University, New York, 1963, pp. 190–216; Charles E. Silberman, *Crisis in Black and White,* Vintage Books, New York, 1964, pp. 249–307.

When it comes to handing out rewards or selecting children to participate in special programs of social as well as academic distinction the upper middle class child will invariably be chosen before his lower-ranking classmates. The upper-middle-class child thus has his parents' positive view of school (its importance and the gratifications to be found in the school experience) reinforced, while the lower ranked child has his parents' neutral or negative view of school similarly reinforced. The upper-middle-class child's interest is intensified by his success while the working-class child's alienation is intensified by his exclusion. Interest in one child confirms the positive assumptions held by the teacher and administrator while alienation from another confirms their negative assumptions. Thus they continue to reward the interested child while they simultaneously withhold rewards from the alienated child. The schools therefore not only differentiate among children but they do so in accordance with preexisting stratification characteristics in the community, and in so doing tend to restrict social mobility and maintain the social class system from one generation to the next. And so, a second unintended function of the educational system is the maintenance of a stable social structure within the community, at least in so far as a relatively closed stratification system supports such stability.[15]

In sum the following should be noted with regard to the functional qualities of the American urban education systems. There are intended consensual functions that appear to be universally endorsed and generally actualized in appropriate measure to the intended purpose. These are (1) enabling training for adult responsibility, (2) enabling training for economic participation, and (3) a quality of technological progressivism and value conservation. Beyond the consensual functions, there are intended functions that are prone to engender controversy and that are therefore dissential. These functions become part of the educational systems in some communities while in others they are ignored, or their proponents are restrained from actualizing them as educational policy. When adopted, their effect seems to be highly variable. These are as follows: (1) the education for the "whole man" functions—preparation for leisure and personal (or self) awareness (2) the intergroup amity function and (3) the compensatory/special education function. There are finally the unintended functions, or those that occur without conscious planning on the part of professional educators or interested laymen. These are (1) the socio-

15 See W. Lloyd Warner, Robert J. Havighurst and Martin B. Loeb, *Who Shall Be Educated?* Harper, New York, 1944.

economic placement function (the school as a distributive mechanism) and (2) the limitation of intergenerational social mobility (the school as a means of stabilizing the social structure of the community).

PATTERNS OF ORGANIZATION AND PARTICIPATION In recent years much of the controversy surrounding urban school systems has focused upon matters of organization and control rather than on curriculum and method of presentation. A debate ever increasing in its intensity and acrimony tests the issue of *who* shall control the schools rather than the immediate issue of *what* shall be taught in the schools and *how* it shall be taught. Those contending for control may be characterized as follows: (1) the *traditionalists,* a coalition of laymen and school administrators who wish to retain the control they already possess and in so doing to maintain the existing organizational personality of the schools, (2) the *militant professionals,* most frequently teachers who believe that the education of children is so complex a process that ultimate control of the schools must rest in the hands of those who possess an expertise that is the product of years of preparation, (3) the *lay militants* a coalition of activists led most frequently by disenchanted blacks and critical intellectuals who deny the value of professional expertise in education on the basis of the presumption that the professionals have little to show for their efforts and who seek to give control of the schools to those laymen who have not previously had much say in the education of their children, the socially dispossessed of our cities, and (4) the *student insurgents,* groups of students who previously have had no rights in the schools—only privileges—who are seeking to have a "student voice" institutionalized as part of the process of educational decision-making. The insurgents have been most active in colleges and universities—but as time goes on they seem to be developing a constituency in the secondary schools as well.

The struggle over the organization and control of community schools is no doubt the most significant controversy in urban education. Its resolution or outcome in any given community will have a profound effect upon the nature of educational output for generations to come. (What is at stake is not merely the organizational personality of the schools but the character of educational output as well.) As the organization of the schools is "up for grabs," so too is the ability to realize some educational intentions while relegating others to the history of education. While in the recent past advocates for one program or another did not generally challenge the decision-making prerogatives of those who were part of the school system, today they often demand a complete overhaul of the decision making process. They have proceeded from the advocacy of educational reform to the advocacy of educational revolution, from the advocacy of change *within* the system to demands for change in its basic organizational qualities.

Ideally the organizational participation patterns of urban school systems are supposed to consist of a balanced mixture of lay interests and professional expertise. The public schools are generally conceived of as one of a number of municipal service organizations and, as such, their character and quality are matters that ultimately are the responsible concern of all the local citizenry. Since the organization of the schools is complex and since it demands sustained attention from its lay stewards, the public at large characteristically delegates its control function to representatives (either by direct election or appointment by an elected official such as the mayor) who make up the local board of education. The board does not manage the school system but, in theory at least, embodies the public interest in the educational process. Members of the board therefore serve, ideally, to protect and improve the quality of education within the community in terms of their reading of the lay public's intentions in this area.

Lay participation in the school systems is not restricted to membership on the board of education, although the board is the only corporate body of laymen (other than the citizenry as a whole when it has a referendum submitted to it—or when there is a school board election) that has decision-making authority vested in it. Lay participation beyond the board of education is expected to be advisory and supportive. Provision is made for parental support of local school programs through Parents Association, that are attached to particular schools and that consist of parents whose children attend those schools.

Such groups as these are (in one sense) particularistic and impermanent in their membership since participation is restricted to the citizens who have children in a given school. Parents whose children have been promoted out of the school or whose children are no longer students in the system must give up their Parent's Association membership regardless of the quality and vigor of their previous participation. In many urban communities it is considered important to have less restricted advisory and support groups. Thus one can expect to find public education associations, which in the communities where they exist, generally function to articulate the interests of those citizens who are more than nominally supportive of the public schools. Beyond the presence of adjunct organizations, open meetings of the school board are mandatory and in theory any citizen or group of citizens may present arguments for or against any issue before the board.

Laymen are expected to have little if anything to do with the day-to-day operation of the schools. Indeed, when laymen attempt to exert their will in operational situations they are likely to meet with intense resistance on the part of the professionals, the teachers, and the administrators who claim the educational process as their very own responsibility, not to be tampered with by the untrained and therefore the unknowing. In theory, at least, all school operations from the disciplining of a wayward 8th grader to the preparation of the annual budget are matters reserved for action by the professional staff. Typically the professional organization is arranged hierarchically, with teachers responsible to the local school administrators who, in turn, are responsible to the central administration for the system. The central administration itself may be organized hierarchically—with assistant superintendents for instruction, business, special programs, community affairs (and their staffs, for example) reporting to the superintendent who, as chief administrator of the system, reports directly to the lay board of education. Theoretically the professional staff is represented by the superintendent in the deliberations of the board, although there are many instances when this expectation is merely honored in the breach.

In sum, the two organizational components—the lay board and the professional staff—are expected to respond to each other in the following manner: the school board, as representative of the public interest in education, sets broad parameters for expected educational output. The professional staff applies its expertise to the realization of this output in day-to-day educational policy and pedagogical operations.

It should be noted that both the school board and the professional staff must operate in terms of externally imposed standards and operational procedures. Regional accrediting associations set standards for the operation of local schools, the violation of which can result in the loss of accrediting sanction. State boards of education also impose upon local systems such things as licensing standards for teachers and, in some instances, norms of achievement for students in given grade levels. In recent years the federal government has similarly imposed itself upon local schools. The federal government has been particularly active in matters related to the desegregation of schools in one community after another.

As matters stand at present, there is considerable variation in the actual organizational characteristics and participation patterns in urban school systems. The first and most obvious dimension of variation is size and its concomitants. Although both New York City and Champaign, Illinois, by definition house urban school systems, the scalar difference between the two communities, and consequently between their two school systems, is such that there is marked differential in their respective organizational personalities. The New York City system employs approximately 56,000 people, and has a regular enrollment of over 1 million. The Champaign school system employs approximately 1000 people, and has a regular enrollment of approximately 12,000 students.

At 110 Livingston Street in the borough of Brooklyn (New York City) there stands a building covering nearly one square city block. This building houses most of the New York City school system's central administration. Anyone who has ever crossed the portals of this "little Pentagon" knows just how imposing that educational bureaucracy really is. The enormity and complexity of it all is apparent with merely a glance at the directory in the main lobby. To illustrate, the following are located there: the office of the superintendent (now called the chancellor) and his special assistants who occupy staff positions; the offices of the deputy superintendents and their staffs; the offices of the associate superintendents and their staffs; and a myriad of divisions, boards, and bureaus such as the Medical Division, the semiautonomous Board of Examiners, which functions as the system's credentials agency, and also the Bureau of In-Service Training, which keeps track of the individual teacher's postgraduate training and his consequent eligibility for salary differentials. A sojourn through 110 Livingston Street invariably brings to mind the surrealistic nightmare of Franz Kafka's *Castle* (or perhaps for those with a more classical turn of mind, Dante's *Inferno*), for not only is one confronted by line bureaucrats—those functionaries who have *some* responsibility, limited though it may be—but also one is questioned, prodded, and ordered about by countless individuals who populate the bureaus and divisions as the guardians of bureaucratic routine and nothing more.

If 110 Livingston Street were all there was to the organization of the N.Y.C. school system it would indeed be overwhelming. But it is actually only one component of this many-faceted multilevel administrative system. Up until recently the administrative outreach from Livingston Street operated through district superintendents whose responsibility it was to manage a number of schools. The district superintendent in turn delegated managerial authority to his principals who in turn delegated certain tasks to their assistants, department heads, and ultimately, to teachers, teaching aids, and clerical personnel. In each district also there was a local school board of laymen whose primary function it was to act in an advisory capacity to the local professional staffs. However, recently there has emerged a major change in the organization of the system. Out of the struggles over who shall control the schools has come a plan enacted into law by the state legislature that increases the autonomy of local school districts, thus giving to the elected lay boards a share in the prerogatives of the old central board and professional staff. District superintendents must be acceptable to the local board, as must be other administrative appointments. According to this plan, local districts will henceforth have greater autonomy in the planning and executing of programs believed to be relevant for the children of a given district. Decentralization has increased the degrees of freedom at the contact level (that is, between the schools and their clients) but the overall system of hierarchy remains reasonably intact. Licensing and appointment remain central administration prerogatives, limited only by the terms of negotiated agreements with the local teachers union.

The advent and growth of the United Federation of Teachers is itself important to note, because the union has become a significant component of the system. Union objections to policy changes cannot be taken lightly, as witness the lengthy New York teachers strike of 1968 when the union resisted the decentralization of hiring and firing prerogatives.[16] The union won and as a result of its efforts the decentralization plan voted into law by the legislature in 1969 deviated markedly from the original plan that would have given decentralized districts almost complete autonomy in personnel determinations. Aside from the U.F.T., other interests have permanent organized representation in the system. Each supervisory level in the school is represented by a federation of associations of school administrators. For the most part, this federation has been the professional element most resistant to changes in the organization of the system.

In spite of recent changes the enormity of the New York system is a social fact that defies mitigation and, consequently, there is probably little that can be done to reduce the frightening complexity of its bureaucratic structure.

In Champaign, Illinois, on the other hand, the situation is not quite

16 The teachers went out on strike when the administrator of a demonstration district, Ocean Hill-Brownsville, in which local control and decentralization was being tried, attempted to have union teachers transferred out of the district without demonstrable due cause. The strike took on a racial cast because Ocean Hill-Brownsville was primarily black, while the U.F.T. membership was primarily white.

so gothic. There is a bureaucracy to be sure, but its scale is at least comprehensible and its complexity is in no way comparable to that of New York. On a characteristically bucolic street, there stands a complex of buildings—one low-slung, of contemporary design amidst two or three older rambling frames—that houses the central administration of Champaign's school district. In the lobby of the newest building, a visitor is greeted by a receptionist—who also mans the main switchboard. The receptionist will invariably ask the visitor who it is he wishes to see and then direct him down one of the relatively short corridors to the appropriate office. In this modest building are located (1) the superintendent, (2) the assistant superintendents for instruction, personnel, and business, (3) the director of the system's physical plant, and (4) various support personnel such as clerks and typists. In the surrounding buildings one will find the remainder of the central administration, the Director of Special Services and his staff, and the coordinator of Primary Grades and his staff, for example. The rest of the administrative staff, the principals, assistant principals, and deans are located, as one would expect, in their respective primary and secondary schools throughout the city. The system is of course hierarchical and centralized, but there are fewer levels and fewer subdivisions at each level as compared to the New York school system or, indeed, as compared to any urban school system located in a metropolitan center.

In the Champaign system, teachers are represented by the local chapter of the National Education Association that, despite its recently acquired assertiveness, cannot be characterized as constituting an effective component in the organization of the system.

The school board is itself a body directly elected and it functions primarily to oversee the budget and related financial matters. Its powers are limited, however, by the fact that important financial matters such as rate changes in the tax law for the schools must be submitted to the local citizenry in general referenda.

Unlike the New York system where it is difficult to fix responsibility for operational conditions because of its complexity, the Champaign system is relatively easy to fathom. Operating authority very clearly resides in the office of the superintendent and appears to be delegated at the prerogative of the individual occupying that office. While theoretically the board of education possesses veto power on basic policy issues, the superintendent, by virtue of his superior expertise in matters pertaining to the operations of the system, in effect is in a position to manage the board. There are limits, of course, to what he may do (a public challenge of the board on his part would not be tolerated), but by the use and practice of a modicum of diplomacy he can usually get the board to go along with his recommendations.

Two urban school systems, but they are two systems whose organizational personalities differ considerably because of differences in scale. What is true of the New York system tends in some measure to be true of all extremely large systems, and what is true of the Champaign system tends to be true of the smaller urban systems. Organizational complexity, internal specialization, multilevel bureaucratic hierarchism, and organized teacher militance tend to be functions of increased size: the larger the city, the larger the system and the closer its approximation to the New York situation.

It must be understood that the characteristic organizational personality of a school system has a great deal to do with the quality of the educational experience available to students, professionals, and interested laymen. As this is true, so it is ultimately true that the size of a community is an "independent variable" in determining the character of the educational (or school) experience available in that community. Before proceeding to a discussion of other community factors that affect the actual organizational characteristics of urban school systems, let us pause to explore some of the implications of scalar-determined organizational characteristics.

The multiplication of organizational levels and the proliferation of divisions, bureaus, and other minibureaucracies within the bureaucracy has the effect of intensifying the individual's identification with his own particular subunit while at the same time weakening his identification with the organization in its entirety. Or stated another way, the more elaborate and intricate the organizational structure, the greater the social distance between actors in any given unit of the system and actors in the other units of the system, while at the same time the social density among members of the same unit is increased.

That this should be so is not difficult to comprehend. When the elaboration of many subunits occurs, there is a concomitant increase in task specialization. Actors assigned to a given division are expected to accomplish what is, from the perspective of the entire organization, a narrow range of tasks. They tend to become expert in these tasks, by virtue of their repetition if for no other reason, while at the same time they have little opportunity to observe the functional relationship between what they are accomplishing and what their counterparts in other divisions are accomplishing. Indeed, when the number of differentiated units within the organization is great the probabilities of any individual in a given unit even knowing what it is that his counterparts in other units are doing are extremely limited. Unless an individual has been rotated through several units it is highly unlikely that he will have an accurate perception of their contributions to the overall purposes and well-being of the organization. In their ignorance of the contributions and operating procedures in other units the commitment they have to the organization as an entity tends to become defined in terms of their own tasks and those of their most immediate colleagues. Because of this understandably narrow basis of commitment the probability of intramural (or intraorganizational) conflict is heightened—a situation that itself serves to intensify the already existing proclivity toward compartmentalization.

The organization as a whole has limited resources available to it. Allocation of these resources intramurally must be made in terms of an evaluation of each unit's needs in terms of its expected contribution to the overall purposes of the organization. Such an evalution must, of necessity, result in a ranking of the constituent units so that some will be allocated resources in excess of those allocated to the others. While this ranking and consequent allocation of scarce resources may be perfectly rational and necessary in terms of the organization's overall purpose, for those who perceive the organization in terms of their narrowly defined tasks, a reduction in their request for resources may be seen as unfair and in some cases the result of the politicking of the other units who have been more successful in having their requests met. Such an experience can engender in the subunits a resolve to "do better" next time, and such a resolve can only be expressed competitively. A self-fulfilling prophecy comes to pass. The relationships among units of the same overall organization become politicized and competitive because of a perception that has held them to be so.

Thus far we have been examining the implications of organizational scale in the abstract. We need now to concretize our comments with particular reference to these organizations we call "school systems." In very large school systems, it is often the case that the highly compartmentalized bureaus, divisions, for example, work at cross-purposes with one another thus confounding the purposes of the system as a whole. Operational traditions build up within each unit, traditions that are in fact counterproductive, but which may not be seriously challenged simply because they exist. Several years ago, a new superintendent of schools in New York City announced that henceforth the system would seek out talented individuals to teach in the schools and that the procedures of the Board of Examiners (a subunit of the system) would be modified to speed the recruitment process. The Board of Examiners persisted in its operational traditions, the superintendent's announcement notwithstanding. The Examiners are still there, with many of their operating procedures and traditions still intact, while the superintendent is long gone. Or recently, when as part of the decentralization experiment (see above) an attempt was made to bring qualified but noncertified people into administrative positions in ghetto schools, the certified but not always qualified administrative personnel, perceiving a threat to their interests, resisted the innovation on the grounds that education could not be left to those who had not proven their capacity to lead in the traditional manner. (This matter is presently before the courts).

Another implication of the proliferation of levels and units within the large scale school system is the fact that events tend to "get lost." Compartmentalization within the school bureaucracy amounts to a kind of sub rosa decentralization of units; a decentralization of units that is ultimately irresponsible because it occurs contrary to expectation and, consequentiy, without concomitant monitoring. Because of the absence of effective monitoring, events that occur in the context of a given subunit, such as a school, but that should come to the attention of a responsible officer who is outside the unit of origin (an associate superintendent for example) often do not come to the attention of the appropriate functionary.

This is particularly true when the event in question involves malfeasance on the part of personnel in the unit of origin as the following incident will illustrate. A few years ago a number of toughs invaded a ghetto school in New York and assaulted a teacher. An emergency meeting of the school's parents' association was called to consider this incident and possible courses of action. The outcome of that meeting astounded almost everyone. Instead of condemning the violence in the school the parents' association actually endorsed the beating! Unbelievable? A parents' association that condoned the invasion of a school and the wanton beating of a teacher? Underlying this strange course of events is a story that was "lost" or that never got beyond the compartmentalized unit (the school) in which it occurred.

Several weeks before the teacher was assaulted, another teacher in the school meted out a fairly typical punishment to an obstreperous child—he locked her in a storage closet. What he failed to do however, was to unlock the closet at the end of the class period, or indeed, at the end of the school day. In the middle of the night he awoke from his sleep, and remembering that he had locked the child in the closet, went to the school and freed the hysterical girl who was then returned to her equally hysterical mother. When the mother, a welfare recipient, came to the school to complain, she was threatened by the principal who told her that if she pressed the matter further he would see to it that she lost her welfare allotment. Fearful of losing her only means of support and ignorant of whom else she should complain to she let the matter drop, but did not forget it, and the incident became common knowledge in the community. The principal did not himself refer the matter to his superiors for possible disciplinary action against the teacher who was responsible. Shortly after this shameful affair, two teachers in the same school decided to discipline a child by holding him down and pouring cold water on him. When the parents of this child came to the school to complain, they were warned by the principal against causing trouble for him or for his staff. Such classic injustice, such contempt for students, for parents and for fair play!

None of this came to light until a teacher in the school was assaulted. Because of the extreme compartmentalizaion in the school system the underlying events—the causes of the assault—were "lost," "buried," so that no action was taken against those who had clearly violated their trust. Can there be a clearer demonstration of decentralization without accountability? The parents' association endorsement of a willful act of violence against a teacher was a public symbolization of the frustration and antipathy engendered by those willing to countenance the victimization of students and their parents.

It should not be inferred from the material we have presented that the "loss of events" is totally uncharacteristic of smaller school systems. As long as the system is organized in a bureaucratic manner, some compartmentalization will take place, which, by its very nature retards interunit communication, and thus a very real possibility of event-loss exists. It is however true that the *probability* of event-loss increases in direct proportion to the extent of unit proliferation and compartmentalization. The less elaborate and complex an organization, the greater is the visibility of action taken in one of its units. Since larger school systems tend to be highly bureaucratized and highly compartmentalized, they contain the highest potential for event-loss.

There are other factors besides scale that affect variations in the organizational personalities of local school systems. Particularly important among these is a factor that is not unrelated to community scale, the demographic characteristics of the community.

Homogeneity of population both in terms of social class and ethnic affiliation tends to be reflected in (1) a more harmonious relationship between the school system and the community it serves, and (2) a reduction of internal (organizational) problems that arise in direct proportion to external pressures and conflicting demands upon the schools. In a community that is predominantly white middle class, the demands upon the system from the public are likely to be consistent in their emphasis upon reasonably good academic programs and preparation for higher education. There may be some dissent on the matters of having to do with expenditures for so-called educational "frills," but on the whole the public will regard the schools as accomplishing their task if they provide the community's children with the requisite skills for reasonable economic and social mobility. This relatively untroubled milieu allows the school system to routinize its operations, allowing things to proceed with a minimum of self-examination and intraorganizational revamping and/or expansion.

On the other hand, a school system that serves a community that is heterogeneous in its composition—a community that houses blacks and whites ranging in class from the dependent under (or welfare) class to the affluent upper-middle and upper classes—will be confronted with a multiplicity of demands for service, some competing with others for attention and some indeed that are mutually antithetical. The upper-middle class wants to emphasize the most up-to-date academic programs and the newest educational hardware; the lower-middle class wants a low-cost educational program, a good one but without unnecessary expenditure, and will not equivocate on its demand. The black population is justifiably unhappy about de facto segregation and the educational neglect of their children. They are demanding a series of remedies, more and better remedial programs, cross-bussing, and/or immediate decentralization that will give them effective control over the schools located in their neighborhoods.

Each of these demands and others like them commands the full-time attention of the professional staff of the system, and in most cases the presence of a differentiated constituency with their variegated claims means the proliferation of units or task forces within the organizational structure of the system. A system with external pressures such as those just described will likely have an office of community relations, perhaps with its own assistant superintendent, a special services division whose task it is to oversee remedial programs, a program evaluation bureau whose task it is to provide the superintendent and the board of education with measurable evidence of the relative effectiveness of the programs undertaken by the schools, a task force on bussing, and finally, purchasing and physical plant divisions. If this were not enough the superintendent himself, now confronted with external interests represented in the structure of his own organization, must surround himself with staff assistants whose loyalties to him are unquestioned and whose task it is to monitor the operations of the increasingly compartmentalized system.

Demographic heterogeneity is not a function of size; a large population agglomeration could be relatively homogeneous. It is true, however, that demographic heterogeneity is *positively correlated* with size of population. It is the great metropolitan cities of America—such as New York, Chicago, Boston, Cleveland, Detroit, Los Angeles, and St. Louis—that characteristically generate *images* of internal differentiation and active competition among the diverse population elements as each attempts to maximize its leverage to prosecute its interests. In such cities, even the numerical minorities are large enough to maintain a political voice for themselves. As the size of the community decreases, there tends to be a concomitant decrease in the absolute number of diverse population elements. Beyond this, moreover, decrease in the size of the overall population of a community means a decrease of numbers within the still existing population categories.

In the extreme, numerical minorities may continue to exist within a community but their size can be such that it is virtually impossible for them to maintain significant political resonance in the affairs of the community (the exception to this occurs when the minority has economic significance, for example, the small group of managers who literally run the company town). Thus it may be argued that population size is a good predictor of the extent of politically resonant, differentiated population segments; and this being so, size of population must also be a good predictor of bureaucratic proliferation and its attendant problems within the school system.

Taken together, the size—heterogeneity combination results in a continuum of negative insulation of the educational process and, in particular, of educational decision making in urban communities. At one polar extreme are those small and relatively undifferentiated communities in which the organization of the school system is reasonably simple—having escaped those social processes that result in a convoluted and compartmentalized bureaucracy. In such communities, the decision makers, the school board, and the professional administrators, tend to be visible and accessible to most of the community's citizenry. Thus, for better or for worse (from the point of view of the functionaries) they are publicly accountable for their decisions and other events occurring in the context of the school system. At the other polar extreme are the many large highly differentiated urban communities in which the organization of the school system—because it is subject to the imperatives of scale and the multiple claims of different publics—is very complex and extremely bureaucratized. In such systems, compartmentalization and sheer size renders the decision makers inaccessible to large segments of the citizenry. The educational professionals have tended to run such systems with a minimum of public accountability; the bureaucratic structure is interposed between the educational professionals and the public they ostensibly serve. The result is a circumstance in which "a small core of school people control decisions for public education in every large city."[17]

In very brief summary, let us enumerate the organizational qualities that are characteristic of education in contemporary urban environments of American society.

1. Ideally there is a balance between lay participation and professional control over the operations of the school system, the public interest in education having its formal statutory manifestation in the election or appointment of school board members. As stewards of the public interest, the board functions to set broad policy for the schools, policy which is consonant with the wishes and mores of the local citizenry. The professional staff is expected to operationalize such broad policy in the specific tasks of managing the school system and of teaching within it.

2. Patterns of organization are in reality highly variable. The two major sources of variability are (a) scale of the community and consequent scale of the school system (b) the degree of demographic differentiation characteristic of the community which houses the system.

3. Scalar variations are directly related to the degree of bureaucratization in the organization of the school system. The larger the system the more highly bureaucratized is it likely to be. The more highly bureaucratized, the greater is the probability of compartmentalization with its potential for the genesis of intramural conflict and event-loss.

4. The more heterogeneous the citizenry of the community the more heterogeneous are the claims made upon the school system. In order to deal effectively with the multiplicity of claims (some of them competing) the school system tends to generate specialized sub-units. The proliferation of such units results in the increased bureaucratization and compartmentalization of the system. Thus demographic heterogeneity, like large community scale, contributes to the organizational complexity of the school system.

17 Marilyn Gittell and T. Edward Hollander, *Six Urban School Districts: A Comparative Study of Institutional Response*, Frederick A. Praeger, New York, 1968, pp. 196.

5. Both scale and degree of heterogeneity taken together influence the extent to which the educational process is insulated from the general public of a given community. The larger and more heterogeneous the community, the greater the bureaucratization of the system, the less accessible are the responsible school professionals to public accountability.

THE SECONDARY INSTITUTIONS: SOME CONCLUDING REMARKS

In this chapter, and in the preceding one, we have concluded our systematic treatment of the ideal and actual characteristics of contemporary American urban institutions. Our analysis has focused in these pages on the family and educational systems of urban America. These institutional orders (together with the religious system) have been labeled the *secondary institutions*, for in spite of their obvious significance in urban communities and in framing the urban experience, they are less significant than is the polity or the economy in affecting the *immediate* social destiny of any given community.

Like the primary institutions of the polity and the economy, the family and educational system vary around a set of ideal normative expectations. Variations in actual family patterns do not generally seem attributable to specific community characteristics. They are rather the variations, which as characteristic of the *American family system,* can be found in most community settings of this society. The family profile of a given urban community is, however, a function of the variations in family organization that tend to be the properties of identifiable population segments within that community.

Variations in the patterns of urban education—both in terms of actual output and organizational "personality"—can be more closely linked with specifiable community characteristics. Such factors as socioeconomic makeup of the community and its size may be understood as having significant impact upon both the character of educational output and the organizational "personality" (inclusive of lay participation) of urban school systems.

PART TWO

The Problems of Urban America: An Experiential Analysis

Men and women experience events; they do not, as the rhetoric of sociology might lead us to believe, experience social institutions. Although we have analyzed the nature of contemporary urban institutions, we must be aware of the crucial fact that we have not analyzed the contemporary urban experience as it claims the attention of American city dwellers.

Institutions are abstractions, concepts created by social scientists to put into some kind of order the behaviors that they regularly observe. On a day-to-day basis, however, most men and women go about their business, initiating behaviors and experiencing events, without ever identifying what they are doing or experiencing in institutional terms. Institutions have an intellectual reality; they are useful orderings of social observation. They represent a language of social analysis. But from the perspective of the actor in his (or her) everyday life, they have no experiential reality.

In the following chapters we shall attempt to analyze major components of the contemporary urban experience in American life. From time to time we shall have recourse to our earlier analysis of contemporary urban institutions. For the most part, however, our attempt will be to capture the urban spirit—or *geist*—as it is manifest in the lives of American city dwellers.

Where shall we begin? C. Wright Mills argued that because most men and women are unable to understand their personal troubles as functions of public issues, the sociologist ought to focus his efforts on illuminating just how it is that the larger social questions of a time and place establish the boundaries of the individual's biographic experience.[1] What men need, argued Mills, is a kind of analysis "that will help them . . . to achieve *lucid summations* [italics mine] of what is going on in the world and of what may be happening within themselves."[2]

It would seem that Mill's exhortation is particularly apposite when we begin to consider the American urban experience. City dwellers are usually troubled people. They are troubled by the quality of life that is theirs by virtue of the fact that they play out their personal destinies within the confines of the city. Rich or poor, black or white, the urban American is discontented. He complains, he is fearful, he feels mistreated, he perceives himself as the victim of circumstances beyond his control and about which he has inadequate knowledge. Few, if any, urbanites will claim that city living is easy. Even those who would live nowhere else love the city *in spite* of the difficulties they experience. Thus, if we are interested in exploring the *geist* or spirit of contemporary urbanism, we would probably do well to follow Mills' suggestion and attempt to isolate those public issues that, in our cities, have come to trouble the individual's sense of self and well-being.

There is no foolproof way of isolating those major issues that trouble urban Americans. Obviously there is going to be some significant variation from one city to the next. Unemployment and the flight of important industry is a great problem in the New England mill town, but it is hardly an issue in those Piedmont communities to which such industry has fled. The organization and control of efficient mass transport is certainly a major public concern in New York City, but it is less an issue for many smaller cities. Air pollution is a crucial public concern in industrial cities such as Gary, Indiana, Chicago, and New York, but in the farm belt cities of the Great Plains, it is hardly an issue which holds the attention of the citizenry. For reasons of location, size, functional specialization (or the lack of it), and institutional structure, some issues emerge as crucial in particular cities, while in others they are only minimally present, if they exist at all.

It would take a book considerably longer than this one to treat all the public issues that trouble urban Americans. Thus, the approach taken here will be to select the issues which have the widest manifestation in American cities, those issues which, although they may show

1 C. Wright Mills, *The Sociological Imagination,* Oxford University Press, New York, 1959.

2 Ibid., p. 5.

up differentially in varying urban contexts, seem to have the greatest importance among the widest range of American urban communities. By doing so we will be able to get at the core difficulties that define so much of the urban experience in the United States.

PROBLEMS OF MAJOR EXPERIENTIAL SIGNIFICANCE

The formula that we shall use for identifying the major problems of urban America is relatively simple. We shall look for the controversies: where there is heat, there is an issue. The more heat, the greater the controversy, the greater the significance.

With intense controversy as our criterion for significant public issues, during the last two decades *institutionalized poverty* and the *racial dichotomy* have been among the most important problem areas in urban America. During this period, hardly a day has passed without mass-media coverage of events, proposals, counterproposals and policy proclamations that have been focused upon the circumstances of widespread economic deprivation and the divisiveness of racial identification in our cities. On the federal, state, and local levels the politics of this period have been characterized by prolonged disputes over the meaning of poverty and the methods of approaching it as well as over the extent of racial victimization and the need, if any, to redress the historic grievances of black Americans. Few urban Americans—black or white, poor or not so poor—have been untouched by these issues, and it seems that we are all about to have our lives altered because of them.

In American cities there has been considerable controversy over the presumed "breakdown in law and order." It too must be added to our roster of public issues that are of major experiential significance in contemporary urban America. Invariably the matter of law and order brings us back to racial controversy and the problem of poverty. In this regard, a brief look at the politics of "law and order" may be instructive.

Recently, "law and order" has been a major political issue in mayoralty contests such as those in New York, Cleveland, Los Angeles, Philadelphia, and Minneapolis. On one hand, there were those candidates who claimed to be for tough law enforcement and who explicitly or implicitly indicated that their opponents were less than sanguine about this issue. On the other hand, there were those candidates who, although supporting the concept of vigorous law enforcement, charged their opponents with indifference to civil liberties and social justice.

In fact, law and order slogans in these campaigns served as a message indicating to all that those who invoked them really stood for resistance to the pressures of nonwhite minorities for a larger share of the civic pie. Those candidates who invoked this slogan were appealing to voters who felt most threatened by militant protest and the aspirations of the poor, particularly the black poor. Those candidates who eschewed or otherwise played down the use of law and order slogans appealed for support from the dispossessed, and if the political context in which they were operating did not always allow them explicitly to present themselves as their champion, it was widely recognized that their sympathies were in behalf of those on the bottom. One would clearly miss the meaning of the law and order issue in recent urban politics if he did not recognize its link with the problems of race and poverty.

Thus there are *three problems* that seem to define the core of our urban troubles. As noted, they are (1) poverty, (2) the racial dichotomy, and (3) law and order. In the following chapters, we shall attempt to create those summations of which Mills wrote so that the experience of contemporary urbanism as opposed to its institutional structure will be better understood.

Chapter 6
The Problem Matrix of the Urban Experience

There is one thing that must be made explicit before we begin our attempt to clarify the problems that appear to dominate the urban scene. While these problems—race, poverty, and law and order—seem to define so much of the urban experience, *they are themselves not strictly urban problems*. We have come to identify these problems with urban life, and in so doing we often assume that they are peculiar to the cities alone. Consequently, we assume that their cause or source is to be found in the dynamics of urban social systems.

On the race issue we cannot forget those paroxysms of violence, the summer riots, that so recently rocked the cities. Poverty scars the urban vista with physical and social blight. The streets of our cities are unsafe, are they not? Even the police have become targets of urban hoodlums, as witness the wanton shootings of officers in Philadelphia, New York, Chicago and other cities.

No one can seriously quarrel with the observation that the first order problems of American social life profoundly trouble the urban experience, but we should be aware that these problems are not restricted to our cities alone, but are rather of *national* scope, symptoms of a *malaise* that permeates the national culture of our present American epoch. Undeniably, these problems have manifestations that are peculiarly urban, manifestations that depend upon the confluence of circumstances and conditions that are *urban* phenomena. But these troubles of the contemporary urban experience cannot be completely divorced from the troubles of our national experience. To separate them thusly would render any casual analysis of their presence incomplete, and indeed misleading, and would also render any projected solutions based on such an analysis inadequate to the task of reform and remediation.

We must, it would seem, accomplish three tasks preliminary to remedying our troubles and brightening our urban future. First, we must understand just how it is that these problems dominate urban man in contemporary America. Second, we must link these problems to the more general cultural malaise of our national life. We must try to understand the sociocultural logic that has brought us all to what might be described as a *national moment of truth.* And third, we must try to isolate those circumstances and conditions of urban life that appear to have particular relevance for the way in which this sociocultural logic translates into the experience of the urban American.

We will address the first two tasks in this chapter, leaving for the following chapter the task of isolating the manner in which the circumstances and conditions of urban life translate the problems of our national malaise into the peculiarly urban experience.

POVERTY AND RACIALISM IN THE CITIES[1]

There are approximately 19 million urban poor in the United States who—using the poverty line established by the federal government—account for nearly two thirds of the nation's impoverished people.[2] The aggregate figure is itself appalling—19 million people—a mass of disinherited Americans greater than the total populations of countries such as Norway, Sweden, Denmark, the Netherlands, Portugal, and Ireland. But it is not sheer numerical magnitude that establishes the basis for the urban poverty crisis; instead, it is the fact that millions of our fellow citizens appear to be *permanently* impoverished.

During the period of transformation from an agrarian-commercial society to an industrialized behemoth, American cities housed a goodly number of poor who paid dearly for the opportunity to be part of the "American Dream" realized. But the poverty of the transformation period was not "dead-end poverty"; for many among the impoverished multitudes the deprived circumstances of their lives were but the first trials in the struggle for eventual success. And for many more who would not succeed, there at least existed the belief that the hard life and tough times were only prologue to better things to come. The

1 Because of their close relationship in the public mind and in fact, these phenomena will be treated together.

2 See *Poverty Amid Plenty: The American Paradox,* Report of the President's Commission on Income Maintenance Programs, Washington, D.C., November 12, 1969, p. 25.

economy was still simple enough for even the poorest man to put some distance between what he might achieve and what he started with, as long as he was willing to bear the burdens of hard work and long hours. The peddler might eventually do well enough to open his own little store. The unskilled workingman could earn enough to give his children a better start in life. In the urban ghettos everyone knew of someone who, in spite of his humble origins, had risen above the depriving circumstances of the immediate social environment.

Not so today. Whereas previous urban poverty could be viewed as transitional, from the perspective of the poor, the conditions of the present leave little room for such optimism. For a host of reasons, it would seem that the urban poor in contemporary America can have but scant reason to believe that the future promises relief from the sorrows of the present. Many of them are black or Spanish speaking (or both) and are subject to a chain of discriminating circumstances that weds them to what seems to be perpetual poverty. Nonwhites, however strong their motivation to work, are traditionally the "last hired and the first fired" in urban America. The unemployment rate among black men in the labor force is double that of their white counterparts, and since the end of World War II this unfortunate ratio has remained remarkably stable.[3] Those jobs to which nonwhites and blacks in particular do have relatively easy access are characteristically the lowest paying opportunities on the vocational market. In many instances, those who accept such employment fall beneath the federal poverty standard even if they work 52 weeks out of the year. The concentration of nonwhites in the least remunerative job categories is the single most important source of poverty among this group.[4]

It is, of course, true that some of this unemployment and undersubsistance employment can be accounted for by the fact that many nonwhites do not possess the requisite skills for more remunerative opportunities. But this in and of itself does not obviate the causal attribution that holds that discrimination is at the source of the widespread poverty that victimizes nonwhites in urban America. The most important agency of work-related skill development in contemporary American society is the public school system. Scholastic accreditation is the basis for expanded vocational opportunity in this society. The

3 As cited in the *Report of the National Advisory Commission on Civil Disorders*, Bantam Books Edition, 1968, New York, p. 253. It should be noted that this is the national ratio; in some urban communities the ratio is even greater.

4 Ibid., p. 255.

better the individual's education, the better are his chances for occupational advancement and increasing economic reward. If nonwhites are unprepared for the better job opportunities—if they characteristically do not possess those educational credentials that attest to their possession of economically valued skills—it is not for want of effort on their part. It is quite clearly the negative product of systematic educational discrimination that denies to them equal opportunities to learn and achieve in the public schools of our cities. Educational discrimination in American cities is manifest in the following indisputable findings.

1. Urban schools are highly segregated. A fairly recent survey of 75 major cities has indicated that 75 percent of all black students in the primary grades were attending schools which were at least 90 percent black. Approximately 90 percent of all black students were attending elementary schools that had a *majority* of black students. Eighty-three percent of the white students in the elementary grades were attending schools that were 90 to 100 percent white.[5]

2. In almost all major cities, the schools that serve a predominantly nonwhite population are overcrowded.[6]

3. The schools that urban nonwhites usually attend are charactesistically the oldest and most poorly equipped in their respective systems. One major study has reported that "Negro [the conclusion holds for all nonwhites as well] pupils have fewer of some of the facilities that seem most related to achievement: they have less access to physics, chemistry and language laboratories; there are fewer books per pupil in their libraries; their textbooks are less often in sufficient supply."[7]

4. As a general rule less money is spent educating the children of the ghetto as compared to children in other urban schools. This obviously accounts for the inadequate facilities and overcrowding noted above.[8]

5. As a result of the conditions we have just noted, schools that serve the nonwhite ghetto children in American cities are generally staffed by teachers who are less experienced and less qualified than

5 United States Commission on Civil Rights, *Racial Isolation in the Public Schools,* Washington, D.C., 1967.

6 National Advisory Commission on Civil Disorders, p. 430, cited in footnote 3.

7 James S. Colman, et al., *Equality of Educational Opportunity,* U.S. Department of Health, Education and Welfare, Office of Education, Washington, D.C., 1966, pp. 9–12.

8 National Advisory Commission on Civil Disorders, p. 434, cited in footnote 3.

those who staff the schools that serve middle-class white children. The U.S. Riot Commission concludes in its report that: ". . . the more experienced teachers normally select the more attractive schools in white neighborhoods, thereby relegating the least experienced teachers to the disadvantaged schools. This process reinforces the view of ghetto schools as inferior."[9]

In light of such conditions as these, it should suprise no one that the nonwhite residents of our ghettos are less than adequately prepared to participate in the economy at the more remunerative levels. The question of discrimination simply cannot be begged by raising the issue of competence.

There are other forms of discrimination that, although less directly related to economic opportunity, are nevertheless significant factors in wedding the urban nonwhites to perpetual poverty. Perhaps the most insidious and damaging of these is the discrimination that leads to severely *restricted housing opportunities* for the blacks and Spanish speaking. Housing discrimination against nonwhites is a fact of life in every American city where there is a visible nonwhite segment of the population.[10] Such discrimination limits the housing options of the nonwhites so that they are literally forced to hover together in the most rundown sections of the city. Thus the problems associated with ghettoization are severely compounded by the fact that the ghettos are also slums. The slum-ghettos are characterized by conditions that cannot fail to contribute to a way of life that, in turn, severely inhibits the ability of residents in such areas to participate effectively in the economy of the city: housing in such areas is seriously substandard, lacking in proper plumbing and sanitary facilities, lacking in windows and insulation that protect against the cold as well as the heat, and lacking in structural soundness, adequate and safe electrical wiring, and efficient heating systems. One survey has indicated that nonwhites are confined to such housing at three times the rate for whites.[11]

The inadequacy of ghetto housing is exacerbated by the fact that limited residential options create a situation in which overcrowding is often the rule. In major urban areas, nonwhites are significantly more prone than whites to reside in dwellings that are overcrowded. Overcrowding is not simply confined to individual dwelling places.

9 Ibid., pp. 428–429.

10 Karl E. Taeuber and Alma F. Taeuber, *Negroes in Cities,* Aldine Publishing Co., Chicago, 1965.

11 Bureau of the Census; data reported are for 1966.

If these rundown units are overcrowded, then the neighborhoods that they constitute must be characterized by human densities that far outstrip those found to be characteristic of typical white neighborhoods. Indeed, neighborhood overcrowding in the slum ghettos can be so severe as to be mind-boggling; for example, the thought that if New York City as a whole were as crowded with people as several of the most overcrowded blocks in Harlem, then the total population of the United States would fill but three of the city's five boroughs, leaving the other two in reserve for population expansion.[12]

Finally, slum-ghetto neighborhoods are victimized by a self-fulfilling prophecy. Neighborhoods in which rundown, overcrowded housing abuts on overcrowded, overused streets are often regarded by public officials as being beyond reclamation. As a result of this view, slum neighborhoods have characteristically been shortchanged in the allotment of public services, such as street sanitation and maintenance of public facilities. The poor quality of such services (when indeed they are provided at all) of course contributes to the continuing physical decay of the ghetto; and this convinces the officials that they were correct in their original judgment about the irreversible decline of the neighborhoods in question.[13]

The relationship between such conditions as those we have just described, and the maintenance of poverty should not be difficult to perceive. An overcrowded, poorly insulated apartment is not conducive to physical comfort—even when comfort is minimally described as the ability to get sufficient rest to be prepared to meet the events of the coming day with normal vigor. Reduced vigor is easily translated into reduced work capacity that, in turn, sustains the impoverishment of those who are so afflicted. Overcrowding, of course, has a deleterious effect on the capacity to concentrate. A child must find it difficult to attend to his studies when, in his overpopulated apartment, he is almost continuously confronted by the disturbing stimuli generated by people who quite normally are engaged in other activities. If John has homework to do and Sam wants to watch television in the living room, while Sarah is listening to records in the apartment's only bedroom and mother is busily preparing dinner in a tiny kitchen—where is he to find sufficient quiet to allow maximum concentration on his studies? Overcrowding can thus be linked to poor performance in school,

11 Whitney M. Young, Jr., *To Be Equal,* McGraw-Hill Co., New York, 1964, pp. 151–152.

13 See Charles Abrams, "The Housing Problem and the Negro," *Daedalus, The Negro American* (Winter 1966), pp. 64–76.

which, in turn, results in the occupational disadvantage that sustains poverty.

Finally, poor housing has a negative effect on the health of those who are confined in it.[14] Health problems are quite evidently related to excessive absenteeism at work and in school. Absenteeism at work limits the earning power of an individual, particularly if he is—as so many ghetto residents are—an hourly wage earner. Excessive absenteeism in school seriously limits the individual's potential for scholastic achievement, which, as we have already noted, reduces his capacity to participate in the economy at the more remunerative levels.

Beyond the specific linkages just noted there is, finally, the general problem of demoralization and alienation that results from the inescapable confrontation that ghetto residents have with physical decay and the rampant personal disorganization that is its persistent corollary. Surely, for those who are continuously exposed to the joyless vistas of decrepit buildings abutting on filthy streets, of stunted men and women looking for momentary forgetfulness in cheap wine and expensive drugs, of prematurely defeated young people finding no outlet for their energies except in those illegal activities that must sooner or later land them in jail or worse, hope for the future and self-belief must be frail indeed.

Thus it is that nonwhites, the victims of persisting discrimination in our cities, constitute a population segment whose many members appear to be doomed to poverty in near-perpetuity.

The saga of the "permanent" poor in our cities does not, however, begin and end with discrimination against nonwhite minorities. You can be white and nevertheless be just as locked into the poverty syndrome as the slum-ghetto residents of whom we have just written. There are no exemptions from poverty based solely upon race. The poor in our cities, black or white, are the *economically displaced persons* of our technologically dominated society. They are the people whose limited range of technological skills (whatever the cause) is such that the market value of their labor consistently falls beneath the level necessary for comfortable subsistence.

The productive basis of the American economy—particularly in its urban manifestations—is *machine intensive* as opposed to *labor intensive*. A machine intensive economy emphasizes the use of mechanical

14 Daniel M. Wilner and Rosabelle Price Walkley, "Effects of Housing on Health and Performance," *The Urban Condition: People and Policy in the Metropolis*, ed. Leonard J. Duhl, Basic Books, New York, 1963, pp. 215–228.

devices in the place of manpower. Characteristically, such an economy replaces unskilled labor by machines that both speed up production and improve the quality of the product because of standardized processing. Automated or machine intensive production has the important implication of skewing the vocational opportunity structure away from the unskilled and the semiskilled toward the skilled and technologically sophisticated. Thus the introduction of a machine-intensive process instead of a labor-intensive process has an immediate dual effect. It simultaneously displaces the *minimally skilled* workers who derived their livelihood from the replaced labor-intensive process, and creates a demand for *maximally skilled* functionaries capable of overseeing the sophisticated technology upon which the machine intensive process depends.

The permanent poor are those among us who have neither the skills nor the credentials to compete for the vocational opportunities generated by the introduction of machine-intensive processes, while the introduction of these processes deprives them of those job opportunities to which they had relatively easy access in the past. A study of major urban areas has clearly indicated the awful validity of this assertion. Typically most of the unfilled jobs in these cities were in the white-collar vocations. At the same time, only a small minority of the unemployed poor had the skills and credentials that would qualify them for white-collar employment. In turn, openings in the operative and laborer categories (those categories for which the poor were most likely to qualify) were relatively few in number.[15]

The contemporary poor constitute an economically *surplus population* in American society.[16] They exist at the periphery of society—far from its economic mainstream—isolated economically, politically, and to a certain extent, culturally, from those of us who have had the good fortune to escape this cruel destiny. The millions of urban poor are the flotsam and jetsam in the wake of our economic development, and it is precisely this circumstance that bestows the imprimatur of a terrible reality upon the poverty crises of our cities. Unlike their predecessors the slum dwellers and ghetto inmates of today are no longer the *mobile* poor. They are not beginning a climb up the ladder of oppor-

15 *Manpower Report of the President and A Report on Manpower Requirements, Resources, Utilization and Training,* The United States Department of Labor, Washington, D.C. (April 1967), p. 82.

16 For a general discussion of *surplus population* see Bernard Farber, *Mental Retardation: Its Social Context and Social Consequences,* Houghton-Mifflin, Boston, 1968, pp. 9–15.

tunity. Indeed, at the present stage of our economic development, access to vertical mobility and to increasingly remunerative vocational participation seems to be limited more and more to those who have already "made it" in some measure. Economic opportunity created by the technological sophistication of the American economy drifts further and further away from the grasp of the poor. Horatio Alger is dead, and his resurrection amidst the decay and rubble of our cities would require a social and economic miracle so awesome as to be revolutionary in character.

In spite of the demoralizing circumstances that confront them, not all of the poor and the black have succumbed to despair. It may be argued that their refusal to accept what appears to be their fate is itself problematic for the rest of us. If the poor and the black in our cities accepted (for whatever reason) their lot and their station, the rest of us would be less troubled by their presence in our midst. Some of us would no doubt suffer occasional pangs of guilt, but moral sensitivities notwithstanding, their condition would not be a problem for us. It *is* a problem precisely because some of the victims of discrimination and progress are not meek: they offer up a vigorous challenge to us all. And because they are neighbors, fellow citizens abiding within our communities, we cannot ignore their challenge and their threat to our too often mindless life styles and moral isolationism.

Their refusal to bow before circumstances that seem overpowering in their negative impact stems from the fact that they, like the rest of us, subscribe to equalitarian values. They have been taught—as we have—that in the United States, all men are supposed to have *equal access to opportunity,* that none should be constrained by an accident of birth from aspiring to the best that this society has to offer and from realizing these aspirations to the limits of their talents.[17] Many of the urban poor cannot resign themselves to their poverty for, like the rest of us, they believe in equal opportunity that they accurately perceive as being denied them. The urban blacks too cannot docilely suffer discrimination because they are American, and are therefore imbued with the values of equal opportunity in an open society.

In recent years American cities have become the settings in which the displaced and disinherited of American society have dramatized their resistance to continued victimization The blacks in particular

17 For a classic functional analysis of the implications of equalitarianism in American society, see Robert K. Merton, "Social Structure and Anomie," *Social Theory and Social Structure,* revised edition, The Free Press, Glencoe, 1957, pp. 149–190.

have been in the forefront of the *urban protest* against discrimination and permanent poverty. As a result of the militant nature of this protest, few city dwellers—black or white, rich, or poor—have been able to isolate their private lives from the public turmoil that it has engendered. Communities have been polarized as the latent antagonism between haves and have nots, between white and nonwhite, has become manifest with an intensity that has destroyed our domestic peace, and renders questionable the confidence we have in the continued habitability of our cities.

The *protest* has taken a number of forms—some organized, some within the limits of "politics as usual," and others beyond these limits. Some manifestations have been reformist in nature, based upon the assumption that true equal opportunity can be achieved in our communities as they are presently constituted. Other forms of protest seem to have rejected the optimism inherent in the reform position, opting instead for a quasi-revolutionary posture which holds that a radical reorientation of community life and of American institutions is the only means by which the poor and the black will cease being victimized. Others still, particularly those of the Black Nationalist persuasion, have foresworn both reform and revolution, holding out for the promise of salvation in the rejection of and the withdrawal from the established community and culture in American society.

The reformist wing of the urban protest consists of two subtypes. First, there are the *moderates* as represented by such organizations as the local chapters of the *National Association for the Advancement of Colored People* (the N.A.A.C.P.) and the *Urban League*. There are also the *reform radicals* represented by such groups as the local chapters of the *Southern Christian Leadership Congress* (S.C.L.C.), the *Congress of Racial Equality* (C.O.R.E.), and various unaffiliated local activist groups, such as those that have organized rent strikes and economic boycotts in a number of communities across the nation.

The *moderates,* by means of litigation, by the sponsorship of ordinances and other locally relevant legislation, and by extending welfare services and educational programs, have attempted to reduce the salience of discrimination with particular regard to those aspects of urban life that result in sustained impoverishment for those discriminated against. In large measure, these groups have approached racism and the victimization of the poor as though these all-too-common facets of the urban scene were harmful to the victimizers as well as the victims. By pursuing their moderate-within-the-system programs, they have attempted to call attention to the grievances of those who are disinherited, and redress them. They have attempted to convince us all that discrimination along racial lines and inattentiveness to the problems of the poor is wasteful of human potential, and that such waste is an impediment to the progress of our communities and nation as a whole. By actively attempting to improve conditions and opportunities for the poor and the blacks, we would all be better off, they claim. We would increase the flow of talent into the mainstream of community life by making manpower resources available that, up until now, have been inaccessible because of prohibitions born of discrimination and mindless neglect; we would reduce the costs of welfare; and we would reduce the costs of crime that poverty and blocked opportunities breed.

The record to date would seem to indicate that the assumption of universal dysfunction (or harm) is questionable. The reform moderates working in terms of this assumption have indeed won many battles, but they have not begun to win the war. In community after community the moderates have moved the sociopolitical system to strike down *formal* restrictions to equal opportunity. In terms of formal success, their optimism with regard to the possibilities of reform within the system appears to have been justified. Nevertheless, it must also be noted that what is now prohibited *de jure* (by law) is still maintained *de facto* (in fact): that formal responsiveness to the grievances of the poor is not descriptive of actual behaviors with regard to these grievances. The poor and the black within our communities are still victimized, are still disinherited.

The persistence of discrimination and of inattentiveness makes the assumption of universal dysfunction a tenuous one. If, in the face of highly publicized and formally successful reform efforts, the victimizing behavior continues almost unabated, should we not then conclude that it serves some vital interest of its perpetrators? If we are aware of the benefits that we all presumably would derive from an end to victimization, and we persist in our established ways, does this not suggest that at some level we do not recognize the dysfunction (or harm) in such behavior? The answer is probably *yes*. Yes, discrimination is not dysfunctional to those who discriminate. Yes, continued neglect of the grievances of the poor works to the advantage of the nonpoor. Later in this chapter we shall attempt to discover the interests that are being served, and the needs that are being met by maintaining the disinherited in their lowly station. Here we simply note that moderate reform has not achieved its goal, and that its operative assumptions must therefore be called into question.

The *reform radicals,* like the *reform moderates* have largely accepted equal opportunity as realizable within the existing institutional framework. The major difference between the majority of the reform radicals and their moderate brethren is to be discovered in the means that the former employ in behalf of their cause.

While confident that equal access to opportunity can be obtained without recourse to full scale social revolution, the reform radicals have not been willing to pursue their ends within the constraints of institutionalized politics. Even while recognizing the importance of judicial decisions to the success of their cause, they have not been willing to rely solely upon the courts. Even while seeking to expand the power of black people and poor people in general at the polls, they have placed little faith in the efficacy of working within the established political parties. They do not subscribe to Gunnar Myrdal's assertion that when confronted with the realization that their behaviors run counter to their values, the victimizers are likely to desist in such behaviors.[18] In the eyes of the radical reformers, normative education must confront the victimizer with the victim's resistance. It must make the victimizer aware that he cannot continue his behavior immune from actions taken by those who suffer injuries. Normative education must teach that the black and the poor can complicate the life of the victimizer, offend his interests, and make him uncomfortable even as he has stolen *their* birthright to equal opportunity.

Operating beyond the limits of institutionalized politics, dissent has largely meant recourse to the stratagems and tactics of *direct action.* The best way to convey the meaning of direct action is to refer to some typical examples that have been characteristic of the reform-radical protest in the cities: when downtown stores do not hire blacks as clerks, they are boycotted and not taken to court, in the hope that economic pressure will teach their management that such a practice is costly. When a local board of education does not remedy the injustices brought about by de facto segregation, a school boycott is organized in the hope that the orderly affairs of the school system will be disrupted to a point at which the authorities will be coerced into action they would not otherwise take. When absentee slumlords turn deaf ears to requests for repairs and rudimentary services in buildings that they own, a rent strike is fomented—not court litigation—to withhold from the slumlords the profits they are reaping from their malfeasance. These and other examples of direct action have been the typical non-institutional instruments of hoped-for reform employed by the reform radicals. They have been minimally successful in achieving their immediate ends, but judging from the facts of continued racialism and

18 Gunnar Myrdal, *An American Dilemma,* Harper and Brothers, New York, 1944.

poverty in urban life, they have not had much cumulative impact upon the long range goal of extending equal opportunity to those who are beyond the range of effective inclusion.

As noted earlier, the victimization of the poor and the black has elicited a *quasi-revolutionary* response, as well as a reformist response within the communities of urban America. The *quasi-revolutionaries*[19] such as the Black Panthers and their white allies (the White Panthers, Progressive Labor, the Yippies, Crazies, the Weathermen, SDS and numerous other groups, some consisting of the victims themselves and others, particularly the white groups, consisting of those who feel impelled to act in behalf of the disinherited) have located their challenge to the American status quo in the cities. Believing, as they do, that poverty and racialism are not the products of historical inadvertence, that they are not therefore remediable by means of reform, and that they are instead symptomatic of a social system that maintains itself by exploiting the many for the benefit of the few, they have become self-styled "urban guerrillas," implacable in their commitment to the destruction of the present order, and resolute in their belief that they will be able to construct a millenial future in its place.

The quasi-revolutionaries represent but a minority of those involved in the urban protest. Nevertheless, because of their militance and their willingness to include violence in their strategic repertoire, they are important beyond their numbers, and the contemporary urban experience is profoundly influenced by what they say and what they do. Although they have not had much success as measured by the extent to which they have destroyed or even weakened components of the existing order, or as measured by the numbers they have recruited to their ranks, they have nevertheless created havoc in the cities. On more than one occasion they have rampaged through city streets in assaults against the property manifestations of the system they have sworn to destroy. They have engaged in shootouts with the police; they have employed bombs and incendiary devices where others have used words; and they have temporarily "liberated" schools, churches, and government buildings in a calculated attempt to disrupt the orderly flow of civic affairs.

Because of all this—because they have translated revolutionary discussion into revolutionary behavior on a scale previously unknown in American cities—they have created a sense of urgency about the protest that no urbanite can ignore. As has been noted, however, the

19 *Quasi* because, their rhetoric and programs notwithstanding, they have not been able to launch a serious attack upon the social structure of the American present.

turmoil they have created cannot be equated with success, if by success we mean the realization of revolutionary goals. If an end to racialism and the victimization of the urban poor depends upon a far-reaching restructuring of American society, then the poor and the blacks can only despair in the lack of progress that this committed vanguard has made. For example, at this writing, the Black Panthers are in a state of disarray, pressured from without by the police in almost every city where they had achieved some visibility, and attacked from within by disputes that threaten to decimate their leadership. And the Panthers, it should be noted, seemed to be the most potent of all the quasi-revolutionary groups. The failure of these groups is attributable in part to their inaccurate reading of their position within the communities of urban America. To the extent that their failure is itself a component of the contemporary experience, we should address ourselves to its source.

If history has anything to teach us about revolutionary change, it is that such change can only come about when particular circumstances *other than* the mere active presence of committed revolutionaries dominate the social landscape. Revolution can only come about when one of the following two conditions is apparent: when the economy and the polity have ceased to function in a predictable and serviceable manner, or when revolutionary communities, having developed in functional isolation of the society at large, become so powerful and attractive that they can undermine in large numbers of people their loyalties to the values and norms of their society.[20] In the first instance, a well-disciplined revolutionary vanguard may succeed by moving into a leadership vacuum that is created when the *economy* fails in its productive and distributive functions, thus depriving the populace of the goods and services that they have come to rely on; when the *polity* can no longer endow those who dominate it with legitimacy; and when the police lack the power to enforce edicts and decisions. There is no evidence that the institutional structure of American society, and therefore of the cities, is in any real danger of breaking down in such a manner; consequently, there is at present no leadership vacuum to fill, nor is there likely to be one in the foresee-

20 The primary example of the former condition is Russia during the latter part of the 19th century and in the years just prior to the Bolshevik revolution in 1917. The primary example of the latter condition is one that existed in the liberated areas of China that the Communists dominated prior to their seizure of national power. For a brief but excellent analysis of conditions that heighten the potential for revolution, see Barrington Moore, Jr., "Revolution in America?", *The New York Review of Books,* January 30, 1969, pp. 6–12.

able future. If disorder does not reign, the revolutionaries have no place to go.

Thus, while the quasi-revolutionaries may create turmoil by their stratagems and tactics, such turmoil, for all its apparent intensity, would seem to be superficial and therefore unproductive of significant revolutionary opportunity. The cities and the society as a whole may suffer through recessions, there may be prolonged racial conflict in our midst, metropolitan areas may seem continuously unmanageable, and a visible segment of the population may become increasingly alienated, but despite these crises there is nothing on the horizon so cataclysmic as to seriously threaten to destroy institutional functioning. The quasi-revolutionaries, local or national, would thus appear to be out-of-step with the sociological reality of our time. To the extent that their success depends upon massive social disorganization, it must be noted that even the most chaotic of American communities—a New York or a Detroit, for example—are simply too well integrated for even the most disciplined revolutionary cadre to seize and hold the power necessary for radical social reconstruction, and even if this should occur in a few communities, a reasonably well-integrated federal polity would undoubtedly take successful counter-action against the revolutionaries.

The urban location of the quasi-revolutionaries itself would seem to preclude the development of powerful functionally autonomous alternative social systems or communities. By definition, such communities must reject the conventional wisdom that is characteristic of the system they seek to undermine. In isolation they might develop to a point, but even then their success would sooner or later bring hostile pressure to bear upon them.[21] In the midst of the conventional precincts of the contemporary city with its aggressive newsgathering and publicity mechanisms, it would seem that they are doomed to premature exposure and consequent failure.

Unless they win over to their cause army and police units, or otherwise develop a sufficient force of their own to fend off repressive measures by the "system's" enforcers, they will be destroyed before they even begin to fire the imagination of the disenchanted. Also, revolutionary proselytizing is a public act. The participants cannot

21 This has been true historically in the United States. For example, no sooner had the Mormons developed in New York than they were forced to leave for Navoo, Illinois, by their hostile neighbors, and no sooner had they developed their community in Navoo when the process was repeated and they were forced to make their great trek into the wilds of Utah. See Thomas F. O'Dea, *The Mormons,* University of Chicago Press, Chicago, 1957.

expect to escape surveillance and consequent action against them if they attempt, as they must, to proselytize. Even today, there is evidence that those who seek revolution through the example of the radical community cannot escape popularly endorsed harassment on the part of those who support conventional norms. The intense pressure on the Black Panthers, and the less focused but obviously hostile action of the police against the white radical communes is evidence of this. The task of alienating the enforcers from the system they serve seems nearly impossible under present circumstances and the revolutionaries have not made this task any easier by expressing hostility toward them. Should the revolutionaries seek to mount their own force against the system they are not likely to succeed. Secret arsenals are one thing: trained urban guerrillas capable of overcoming the organized forces of the army and the police are quite another. A revolution that depends upon the autonomous community strategy will fail unless the system comes apart at its institutional seams.

The *urban protest,* it would seem, affects the contemporary urban experience in two ways. First, in its increasing vehemence, it is profoundly troubling to the white nonpoor who must live with the manifestations of its challenge to their privileged position. They have been put on the defensive, and they can no longer rest easy. Hostility surrounds them. They are challenged in the courts and at the polls. They are threatened in the streets, in their places of business, and even in their own homes. They may maintain their privileges, as the evidence suggests they are doing and they may fend off the challenge, but only at some cost to their peace of mind and sense of normalcy within their communities.

Second, for the disinherited—the blacks and the poor—the emergence of the protest has had the effect of increasing their engagement with those elements in their communities that do indeed victimize them. In the immediate present and the near future, this has positive portent. For, at least, some among them the protest in all of its forms sustains a sense of hopefulness, a sense that something can be done to escape the treadmill of poverty, and a sense that the ideal of equal opportunity may yet be realized. But it must also be noted that if these present hopes are not confirmed in measureable and obvious progress, the disappointment of the disinherited may be all the greater, for their dreams have been fired, and the protest has encouraged them to hope, If that should come to pass, their embitterment would be enormous, and their alienation from the American dream might very well be irrevocable.

The problems or issues of poverty and race have undoubtedly had a profound effect upon the quality of the contemporary urban experience. For the poor and the blacks, city life is bleak indeed. They are the disinherited in our midst. They suffer defeat as a daily experience. The economy has little use for them, and even where they might be useful many are denied opportunity because they are not white. The schools ill serve their aspirations. They live in impacted slum ghettos that are hardly habitable. It is a wonder that they have not completely succumbed to bitter despair. Yet in fact they have not done so. With their faith in the values of equal opportunity and equal treatment, they have enlisted in a protest against continued victimization and defeat. The protest in turn has extended hope in the immediate context, but it must also be noted that *none* of its manifestations has *significantly* changed the life conditions of the disinherited. As this is the case, we must be forewarned of the possibility that the unrealized hopes of the present may portend almost indescribable alienation in the future. Should this come to pass, the consequences will be ominous not only for the victims, but for the victimizers as well. In this light, we must ask whether any community system can remain viable while carrying such a heavy burden of disenchantment among a numerically significant segment of its populace.

For the nonpoor and the white majority, the protest has destroyed the peace and normalcy of urban life. And while they cling to the perquisites of their advantaged station, they do so at considerable cost to themselves. Their resistance to change, to the redress of just grievances is, in fact, destroying their freedom. There are places they may not go within their own communities and times of day when they dare not leave their homes. They are no longer free to pursue their private interests in isolation from strife and turmoil—and it may get worse.

Optimism is a scarce commodity when we view the impact of poverty and race on the urban experience. One wonders why the victimizers persist in a course that seems counter to the desire for an unproblematic existence—why indeed? We shall try to find an answer in our examination of the national cultural malaise, but first let us characterize the import of the issue of law and order for the experience of the urban American.

LAW AND ORDER IN THE CITY

Cities are made up of strangers. For any given individual, the overwhelming majority of his fellow citizens are literally unknown. They have no biographic reality. Such a circumstance, when you think about it, has considerable potential for generating tension and fear among the citizenry. The urbanite is continually put into contact with people he does not know, and without biographic information about such people he must continually confront the possibility that they may wish to harm his interests or his person.

There are highly structured situations in which this possibility is mitigated (but not completely) by the fact that even without biographic information, it is assumed that the contact between unknowns occurs for some legitimate purpose, as when strangers sit side by side at a lunch counter, or when laden with groceries they wait their turn at the checkout counter in the local supermarket. But there are other situations common to city life that are far more ambiguous and that therefore make the appearance of the stranger a potential threat. A woman alone in an apartment does not open the door to a man she does not know. Walking in the streets after dark, particularly late in the evening, one is wary of the presence of other such strollers; waiting for a subway train one shuns contact or casual conversation with another.

In all cities the fact that most people are strangers to one another has always made unstructured situations somewhat threatening. In recent years, however, the threat posed by the stranger seems to have become more pronounced, so that his presence even in presumably well-structured situations is something to be wary of. The taxi driver, who in the past assumed that the strangers entering his cab did so for the legitimate purpose of being conveyed to their destinations, no longer makes such an assumption without some reservation. After a rash of robberies and murders in which passengers victimized drivers, New York taxi owners have installed bullet-proof partitions between the driver and the passenger in their cabs. Whereas one used to assume that the strangers encountered in a park were there to take some leisure amidst pleasant quasi-bucolic surroundings, one no longer does so. Does the stranger who enters the clothing store really intend to purchase something or is he a holdup man? In many areas of the city, retailers no longer assume legitimate purpose in their encounters with strangers who in the past would have simply been presumed potential customers. The stores are now equipped with emergency alarm systems and many shopkeepers never move from within reaching distance of the firearms they have registered for their protection.

Whether urban crime rates have actually risen significantly or alternatively whether the urban awareness of crime has become more pronounced, it cannot be denied that the fear of crime in the city—the fear that the omnipresent stranger may have criminal designs on people and property—appears to be a predominant social aspect of the urban experience. The American city dweller lives with more fear of his fellows today than at any other time in American urban history. It is not surprising, therefore, that the issue of law and order should be a pervasive concern of those who reside in any city of more than minimal size.

On the surface, the issue of law and order seems quite straightforward. It is easy enough to see the apparent connection between the increment in fear of crime, and the demand for more vigorous police action and tougher judicial treatment of presumed criminals—all of which define what seems to be the preeminent hardline interest in law and order. A more penetrating examination of the law and order issue, however, reveals considerable complexity and affirms our earlier assertion that, to a very great extent, the issue of law and order in our cities is closely bound to the issues of race and poverty.

Those who take what might be called the hard line on law and order, those who demand more and tougher police action against the criminal elements, and those who demand that the judiciary mete out harsh punishments to convicted criminals on the presumption that such a course will serve as a deterrent, are, generally speaking, overrepresented among the white nonpoor of our cities. This is a curious state of affairs for the available evidence suggests that these are the very people who are likely to be the *least* affected by encounters with serious crime. While the validity of crime statistics is a matter of some debate, available indicators would seem to demonstrate that low income groups, among whom nonwhites are overrepresented, suffer disproportionately from the commission of serious crimes. A study of serious crime in Los Angeles has, for example, indicated that an individual has six chances per 1000 population of being victimized by violent crime if he lives in parts of the city where the median family income is under $5500 per year, while his chances are less than one chance per 1000 if he lives in areas where the median family income is over $8000 per year.[22] Another study has indicated that lower class areas, as compared to more affluent areas, have higher rates of juvenile offenses and, more importantly, that they have higher rates of the more serious types of offense in particular.[23] Still another study points up the positive correlation between homicide and assault, and

22 James Q. Wilson, "Crime in the Streets," *The Public Interest,* Fall 1966, pp. 26–35.

23 John P. Clark and Eugene P. Wenninger, "Socio-economic Class and Area as Correlates of Illegal Behavior Among Juveniles," *American Sociological Review, XXVII* (December 1962), 826–843.

such factors as low income, overcrowded dwellings, and the high percent of nonwhites in the population.[24]

If this is so, we should ask why those who suffer the least from the threat of serious crime in our cities take the hard line on the issue of law and order. It may, of course, be suggested that the demonstrable difference in rates of victimization that favors the more affluent (non-poor) whites within any community is not germane to the question, for if men define a situation as real, it is real insofar as they act in terms of their definition, without regard to whether or not their reading of the situation has empirical support. Thus, it may be argued that the fact that the relatively affluent or advantaged whites within a community suffer less from the misfortunes of crime than do low-income nonwhites has little bearing on their *belief* that they are, in fact, seriously threatened by the criminal element. And as long as they believe that they are threatened, they will act in a manner that they assume will increase their protection. Cracking down on crime, and on those who appear likely to perpetrate crime, would seem to be a course of action consonant with the belief that they are in need of increased protection.

This is a reasonable argument, but it has a serious flaw. If adherence to the "hard line" is a function of fear, empirically grounded or not, then one should expect to find that those who are *really* threatened by criminal behavior on a daily basis—the poor and the nonwhite in our cities—would also subscribe to the "hard line." If those who have less to fear translate their concern into a "get tough" policy, it is only reasonable to assume that those who have the most to fear would likewise translate their concern into a predisposition to "crack down." *The fact of the matter is they do not do so.* The fear of crime is no less real in the slum-ghetto of the city—and it is fear based upon actual experience—but the response of the nonwhite poor to their situation is far removed from the so-called hard line.

To begin with, the poverty-stricken inhabitants of high crime areas see a need for the extension of publicly supported social services in their crime-ridden neighborhoods. They demand, or support demands, for considerably more in the way of drug rehabilitation programs, mental health facilities, child guidance centers, and organized recreational programs than presently exist in their neighborhoods. They argue that inroads can be made against the high incidence of crime by the extension and intensification of services such as these. Beyond

24 Karl Schuessler, "Components of Variations in City Crime Rates," *Social Problems, IX* (1962), 314–323.

this, however, they often tie the high incidence of crime in their neighborhoods to restrictions on their opportunities in the economic and social mainstreams of their respective communities. In this view, crime is a product of *"blocked access"* to opportunity. Thus they maintain that only social reform, the lifting of the barriers to their full participation in society, can be expected to markedly reduce the incidence of urban crime. The ghetto criminal in their view, will persist in his behavior despite increased threats to his freedom, as he believes that he is not *free* to begin with, given the restrictions upon his legitimate opportunity. This argument holds that a man cannot be deprived of something he does not believe he possesses. The ghetto criminal simply has nothing to lose in continuing his criminal career if he has no real legitimate alternative—the "hard line" notwithstanding.

If the hard line were merely a function of fear of crime, empirically justified or not, we should expect its nearly *universal* adoption within any given urban community. The fact that this is not the case must lead us to seek another explanation of its characteristic presence among the nonpoor whites who, as we have seen, actually have less to fear than the poor whites *and* nonwhites who do not characteristically subscribe to it.

Earlier in this chapter, we took note of the fact that the urban protest on the part of the poor and the nonwhite had destroyed the peace of mind and sense of community normalcy of the white nonpoor in urban America. We suggested that the nonpoor whites feel increasingly threatened by those who are challenging their prerogatives, that they are threatened in the streets, and that they are uneasy even in the privacy of their homes. With this circumstance in mind, it may be suggested that the characteristic endorsement of the "hard line" on the part of white nonpoor is less a reaction to the fear of criminal injury than it is to the very real threat that is posed by the urban protest of the poor nonwhites. *For the white nonpoor, law and order is less a matter of the need to deal with crime than it is of the need to deal with the "criminal element," so-called, who are typically conceived of as poor and nonwhite.* For the whites, the threatening stranger is almost invariably black; for the nonpoor he is almost always impoverished.

By linking the protest to criminality the white nonpoor are able to resist the challenge that the protest offers without qualm: the "criminal element" in its nefariousness wants something for nothing, and wants what others have earned by virtue of their hard work and self-discipline. The "criminal element" riots in the streets, vandalizes property, loots stores, burns, and plunders. Their vice-ridden neighborhoods are full of prostitution, narcotics, and the numbers. The protest itself becomes criminal; it is a threat to law and order. It must be restricted because it is a mask for criminal inspiration, for nefarious intent. When the nonpoor whites in any community inveigh against the coddling of criminals, when they demand a "get tough" policy on the part of the police, and when they insist that the law is being used to protect the "criminal element" with little or no consideration given to the rights of their victims or potential victims, they are crying out (albeit in code) against the challenge that inheres in the protest of the poor and nonwhite in their communities.

There is evidence that can be cited to sustain such an interpretation. In Chicago, during the mid-1960s, civil rights demonstrators were set upon by unruly white mobs who pelted them with bricks and bottles, assaulted them with baseball bats, and burned their automobiles. While many condemned this behavior, few whites saw in such lawlessness a threat to law and order. On the other hand, riots in the ghetto areas on Chicago's South and West sides were seized upon as examples of criminal lawlessness that supposedly threatened all the good citizens of that city. One need not deny that the ghetto-riots were lawless to observe that in the differential definition of similar behaviors the whites were not responding to the threat to law and order. Were they responding to such a threat they would have condemned each situation equally for the behaviors in question were indeed equal in their affront to the law. But they did not do so. The rioting of the white mobs was described as "unfortunate" not to be "condoned" by people of good will; the rioting of the poor blacks was "criminal," a "threat to life and liberty," and reason enough to crack down on the "criminal element."

The differential response would seem to be indicative of the fact that the white nonpoor are not so much frightened by crime in the streets as they are by threats to their prerogatives within the community. The blacks are depicted as the "criminal element" and in such stigmatization all facets of their protest are discredited. Not only are the riots a threat to law and order, but so too are their orderly demonstrations, and their economic boycotts, as well as all their militant challenges to the inequities of their life-space conditions.

In the spring of 1970, demonstrations against the allied invasion of Cambodia were set upon by a contingent of construction workers in the streets of New York. The action by these "hard hats" was denounced by many, but it was endorsed explicitly and implicitly by many others including the President of the United States. Clearly the assault upon the demonstrators who were doing no more than exercising their right to assemble freely was an example of collective lawlessness. Few indeed were explicit in their denunciation of such behavior as a threat to safety in the streets, as a criminal threat to lawful order in the city. Let us suppose that these construction workers had been a disorderly mob of black and Puerto Rican assailants in the streets of New York. Is there any doubt that they would have been condemned unequivocably, that their behavior would have been used as prima-facie evidence of "lawlessness," and of the need to give the police a free hand in ridding the streets of the "criminal element"? Blatant lawlessness is not characteristically defined as such by the white nonpoor so long as it is perpetrated by their own kind. Thus it must be that lawlessness itself is not the issue. The *lawlessness of the poor and the nonwhites is the issue,* and can therefore be used to discredit even their lawful actions taken in order to redress their grievances within the community.

Finally, it should be noted that the white nonpoor in our cities do not characteristically condemn the unlawful acts of whites against nonwhites. Even as they condemn the vices of numbers and prostitution in the "bad neighborhoods" (the ghettos) of their cities, they evidence little concern about the clearly unlawful acts of the slum lords and building inspectors who conspire to flout building codes, little concern about the unlawful acts of untrustworthy white storeowners who foist shoddy goods upon an unsuspecting ghetto clientele, and little concern about police actions that on occasion victimize the people they are sworn to protect. Clearly, law and order are undermined by such behaviors as these. If the issue for the white nonpoor was really the breakdown of law and order, they would voice the same indignation at these violations as they do about the vices of ghetto life. The vices of ghetto life elicit moral indignation on the part of many of the white nonpoor because they can be used as justifications for their resistance to the protest of the disinherited, which is the real threat to them. The vices of those who victimize the nonwhite poor serve no such purpose and consequently they do not engender such a reaction.

All told, it would seem that the hard line is not a hard line on law and order, but a defense against the threat that the protest of the underclass poses for those who have had the good fortune to avoid being among them. As noted earlier in this volume, recent urban politics has focused to a great extent on the issue of law and order. The politicians taking the hard line have made it abundantly clear that they stand for resistance to the challenge mounted by those on the bottom, while those who have attempted to play down the issue invariably seem to have a more liberal position on the need to address the grievances of the poor and the nonwhite. It is not by chance that the hard line on law and order is allied with a hard line on protest, or that the more flexible, less rigid position on the law and order issue is tied to the more liberal stand on redressing the grievances of the underclass. The law and order issue is more than anything else a justification for resistance to redress. Those who support such resistance make the most of the issue; and those who see the need for change reject its presumed importance.

Later in this chapter we shall explore the nature of the threat posed by the poor and the black. When we specify those white nonpoor interests that are being threatened in the urban protest, the symbolic meaning of "law and order" for such people—the meaning underlying the link between protest and crime—will be developed further. For the moment, however, let us note the fact that to divorce the law and order issue from the race and poverty issues in urban America would be to distort its experiential meaning for white and black alike, for the poor of our cities as well as for the nonpoor.

Having characterized the core problems that profoundly affect the urban experience in contemporary America, we now turn to an examination of the cultural malaise that has generated these problems. What is it about our *national* culture that has resulted in the synchronic and obviously related manifestation of these three problems—race, poverty, and law and order—in our cities? Why are these three so central to our troubled urban life styles? Why do they persist? Why do they seem so pervasive throughout urban America? The following thesis is offered as a tentative answer to these questions.

THE PARADOX OF NON-INSTITUTIONALIZED INEQUALITY: THE RESIDUAL SEARCH FOR PERSONAL VALUE, AND ITS IMPLICATIONS

In American society all men are encouraged to have great expectations for their futures, to believe that they need only apply themselves to succeed or be winners in the mobility game.[25] There is a normative imperative in American society to the effect that we should all strive

25 Merton, cited in footnote 17. See also, Michael Lewis, "Structural Deviance and Normative Conformity: The Hustler and the Gang," *Crime in the City*, ed. Daniel Glaser, Harper & Row, New York, 1970, pp. 176–199.

to better ourselves, that the meaningfulness of our lives depends upon how assiduously we apply ourselves to the tasks of self-improvement, and upon the extent to which our efforts are recognized and rewarded by our fellows.

On the surface, at least, it would seem that such universal encouragement to improve one's station by individual effort and personal dedication is a positive social fact in American life. In the history of mankind there have been few societies in which this has been the case. For most people in most places, there have been institutionalized limits that fixed individual mobility, irrespective of personal endowments, and their willingness to expend the necessary effort. If a man was born a peasant, peasant he would remain until his maker claimed him. No burgher might aspire to the nobility, and few noblemen might seriously harbor illusions of elevation to royalty. There were more successful and less successful peasants, substantial burghers and those who were marginal in their communities, powerful barons and those who were politically and economically dependent. The lesser men might aspire to the eminence and power of their betters, but only of those betters whose social identity was basically the same as theirs, of those who belonged to the same social estate.

In most societies of historical record, *inequality* (social, political, and economic) has been *institutionalized*. The fact that some men could press their claims to wealth, power, and prestige as a matter of right while others were permanently consigned to the travails and sorrows of society's nether reaches, was rarely if ever challenged. Both those who flourished and those who suffered in such a system jointly accepted the legitimacy of their disparate personal destinies. In the American present we have a different situation indeed. In place of institutionalized inequality, we accept as legitimate only those values, plans, or proposals that conform to the *ethos of equalitarian mobility*, in which the only recognized limitations upon a man's aspirations are the limitations imposed by the extent to which his personal endowments are appropriate to his ambitions. Every newborn is a potential President or First Lady, every corner boy is a potential Senator, Governor or head of General Motors, if only he possesses the necessary talents and the will to put such talents to maximum use.[26]

So pervasive is this ethos of equalitarian mobility, that even those

26 For a discussion of the development of this ethos as well as the extent to which it has been realized historically, see Michael Lewis, "Social Inequality and Social Problems", *American Social Problems in a Revolutionary Age*, ed. Jack D. Douglas, Random House, New York, forthcoming.

who in private would subscribe to more restrictive conceptions rarely if ever do so in public. No American politician, including the most conservative among them, dares to be so explicit as to argue publicly that a particular group or people should be prevented from aspiring on high or from acting upon such aspirations. (Even such avowedly racist politicians as George Wallace, Lester Maddox, and James Eastland shrink from stating that *as a matter of principle* the aspirations of Negro Americans should be limited *de jure*.) To do so would invite public censure for being undemocratic, for violating one of most cherished of our ideals—an ideal which marks the 'American way' as different from and superior to the political cultures of other nations.

In spite of its apparent historic progressivism, the ethos of equalitarian mobility—the universal imperative to be mobile, unrestricted by extra-individual impediments—has certain implications, or as Melvin Tumin has phrased it, certain "unapplauded consequences,"[27] which at the very least are problematic and constitute the context in which the core problems discussed above are generated.

To begin with, the emphasis upon equalitarian mobility has been extremely potent in limiting the importance of *social class* as a meaning context in American society. The openness engendered by the belief in equal opportunity to be mobile, creates a situation in which people conceive of mobility as an *individual* rather than a *collective* experience. For example, the working man does not view the realization of his dreams as a function of the triumph of the proletariat. Even when the proletarian realizes that his dreams are being denied by conditions that exist beyond his personal control, his attempts to change this circumstance do not usually rest upon a belief that he is fighting for the collective triumph of all those similarly denied. Instead, he works to *reform* the system so that people like himself will have their promised opportunity to improve themselves *as individuals*.

The sense of class identity and collective social destiny is undermined by the ethos of equalitarian mobility in yet another way. The belief in the possibility of unrestricted personal mobility encourages people to regard their present class affiliations and the life circumstances attendant to them as impermanent. The presumed ephemeral nature of the present, the feeling that current conditions are only a prologue to the future makes it difficult to develop collective interests. When individual horizons seem limited, when an individual clearly perceives the class boundaries within which he must live out his life,

27 Melvin Tumin, "Some Unapplauded Consequences of Social Mobility in A Mass Society," *Social Forces, XXXVI* (October 1957), 32–37.

he is likely to pay attention to the collective interests of his similarly situated cohorts. When, on the other hand, the limits to personal mobility are vague, or are presumed to be nonexistent, the individual does not feel constrained to realize his dreams within a class context and will find little meaning in his class identity. The net result is the substantial weakening of social class in America as a context in which the individual finds meaning for his existence.

A second problematic implication or "unapplauded consequence" of the ethos of equalitarian mobility may be depicted in the following manner: in a society where there is strong belief in personal mobility, there is every likelihood that a mass *status market* will develop. The status market is a device that caters to widespread aspirations for individual mobility by literally *selling* the illusion of personal success without regard to the quality of actual individual achievements. The status market makes available to a mass public relatively cheap copies of those appurtenances and perquisites that are usually associated with high status. If the sales clerk cannot afford a Dior original, she can easily afford the mass-produced copy offered by the garment center. Not everyone can own a new Cadillac or Lincoln Continental, but almost everyone can find a Ford or Chevrolet in his future. And these motorized conveyances are tooled in such mimicry of their expensive prototypes that it is often difficult to tell them apart, particularly at today's high speeds. If a Park Avenue address is beyond one's means, a less expensive, but nevertheless equally pretentious neighborhood will be found. (The name will be fancy as will be the doorman, all decked in livery with gold braid.) It's true that not everyone can vacation at Newport or Key Biscayne, but there is always the Catskills with its conspicuously ornate hotels. All this and much more is available on a mass basis to those who are willing to spend what they have and incur debts for the rest.

The status market operates on the assumption that the mobility aspiring have need to legitimate their status—their "up and comingness"—by means of conspicuous consumption of those things popularly conceived of as marks of success. And, indeed, the assumption seems to have been proven correct. But, paradoxically, the mass distribution of possessions that are presumably status conferring has made their ownership of questionable psychic value: if status-conferring appurtenances are possessed by large numbers of people whose actual locations in the stratification system are dispersed, and if those who possess such objects are in fact quite heterogeneous in their social characteristics, then in any given instance, the possessors of the objects in question cannot be secure in the belief that their ownership does indeed signify personal distinction. The mobility-aspiring American (and that would seem to include the greater part of the total adult population) chasing after the perquisites of distinction, finds himself constantly disappointed in their possession. He is forever unsure that his possessions attest to the "fact" that he has "made it," the "fact" that he is "up and coming." Thus, the status market that only exists on a mass basis where the ethos of equalitarian mobility is widespread, in its very success as a mass phenomenon induces widespread *status insecurity*.

The problematic nature of these implications of our extensive commitment to the ethos of equalitarian mobility, may be described as a *crisis of personal meaning and self-worth*. The life of the peasant in traditional societies (those societies in which inequality is institutionalized) may have been hard—perhaps even brutal; but in the daily round of his activities, in his relationship to the land, which was as it had been for endless generations past, in the ageless ritual incantations of his religion, and even in the fears and superstitions that troubled his waking hours and disturbed his sleep, the peasant could find constant affirmation of his way, and constant support for who he was and why he was. His personal meaning and his place in the scheme of things was fixed and sure. In societies where inequality was institutionalized, where class affiliation consequently provided meaningful boundaries within which the individual acted out his personal destiny, where there could be no insecurity about a personal status or social location for this was more or less fixed at birth, the matter of personal meaning was hardly, if ever, problematic except in the metaphysical sense. And since relatively few people have ever been troubled by the metaphysics of existence, it is probably safe to conclude that in such societies the matter of personal meaning was simply nonproblematic for most people.

But in contemporary America, how different and how perplexing it is. Class affiliation, as we have seen, is nearly meaningless in establishing the boundaries of our consciousness of life-style and personal possibilities. And because of the establishment of the status market on a mass basis, even the external marks of rank and social value have lost much of their symbolic potency. In such circumstances as these, how is a man to know who he is or what he has become? How is he to be secure in the belief that he has really followed the imperative to be mobile, that his efforts to "better himself" have really counted?

Given the personal or subjective meaninglessness of class affiliation (that is, the fact that social class does not provide a meaning-context for the individuals), and the ambiguity of possessions that were once presumed to be status conferring, large numbers of Americans can be secure in their mobility achievements (such as they are), not by perceiving *who or what they are*—for this has become increasingly difficult to do—but by perceiving who and what *they are not*. Their definition of self, their sense of personal meaning and self-worth, is increasingly *residual*. They are what is *left over* after they decide what it is that they are not. Even such residual definitions of the self, however, are difficult to come by in the context of blurred class distinctions and ambiguous status symbols. Thus, they are forced back upon the grossest and most obvious indicators of difference, and more than this, they are forced to create meanings for these indicators which in residuum confirm their own sense of personal self-worth.

To begin with the indicators of poverty are particularly suitable raw materials for this manufacture of the residual definition of self. As we have seen, poverty is not merely the absence of sufficient economic wherewithal, but it is also intimacy with physical and social decay, despondency and disaffection, and personal and social disorganization. In themselves, these indicators of the poverty experience have no social meaning. They are simply the categories of experience that frame the common events in the lives of the poor. Their social meaning must be supplied or created from the perspective of those who for one reason or another are compelled to take them into account.

Meaning is the offspring of need. A great many of the nonpoor in American society need to *stigmatize* the poor so that by comparison they, the nonpoor, appear to be successful in living up to their potential. They thus endow the indicators of poverty with meanings that reflect unkindly upon the poor, and in residuum, favorably upon themselves. This is accomplished by means of a fairly widespread cultural syllogism that itself is an outgrowth of the ethos of equalitarian mobility.

For many in American society the *ideal* prescription that holds that no person should be constrained from making the most of his natural endowments is easily transformed into a statement that purports to describe an actual or real state of affairs. Our earliest educational experiences—and perhaps even those which follow when we are more mature and presumably capable of making distinctions between *ought* and *is*—tend to obfuscate or cloud the distinction between our lofty social ethics and the imperfect approximations of these ethics in our daily lives.

All of us have been exposed in our schools to the mystique of opportunity. We have all learned at one time or another that the "American way" is to reward talent and effort in true measure. Abe Lincoln was the son of an obscure mountaineer, was he not? Andrew Carnegie had naught but his wits when he started out. Then there was Booker T. Washington, born in slavery, who rose to become a great educator and "leader of his people," a "credit to his race," who was invited to the White House by President Teddy Roosevelt himself. And it is not just the success stories of Bunyanesque dimension that seduce us into believing that *ought* and *is* are in fact one and the same. We have also learned of those immigrants who came to our teeming cities so that their sons could become doctors, lawyers, teachers, engineers, and businessmen. Our education has tended to emphasize the close, real approximations of the *ought* to the general neglect of those manifold instances when these approximations have fallen far short of the ideal.

It is easy therefore to allow ourselves to ignore those social artifices that we have constructed to impede the full flowering of potential. And it is not an exaggeration to maintain that this is done more often than not. It is this conclusion that in recent years has obviously motivated various Presidential fact-finding commissions to give wide publicity in their reports to those facets of our social life which bring into bold relief the disparities between the ideal and actual, between *ought* and *is*.[28] If the general public did not tend to ignore these disparities, the tone of these reports would have been quite different. As it is, they have generally exhorted us all to be cognizant of how far we have yet to go before the mystique of equal opportunity is realized.

Once the distinction between *ought* and *is* has been obscured, the cultural syllogism that stigmatizes the poor out of the need of the non-poor for assurance of their personal self-worth is played out in the following manner.

1. We assume that all men in American society have equal access to opportunity, that reward is justly correlated with degree of talent and expenditure of effort.

2. We observe the indicators of poverty—economic insufficiency, intimacy with decay, and personal and social disorganization.

3. We interpret the indicators of poverty in terms of our assumptions about opportunity and just reward; and we therefore conclude

28 We refer to commissions such as (1) The National Commission on Civil Disorder, (2) The U.S. Civil Rights Commission, (3) The National Commission on the Causes and Prevention of Violence, (4) The President's Commission on Income Maintenance Programs.

that these indicators *mean* that the poor are poor because of their ineptness, their laziness, and their general lack of moral fiber. Their condition is thus perceived as the product of their own characterological infirmities.

The syllogism that gives meaning to the indicators of poverty and establishes a stigmatized identity for the poor also establishes, in residuum, a sense of personal meaning and self-worth for the nonpoor. We *are not poor.* We are not slum dwellers, we do not live in filth, we are not on welfare, we are not perennially unemployed, we do not have children out of wedlock, we are not forever intoxicated, and we do not run out on our families—all the things that the poor are and do because of their "characterological infirmities." Thus we must be good, energetic, assiduous, competent; and we are successful when we define our successes in a residual manner relative to the poor.

If this formulation can be sustained as accurate, we will have taken a major step in the direction of explaining why poverty persists in American society, and particularly within our cities. If the crisis of personal meaning and self-worth results in our making of the poor a negative reference group (a group of individuals against whose ostensible characteristics we evaluate ourselves) in the process of our residual search for self, then the poor are our psychic hostages against personal meaninglessness and devaluation. Their continuation in poverty is thus a matter of importance to us, for if visible poverty should cease to exist, we should be deprived of our hostages and left to confront the terrifying possibility that our successes *are more image than identity,* that we may not be what we presume to be, and that at the very least we can have no security in our self-conceptions. We must therefore keep the poor in their place.[29]

The persistence and intensificaion of racialism, like the maintenance of poverty, can also be explained as a function of the residual search for personal meaning and self-worth, and ultimately, therefore, as a function of the noninstitutionalized character of inequality in American society. If the mobility aspiring American is forced back upon the grossest indicators of difference in his need to establish his sense of self-worth residually, blacks and other nonwhites (who are overrepresented among the poor) are particularly useful as negative references, or psychic hostages. They are easily identified by the way

29 For a stimulating treatment of this circumstance, see Adam Walinsky, "Keeping the Poor in Their Place: Notes on the Importance of Being One-Up," *The New Republic,* July 4, 1964, pp. 15–18.

they look and sometimes by the way they sound. Then, because of the nature of their history in the United States, blacks in particular are well suited as objects of unvalidated projections of stigma.

Slavery, the peonage that followed, and an unfortunate migration pattern that brought them northward to the cities belatedly have all contributed to the blacks' burden in American society. Slavery literally destroyed their family system of African origin, replacing it with extensive matrifocality (the mother-centered family), which although well-adapted to the rural poverty, is disorganizing in the urban industrial context.[30] Peonage in the form of tenant sharecropping simply sustained the family patterns created in slavery. Late migration to the urban-industrial areas relegated the blacks to the bottom of the industrially based vocational pyramid.

These conditions of their experience, these indicators of their historic victimization in American society, have rendered the blacks vulnerable to white projections of inferiority. By means of the cultural syllogism described earlier in this section, the indicators of victimization—economic insolvency and family disorganization—are transformed into indicators of moral infirmity, and in residuum, into indicators of the personal self-worth of those whites who are desperate in their need for assurance that they have in fact lived up to the imperatives of individual mobility. The black man is thus made to symbolize the worst aspects of the human condition; he is made the representative of all that a man might be if he did not possess the "strength of character" and the "moral fiber" to overcome his worst proclivities and make use of those opportunities "guaranteed in the American system," to improve himself, to be mobile. Ultimately, the white American who is mobile or aspires to mobility, knows that he is worthy, that he is a man of value simply because he knows that he is not black.[31]

If this is true, then it is easy to understand why so many whites resist

30 See E. Franklin Frazier, *The Negro Family in the United States,* University of Chicago Press, Chicago, 1939.

31 It is important to remember that social mobility is a reality in American society. Sociologists have indeed been able to operationalize this concept and measure it. See, for example, Peter M. Blau and Otis Dudley Duncan, *The American Occupational Structure,* John Wiley and Sons, New York, 1967. However, its objective reality does not make it any less problematic from the point of view of those who are mobile or who aspire to mobility. This problem, given the conditions we have described, is a subjective or personal one. Mobile or not, it is difficult to tell whether you really are living up to the mobility/success imperative. This is particularly so when, as is often the case, one has only been slightly mobile, when, in an objective sense, one has moved up only a bit.

any real change in the condition of the blacks, any reform that promises to make the blacks less distinguishable as a pariah caste—or indeed any suggestion that the blacks are and, in fact, have been mistreated in American society. Change would mean that the blacks could no longer serve as psychic hostages against intimations of personal unworthiness or meaninglessness. Even the suggestion that blacks are "disinherited Americans" is threatening, because to recognize the legitimacy of such a suggestion would mean that such characteristics as economic insolvency and family disorganization are *not* volitional, and are *not* the responsibility of those who are so afflicted. Such recognition would render them useless as *residual* indicators of the personal value of mobile whites. If the blacks are not responsible for their lot, then *not* being plagued by disorganization and insolvency may simply be a product of a more advantaged position in society—a matter of good fortune as opposed to a sign of individual effort and achievement. For these reasons, we may suggest that the crisis of personal meaning and value (we are troubled by our inability to find distinctive success in our lives) born of the noninstitutionalized character of social inequality in the American experience functions to sustain racialism as it does to sustain poverty.

Earlier in this chapter we suggested that the law and order issue in the cities is related to the problems of poverty and race. We argued that the hard line on crime so characteristic of the white, middle-American is, in fact, a hard line response to the urban protest of the poor and the black, and that it is a code for militant resistance to demands on the part of the disinherited for greater equity within their communities. The residual search for self-worth underlies, as we have seen, the militant resistance to the protests of the poor and the nonwhite. It may, therefore, be reckoned as having causal importance in explaining the emergence of the law and order issue. The white nonpoor must keep the poor and the nonwhite in their place in order to insure that they will continue to serve as negative references or psychic hostages in their residual search for personal value and meaning. (Their need to do so is, of course, not a conscious need.) In doing so, the white nonpoor equate criminal intent with the protest against continuing inequality, thus allowing militant resistance to the protest to continue with impunity. While it may be morally difficult to defend privilege—the privilege of being white, of not being poor—it is certainly justifiable to defend one's business, home, and family against those who, with no better reason than criminal malice, would harm them. Therefore, if the law and order issue, as we know it, is inconceivable without the problems of poverty and race, and if these problems are themselves the product of the crisis in personal meaning and the concomitant residual search for self-worth, then we must conclude that the law and order issue, as we have described it, is yet another implication of the residual quest for personal value on the part of the white nonpoor.

Beyond this, however, the law and order issue is of particular symbolic importance when considered in terms of the residual value, noninstitutionalized inequality thesis. Consequently, it may be argued that there is an even closer causal association between the residual quest for personal value and the emergence of the law and order issue than the one just described. This association may be explained as follows.

We have suggested that in order to derive a residual sense of self-worth or personal value, the white nonpoor have to keep the poor and the nonwhites "in their place." This "place" is characterized by status stigma, so that to be poor and black means that you are perceived by others as being morally disreputable, as being without the necessary qualities of character that allow a man to make his way in the world. But keeping the poor and the black in "their place" is no mean task, for if they are to be stigmatized—their stigma in turn conferring a residual sense of personal worth upon those who create the stigma—it must appear that they are *not* being *kept* in their place, but that quite the contrary, given the opportunity to succeed, they characteristically fail of their *own volition,* that they are where they are because they have neither the character nor the competence to make the most of their opportunity to be mobile. If it were otherwise—if those who desperately need to keep them in their place had to confront the fact of their own unfair and discriminatory behavior where the poor and the black are concerned—then apparent failures could not be used residually to generate a sense of self-worth among those who engage in the conferral of stigma. If, as we have seen, the visible failures of the poor and the black are not their own responsibility, they are not indicators of moral frailty and personal incompetence and, consequently, they cannot be taken as residual indicators of personal value. The trick, therefore, is to keep the poor and the black in their place while at the same time deluding one's self into believing that no such thing is occurring.

Theoretically, the *law* is the guarantor of equal opportunity for all in American society. The Fourteenth Amendment to the Constitution promises equal protection to all. We take for granted that the *law* is the great leveller of men. Whatever inequalities exist among them, we presume that all men are one in their relationship to the law. The law in all its majestic fairness is assumed to be insensitive to everything save the relative merits of competing claims to justice. The law, therefore, is the penultimate symbol of equal opportunity in American society.

The assumption that the law is fair, that all men are equal before the bar of justice, serves at least two meaning functions in society that enable the nonpoor whites to keep the poor and the blacks "in their place" without confronting the fact *that they are doing so.* In the first place, this precept is itself a formal extension of the widely held belief that all men are entitled to equal access to opportunity. Justice may be understood as a form of opportunity. When justice is done, a man has presumably exercised his formally specified opportunity to present his best petition and to receive impartial and honest judgment of his case. Equality before the law, so long as it is believed to be operative, thus affirms normative equalitarianism in American society. In the second place, equality before the law—as long as it is deemed operative—affirms equal access to opportunity in areas beyond the legal system itself. A belief in its viability serves to reassure us that arbitrary restrictions upon the individual's right to better himself economically and socially—his right to be as socially mobile as his talents will allow—cannot operate extensively. A man confronted with such limitations can seek to have them lifted, and, if it is found that he has a valid grievance, the law will intercede in his behalf. If a man really has equality before the bar of justice, he must eventually have equality of social and economic opportunity, for the law guarantees an equal right to life, liberty, and the pursuit of happiness.

The symbolic importance of *the law,* as manifest in the meaning that the belief in its fairness has for the white and the nonpoor, is central to the drama that we have come to recognize as the "law and order" issue in our communities. The poor and the nonwhite, together with their liberal and radical allies among the nonpoor whites, have as part of their protest challenged the reality of equality before the law in the United States. They point to laws that intentionally discriminate against the blacks, to laws and judicial proceedings, that although fair in intent, work a special hardship upon the poor, and finally to inequalities in the way the law is characteristically administered,[32] inequalities that deprive the poor of access to first class legal services

32 For documentation of discrimination and inequality within the legal system, see Loren Miller, "Race, Poverty and the Law," *California Law Review, LIV* (May 1966), pp. 62–82. Also see *The Report of the National Advisory Commission on Civil Disorders,* Bantam Books, New York, 1968 (The Kerner Report); Jerome H. Skolnick, *The Politics of Protest,* Ballantine Books, New York, 1968 (a report submitted to the National Commission on the Causes and Prevention of Violence).

and that deprive blacks of adequate protection on the part of the police. The activists have recently taken to challenge the legitimacy of a legal system that, they maintain, so clearly discriminates against them to the benefit of others. They demand reforms so that the ideal of equal access to justice can be approximated in reality.

The challenge to the legitimacy of the American legal system has met its stiffest resistance among those who are often identified as the white nonpoor middle Americans. They link demands for legal reform to the presumed rise in crime, and attack those who stand for change as being motivated by nefarious desires or, alternatively, as being soft on crime and the "criminal element." They decry the movement for legal reform as a threat of significant dimension to the rights of the "law-abiding majority." The issue is thus joined. On the one side, the poor, the black and their allies press for reform, on the other side, the middle-American resists even the mere proposal of reform as subversive to the American system.

We may legitimately ask why is it that such resistance emanates from among the white nonpoor (the middle Americans) particularly if, as we have seen, they are least afflicted by the scourge of crime. Why is it that they perceive the challenge to the reality of equal justice as subversive to the 'American way'? Why do they so often attempt to discredit reform efforts as springing from nefarious motives? If they really believe in equality before the law, why do they not join forces with the reformers to rectify whatever needs to be set right in the American legal system? These questions can be answered in terms of the residual self-worth argument.

The need to find personal value residually leads to discrimination against the poor and the black so that their "failures" can validate the "successes" of the white nonpoor. However, in order for the apparent "failures" of the poor and the nonwhite to do so, it must appear that these "failures" are volitional, that they are not the results of obvious discrimination and inequality of opportunity. By assuming that the law indeed guarantees equality of opportunity, the white nonpoor are able to convince themselves that discrimination and limited opportunity have no bearing on the condition of the poor and the life circumstances of the nonwhites in their communities. (After all, the law in its fairness would not permit any citizen to be unfairly deprived of his right to a fair chance of self-improvement and mobility.)

When the disinherited and their allies challenge the reality of the notion that all men are equal before the law, they are, in fact, questioning the reality of the belief which allows the white nonpoor to avoid confronting their own culpability for the presumed "failures" of the poor and nonwhite. In doing so, they are threatening to upset the social-psychological logic that allows these "failures" to be used as residual indicators of the nonpoor "success" and personal value. The white nonpoor thus resist mightily any challenge to the presumed reality of *equality before the law*. The challenge to the reality of a truly equalitarian legal system is indeed subversive—not to the ideals of the "American way," but to the psychic equilibrium of those who tragically must find personal meaning and esteem in the misfortunes of their fellow citizens.

Given this psychic investment in *the law* as a symbolic guarantee of equal opportunity, the white nonpoor must resist the challenge proffered by the disinherited. By linking the challenge to the presumed rise in crime, they can convince themselves of its illegitimacy, and circular though it may be, the demand for reform can be seen as an indicator of the "breakdown in law and order," while those who support reform can be further stigmatized as representing the interests of the "criminal element." The protest against inequities in the law and its administration becomes itself an indicator of the moral frailties of the poor and the nonwhite and, residually, an indicator of the self-worth of those who "take a stand" in behalf of the law and the just order it sustains.

We have argued that the major problems that frame the contemporary urban experience in American society are the synchronic products of a paradox that defines what might be termed the *malaise* of our national culture. Because inequality is not institutionalized in American society, we live in a normative context that encourages us to be as socially mobile as possible. "Making it" is the test of a man and, to a lesser extent perhaps, of a woman. The imperative to be personally mobile has resulted in loss of positive conceptions of personal value and meaning, (the crisis of meaning and self-worth), that in turn results in the *residual* search for self-worth. The residual definition of self so characteristic of the white nonpoor in American society underlies the maintenance of stigmatized poverty, makes racialism necessary, and nurtures the insecurities without which the law and order issue as we know it would probably not exist.

Thus the paradox: on one hand we should regard the fact that inequality has not been institutionalized—or conversely that individuals have been encouraged to aspire without limit—as positive or progressive. This quality of American culture may indeed have been responsible for the rapid development of American society. By encouraging everyone to be mobile, the culture has worked to maximize the use of existing talents within the society. Such a circumstance, it would seem, increases the developmental potential of a society as compared to societies in which caste and class, as principles of social structure, severely restrict the task-rational distribution of human resources. (By task-rational distribution we mean matching appropriate talents with social and economic tasks in need of accomplishment.) On the other hand, the insecurity and problems of personal meaning and self-worth generated by the imperative to be individually mobile (the progressive imperative) would appear to be responsible for the persistence of some of our most grievous public troubles. And when one considers just how ingrained is this propensity to endorse personal mobility as an unadulterated good, it is not easy—given its causal role in the generation of our troubles—to be anything but pessimistic about the resolution of our difficulties in pursuit of maximum human serviceability in society.

We began the discourse of this chapter by noting that much of what is problematic about the contemporary urban experience is a function of a malaise in our national culture. An attempt has been made to indicate the parameters of our troubled urban experience, and to link these troubles to the contradictions that characterize a central aspect of our national culture. In the following chapter we shall attempt to develop a model of the manner in which the underlying cultural problem is manifested differentially in different urban settings, thus resulting in variations in the experience of urban troubles in contemporary America.

Chapter 7
Varieties of the Urban Experience: A Model

Let us attempt to posit a model that orders and accounts for the variations to be found in the extent to which the poor and the nonwhites are stigmatized in contemporary urban communities and, consequently, the extent to which the law and order issue is likely to be a significant component of the urban experience.

If the stigmatization of the poor and the nonwhite is a function of the need to use them as a negative reference for the white nonpoor's sense of self-worth, then the extent to which stigmatization occurs in any given community must be a function of the strength of that need in the community. The need to stigmatize the poor and the black is a product of the "crisis of personal meaning and self-worth" that, as we have noted, emerges out of the devaluation of social class as a meaning context and the status insecurity caused by the paradoxical success of the *status market*. Thus the potency of the need to stigmatize in any given community must be directly correlated to (1) the degree to which social class affiliation is devalued, and (2) the extent to which the *status market* is a factor in the social life of the community.

If it should be the case that social class affiliation is universally devalued as a basis for self-evaluation in all urban communities irrespective of their varying characteristics, and if the status market is equally important in all urban communities, then we should expect the crisis of personal meaning to be equally important in these communities and the need to stigmatize the poor to be constant in its high degree of potency. On the other hand, if variation in the characteristics of the array of urban communities in American society implies some real variation in the degree to which class affiliation is devalued as a meaning context and the degree to which the status market is important in these communities, then we should expect that the salience of the "crisis of personal meaning and self-worth" will vary accordingly and the need to stigmatize the poor and the black will be more or less potent according to the degree of salience which the "crisis" possesses in any given community.

On the assumption that variation in community characteristics implies a corresponding variation in the potency with which the crisis of personal meaning and self-worth is experienced, our major analytic task is to indicate just how this implication is realized.

THE IMPLICATIONS OF ECONOMIC VARIATION The nature of a community's economy has much to do with the extent to which the need to stigmatize the poor and the black is experienced by the whites and the nonpoor within that community, for the character of the local economy is a major determinant of the degree to which social class affiliation can provide a personal meaning context for individuals and the extent to which the status market is a factor in the social life of the community.

The local economy influences the extent to which social class affiliation is personally meaningful in the following manner. Where the economy is highly developed, where it is a complex of heterogeneous functions involving both the export and the local sectors, it generates a multiplicity of job categories and vocational opportunities.

In such an economy, a working man might be an unskilled or semiskilled factory operative or a highly skilled technician who regularly oversees a complex of machinery. Those who are part of the great and amorphous American middle class may be self-employed professionals, proprietors of small or moderate sized businesses, salesmen, white-collar clerks, and dependent or salaried professionals, for example. By generating this plethora of vocational categories the highly developed, heterogeneous urban economy presents a vista of nearly limitless opportunity to those who live within the community—and no matter where one is located vocationally it must seem that there is always that possibility of doing better, of getting ahead. There is enough actual job mobility so that the great variety of economic opportunities is something more than a cultural illusion.

In urban communities characterized by highly developed economies, the present-as-prologue-to-the-future is reinforced by virtue of the fact that from the perspective of the gainfully employed worker, there seem to be few economic dead-ends. The cultural emphasis on becoming, on moving from one opportunity to the next, we have noted, weakens social class as a personal meaning contest. When we emphasize the working out of our economic destinies *as individuals*—as is the case where the local economy is highly developed—we are hardly likely to pay very much attention to the collective meaning of our present economic location and its personal impact upon us. *Thus we can expect that social class as a meaning context will be weakened in direct correlation with the degree to which the community's economy is highly developed and heterogeneous.* This is not to say that social class is very meaningful for the individual even in those communities in which the economy is not so highly developed. Social-class-as-a-meaning context is devalued throughout American society because of our peculiar brand of equalitarianism. Nevertheless the potency of this devaluation varies according to the extent to which the local economy is able to sustain the belief that an individual has within himself the ability to move on to bigger and better opportunities. The more developed the economy, the easier it is to sustain such a belief.

The character of the local economy influences the potency of the *status market* in two ways. In the first place, by reinforcing the American predilection for personal mobility and personal distinction the highly developed economy invigorates the motivational base upon which the status market operates. When the local economy is relatively undeveloped, when it is homogeneous, and when vocational opportunities are limited for almost everyone in the community, the predilection for personal mobility—while no doubt present—is likely to be played down if only because the chances for such mobility as evidenced by the range of economic opportunities seem relatively remote. In such instances the needs that the status market serves will be manifest with less intensity than they are where the local economy is highly developed.

Second, the character of the local economy itself governs the accessibility that people in a given community have to the goods and services that are characteristic of the status market. When an economy is highly developed and diverse, it is much more likely to offer a wide range of goods and services that are generally purchased because of status needs than an economy that is relatively underdeveloped and organized around a narrowly defined set of functions. The difference is significant. In the former situation people are inundated with newspaper and television advertisements that constantly play upon their status needs, ads that promise the conferral of personal distinction with the purchase of the new car, the new coat, and the "best" in hi-fi equipment. And then there are innumerable shops whose sophisticated window displays constantly remind the casual strollers in the downtown area of the goods and services that will bring their possessor new esteem in the eyes of his fellows. In the latter situation (the less developed economy), however, the delights of the status market are likely to be much less obvious. When the local economy is a limited economy the presence of the status market is likewise limited. This limited presence of the status market can be understood as meaning that the residents of the community in question will not be as intensely aware of their status needs as are their urban brethren who live in communities where the highly developed local economy is accompanied by a highly developed status market presence.

Given this analysis of the impact of variations in the local economy upon the degree to which social class is devalued as a meaning context, and the degree to which the status market is likely to be significant in the social life of the community, what can we say with regard to the range of urban communities in American society and the meanings of poverty and racial difference that we are likely to find within them? Since there is a general correlation between size of community and the character of its economy—the larger the community the more complex and heterogeneous is the economy likely to be—that same correlation should extend to the relation between size and the degree to which social class is devalued and the status market is significant within the community. Thus if the economy is likely to be more complex and heterogeneous as size of city increases, it follows on the basis of the foregoing analysis that as size of city increases, the devaluation of social class as a meaning context will similarly increase in intensity, and the degree to which the status market plays an important part in the social life of any given community will also increase. Therefore, to the extent that the degree to which social class is devalued, and the degree to which the status market is important in a community indicate the intensity of the need of the whites and the nonpoor to stigmatize the nonwhite and the poor, *we should conclude that the greater the scale of the urban community the greater will be the potential for the stigmatization of poverty and racial difference.*

The logic underlying such a conclusion is clear and simple. Unfortunately, clear and simple logic when applied to the affairs of men and women in society has a way of being confounded by factors and conditions that are extrinsic to the assumptions from which it flows. And so it is in this case. A rank ordering of American cities would probably generate a rank ordering with regard to the need to stigmatize the poor—*all things being equal.* However, *all things are not equal* and so the ranking and the logic that underlies it would be confounded, at least in part. An examination of this state of affairs will lead us to clarify this matter by concluding that when cities exist in a metropolitan network, the network itself, and not its component municipalities, should be conceived of as a single community for purposes of relating institutional structure to the varying intensity with which the nonpoor and the whites feel the need to stigmatize the poor and the black.

The logic we have been using in developing our thesis to this point has assumed that each community has an economy that can be analyzed as a discrete unit separate from the economies of other communities. We have conceived of the local economy as an encapsulated entity separate from similarly encapsulated local economies of other cities. This is often *not* the case, however. Urban communities irrespective of their size may be independent central cities, suburbs, or satellite cities. A suburb exists on the periphery of a central city (usually a fairly large central city), while a satellite city is conceived of as a community beyond the suburban ring, but nevertheless still within the dominating orbit of the central city. Both the suburb and the satellite city have their local economies inextricably woven with the economy of the central city in whose orbit they exist. In the case of the suburb, it may even be that the community has no independent economy to speak of. The so-called "bedroom suburb," for example, may be an incorporated municipality—but except for a few local stores clustered together in shopping centers and a modest range of professional and service activities, it has no enterprises. Those who live in such a community generally derive their incomes from jobs located in the central city or in a satellite city, they are the legendary commuters. The size of such communities is irrelevant to the character of their local economies; their local economies *are the economies of the central cities which dominate them.* Thus both a small and large bedroom suburb are characterized for the purposes of our consideration by an economy whose degree of development and *heterogeneity* is a function of metropolitan area organization, rather than discrete community characteristics. Consequently the degree to which social class is personally meaningful, and the extent to which the status market has presence in these communities is a function of the degree of complexity and heterogeneity present in the metropolitan economy.

Community size, therefore, need not of necessity be correlated with the degree of economic development and as a result of this, size alone cannot be taken as an indicator of the extent to which social class is

1 This classification is a reformulation of a similar classification that first appeared in Grace Kneedler, "Economic Classification of Cities," *Municipal Year Book,* International City Managers' Association, Chicago, 1945, pp. 30–38.

devalued and the status market is operative. The small bedroom suburb and the small independent city are both small municipalities. But while the latter would no doubt rank relatively low on a scale of social class devaluation and the presence of the status market, the former, because of its tie-in with a highly developed economy of a metropolitan area, would rank relatively high on the very same scale. Thus, there is at least one major *caveat* to the logic of our earlier analysis in which community size is correlated with the degree of class devaluation and the potency of the status market, and consequently with the extent to which poverty and racial difference is stigmatized: community size can only be taken as an indicator of the degree to which poverty and racial difference is going to be stigmatized when the community in question is an independent central city. Even then care must be taken because a central city that is the heart or core of a metropolitan complex might very well house an economy far more developed than its physical scale would indicate. When such a city is the hub of a metropolitan area, its economy will likely have developed in response to an areal need that will include demand factors arising in its suburbs and the satellites.

Taking this second *caveat* into account leads us to a modification of our earlier analytic projection: the greater the community size, the greater will be the propensity to devaluate class as a personal meaning context, the more intense will be the presence of the status market and, as a consequence, the greater will be the need to stigmatize the poor and the nonwhite. Or, to restate: the larger the city and the more highly developed the economy, the greater the propensity to devalue social class as a meaning context, and the more potent the status market in the social life of the community. In consequence of this, it may be argued that the need to stigmatize poverty and racial difference will be more intense in larger cities as compared to smaller cities. When, however, the cities exist in a metropolitan network the *network itself* and not its component municipalities should be conceived of as a single community for purposes of relating institutional structure to the varying intensity with which the nonpoor and the whites feel the need to stigmatize the poor and the blacks.

Among the "other things not equal" that can confound the logic of the formulation just explicated are *regional* differences. Regional culture may very well have a countervailing effect upon the size function with regard to the stigmatization process. This is probably true in the South. The peculiar history of that region in which the value of racial separation based upon the belief in the natural or biological inferiority of blacks has dominated white consciousness, no doubt renders size of community relatively unimportant when we consider the stigmatization process insofar as blacks are concerned. Given the intensity of characteristic white-Southern racial beliefs the stigmatization of blacks within the region is probably more or less invariant from one community to the next regardless of their size. If anything, it may very well be that stigmatization is somewhat abated in the largest Southern communities that are more heterogeneous in population[2] and more cosmopolitan as a result of their economic and cultural links that extend beyond the Southern region.[3]

In any case the social-psychological logic we are posing as the basis for the stigmatization of poverty and racial difference may well have to be modified according to cultural differences that are specific to different regions within the United States. A systematic exploration of this factor would take us too far afield here, but it is necessary to note that such difference may have implications for the manner in which stigmatization occurs. If our basic thesis is deemed to have merit perhaps others will attend to questions such as these: Does the cultural emphasis upon individual effort so characteristic of the Great Plains and the far West intensify *overall* the need to stigmatize the disinherited? Holding community size constant, is the need to stigmatize intensified in these areas because of such a cultural emphasis? How does the overrepresentation of elderly people affect the manifestation of stigma in the retirement centers of California, Florida and Arizona, for example?

THE IMPLICATIONS OF POLITICAL VARIATION It is, of course, necessary to remember that communities vary significantly in non-economic characteristics and that these variations may have an effect upon the extent to which the need to stigmatize the poor is manifest within them. In an earlier chapter (Chapter 2) we examined the ways in which urban polities differ from one community to the next. The differences in these polities must be counted among those factors that have an impact upon the manner in which the need to stigmatize the poor and the blacks is realized from one urban community to the next.

Stigmatization can be mitigated to the extent that the poor and the

2 The population of cities like Atlanta, Miami and New Orleans have segments of non-native whites, whites from other regions of the United States who are less likely to be imbued with the Southern racial credo than are native Southerners.

3 For a sensitive treatment of the white Southern racial credo, see Lewis M. Killian, *White Southerners,* Random House, New York, 1970. Also see W. J. Cash, *The Mind of the South,* Alfred H. Knopf, Inc., New York, 1971; and James W. Silver, *Mississippi: The Closed Society,* Harcourt, Brace and World, New York, 1963.

blacks in any community are able to mobilize in behalf of their interests. Wherever the poor and the black constitute even a minimally politically significant segment of the local population, the action implications of stigmatization—the events of the poverty experience—take on meanings that are less pernicious than would otherwise be the case. The following may be taken as a case in point. In communities where the poor and the black have political presence the public rhetoric and public policy does not usually emphasize their presumed disreputability. The whites and the nonpoor may continue to hold them in disrepute, but there is likely to be some reticence in the translation of such belief into public statements and public policies that appear to represent the community's collective orientation toward the problems of poverty and racial difference. In Los Angeles, for example, the McCone Commission report on the Watts uprising takes a view that is less than complimentary to the city's ghetto residents, but the criticism of the blacks (which probably reflects the private feelings of a great many white and nonpoor "average Angelinos") is nevertheless masked in a rhetoric that gives the appearance of proposing extensive reforms intended to better their lot.[4]

The fact of the Watts uprising itself was a graphic if inchoate demonstration of political presence, and the McCone Commission, for all of its obvious predisposition to blame the black poor for that massive disruption of civic routine, knew better than to do so without at the same time paying lip-service to their grievances and making recommendations that ostensibly are intended to rectify at least some of the wrongs that, according to Watts residents, led to that social explosion in the summer of 1965. To blame the black poor of Watts without admitting to the legitimacy of at least some of their grievances would have been to invite increased political mobilization and action, perhaps even a sequel to the original disturbance. Undoubtedly the commissioners were astute enough to realize this, thus their ambivalent report. Consciously or not the commission took the potential of the black poor for political presence into account when they drafted their public analysis of what had occurred.

As further illustration we can take the case of Baltimore, Maryland, a city little-known for its social progressivism. Things have been happening in Baltimore. Although the poor—and particularly the black poor—have a long way to go before they can rid themselves of the burden which their "identity" has brought them, the intensity with

4 For a critical analysis of the McCone Report, see Robert Blauner, "Whitewash Over Watts," *Trans-Action, III* (March/April 1969), pp. 3–9, 54.

which they are stigmatized (as measured by the action or policy implications of that stigmatization) seems to be on the wane. When Baltimore's black poor demonstrated their political presence by winning a battle over reapportionment, they found that a previously recalcitrant city council approved a self-help housing program and increased rental allowances for welfare recipients. When black leaders demonstrated their authority in the political arena, they found that their white opponents began to "give some ground" and that those whites who shared their concerns began to have some resonance in "key decision-making centers" of the city's polity. In Baltimore the days of almost unabated stigmatization seem gone forever.[5]

It must be noted that political presence of the poor and the black does not necessarily mean that measurable progress will be made in redressing their grievances, nor does it mean that the reforms undertaken as a result of this presence are appropriate to the remediation of the victimizing conditions that are their lot. In the previous chapter we took note of the fact that the *urban protest* has not yet effected significant changes in the life conditions of the disinherited. The reader should not be misled by our suggestion that political presence reduces the intensity of the stigma visited upon the poor and the black. In the first place, it *only* reduces the intensity of stigma as it is manifested in public rhetoric and public policy, it does not *completely neutralize* the stigma. In the second place, while the reduction of stigma (or the intensity of stigma) must be considered positive, it does not of itself signal significant inroads against such conditions as job discrimination, educational discrimination, and inadequate housing that make victims of the poor and the nonwhite in our cities. The reduction of the public manifestations of the need to stigmatize the poor and the black is a necessary first step to significant change in the life conditions of the disinherited—it is nothing more.

If political presence (or significance) reduces the extent to which the stigmatization of the poor and the nonwhite is woven into public rhetoric and public policy, we must face up to the following questions: What factors in any given community are likely to generate such presence on the part of the poor? In what urban communities are these factors most likely to be present?

Answering these questions is no mean task, and what follows is not intended to be definitive. Quite the contrary the answers developed

5 See Peter Bachrach and Morton S. Baratz, *Power and Poverty: Theory and Practice*, Oxford University Press, New York, 1970, pp. 67–103.

below should be understood as tentative, theoretical approximations of what is really happening in our cities.

The poor and the nonwhite can achieve a modicum of political presence within their communities either by using the machinery of *institutionalized politics* or by engaging in behaviors that are examples of *noninstitutionalized dissidence*. (*Radical reform and revolution* are examples; see Chapter 6 for a discussion of these facets of the *urban protest*.) By using *the machinery of institutionalized politics* we mean developing control over some portion of the local apparatus—usually a political party—by means of which public policy is enunciated and developed as a matter of course. By *noninstitutionalized dissidence* we mean behavior that disrupts the social order of a community in a coercive attempt to influence the direction of public policy. Examples of such dissidence can range from a sit-in at the local welfare office to the violent insurrections in Watts, Detroit, Newark, and New York City. Such dissidence may be planned and executed in rational pursuit of a specific objective, for example, the welfare sit-in for better treatment of recipients (radical reform), or it may be more or less spontaneous and diffusely focused against the evils and frustrations of ghetto incarceration, for example, the massive insurgencies in the cities. Such dissidence is ultimately political because it announces that the poor and the black are a segment of the community that must be taken into account in policy deliberations. It is noninstitutionalized because the acts by which this announcement is made are likely to be regarded as illegitimate or beyond the limits of acceptable political expression.

The distinction between the two options of institutionalized politics and noninstitutionalized dissidence is not hard and fast, for it may be that the practice of dissidence is intended as a lever by means of which the disinherited hope to gain control of a segment of the local political apparatus. For purposes of clarity in our analysis, however, we will regard the alternatives as distinct options, each in need of independent clarification. In short the question as regards those factors that generate a political presence for the disinherited must be subdivided so that we may on one hand explore those community factors which generate institutionalized politics, and on the other those factors that generate dissidence.

In order for the disinherited to achieve political significance through control of local political machinery (or party apparatus), a number of structural components have to exist in the local polity. The community must have a polity that is characterized by the practice of *partisan politics*. The absence of a well-defined party apparatus puts the disinherited at a decided disadvantage in their attempt to gain a foothold through institutionalized channels. When the municipal polity is characterized by nonpartisan politics (for a discussion of partisan versus nonpartisan municipal politics, see Chapter 2, pp. 34-38), the salience of the *parapolitical* structure, or the alignment of stable interest groups in their voluntary association manifestations is increased.[6] The intensification of the importance that these associations and other informal interest groupings have in the local polity decreases the probability that the poor and the nonwhite will be able to elect government functionaries on a regular basis who represent their interests, or even the probability that their interests will be taken into account when candidates for public office are slated. The following case is illustrative of this circumstance: the city of Chalmers is the home of some 130,000 people located at the eastern edge of America's Great Plains. Approximately 10 percent of the population of Chalmers are black, the vast majority of whom are poor by any measure. There are, moreover, several thousand poor whites of Appalachian stock who live in ghetto-like neighborhoods at the periphery of the city. Chalmers has a nonpartisan form of polity and a council-manager form of municipal government. The black poor and their white counterparts are rarely, if ever, represented on the city council or on any of the policy commissions (police, fire, for example) that the council appoints. In fact, representatives of the poor—black or white—rarely get enough signatures on nominating petitions to gain a place on the municipal ballot. It is an open secret in Chalmers that "slating" for the municipal elections takes place at a series of Chamber of Commerce meetings. Members of the Chamber are invariably members of voluntary associations like the Rotary, the Exchange Club, the Board of Realtors, the local bar association, and the local chapter of the American Medical Association. Thus the slate that emerges from the Chamber's deliberations represents the business and professional interests in the community. After the slating process has been concluded, each candidate runs as an independent in the elections for councilman-at-large. The electorate chooses from among this group of individuals, but whatever the outcome the business and professional interests in the community are overrepresented in the local government.

Some may suggest that in the case just noted there is nothing to prevent the poor and blacks from running their own candidates against

6 For a discussion of the relationship between the parapolitical structure and the practice of nonpartisan politics, see James S. Coleman, *Community Conflict,* The Free Press, Glencoe, 1967.

the "slate." Theoretically this is, of course, true but a closer look at the political realities inherent in the Chalmers situation indicates just how difficult such a course of action would be.

Because there are no preexisting political organizations, any candidate for—let us say—the city council has to start from scratch. He has to have the resources to develop an organization that is capable of collecting enough nominating signatures to put him on the ballot. This is not so easy as might be presumed. The signers must be registered voters who are residents of the city, and their signatures on the nominating petition may be challenged for a variety of reasons. If he should succeed in his attempt to get on the ballot the candidate must then raise enough funds to campaign and to build organizational support so that he can maximize his potential vote. Financial insufficiency or organizational failure will rule out any chance of his being elected. In such a situation it is clear that "slated" candidates have a decided advantage. They have ready made organizational support: the presumably nonpolitical organizations whose interests they represent mobilize their members to work in behalf of the slated candidates (the parapolitical structure), and they are not likely to be bereft of adequate financial support.

On the other hand, perhaps the candidate who represents the interests of the poor will put an effective organization together, or perhaps he will not since the voluntary associations of the poor tend to be less stable than those of the nonpoor. He will surely have difficulty raising a campaign chest sufficient to give him a real chance for elective office. His major supporters *are poor;* they do not have the financial resources to compete with the resources upon which the "slated" candidates can draw. It is no wonder that Chalmers has rarely seen a representative of the poor elected to municipal office.

Whether or not the local polity is organized along partisan lines is important for yet another reason. Polities organized along partisan lines are generally characterized by ward politics. In communities where this is the case, elections for the city council are held on a district basis. Because of this, each party has to develop an infrastructure that is composed of district-based, or areal, subunits. Each party within the community is thus a federation of district organizations. In such a situation the practice of politics often resembles a negotiated exchange process: in exchange for maintaining their solidarity with the party as a city-wide organization, the leaders of the areal districts (or subunits) receive such political amenities and rewards as campaign funds from the centralized party war-chest, patronage in the form of an allocation of appointive city (government) jobs, and a receptive ear in city hall to the problems of the district, provided that grievances and requests are forwarded through party channels.

On the other hand, in cities where the local polity is theoretically nonpartisan, elections for the city council are often at-large elections as in the case of Chalmers.[7] This does not mean that the political parties have no real organization within the city. Because the city is part of partisan national and state polities, they obviously must organize to elect candidates to office at the state and national levels. Nor does it mean that the parties will have no district-based "infrastructure" within the city. There are district elections for such offices as state legislator and state senator that may, depending on the size of the city in question, generate such subunits of the party. But it does mean that since the parties play no official role in the electoral process, and since the municipal legislative branch is elected at-large, local district units will be little-related to municipal decision making and the processes of local government. Party solidarity vis-à-vis local government is not highly significant in such situations, and the kinds of exchange characterisic of ward politics as generally practiced in communities where the local polity is partisan and organized on a district basis are, therefore, largely absent.

The implications for the poor and the nonwhites stemming from the presence or absence of partisan politics—and its usual correlate ward (or district) politics—in the cities where they reside are quite clear. Where the local polity is organized on a partisan/ward basis, they are likely to develop some presence within boundaries of institutionalized politics; and where the local polity is organized on a nonpartisan at-large basis the disinherited are likely to be at a considerable disadvantage in their attempts to establish such a presence.

We have already taken note of how the nonpartisan polity weights (economically and organizationally) the chances that the poor and the nonwhites have of electing sympathetic representatives in the municipal government. The association of at-large electoral processes with the nonpartisan municipal polity further disadvantages the disinherited in their efforts to gain sympathetic representation. In at-large councilmanic elections, their candidate must stand before the total electorate of the community. Not only must he, therefore, have the solid voting support of the poor whites and blacks themselves, but he must also be able to attract substantial support from white nonpoor

7 See Edward C. Banfield and James Q. Wilson, *City Politics,* Vintage Books, New York, 1963, p. 151.

voters if he is to have any real chance of being elected. The chances of any candidate being able to do this are minimal, for the white nonpoor voter will usually perceive the interests of the poor and the black as inimical to his own.

In such a situation the candidate of the disinherited is caught between the horns of a significant and perhaps paralyzing political dilemma. If he is outspoken in behalf of the interests of his poor supporters, he will probably alienate enough of the nonpoor electorate to insure his defeat. If, on the other hand, his tone is moderate in support of these interests, he may attract some nonpoor votes (although there is no guarantee of this particularly if his opponents are successful in labeling his candidacy as radical or liberal, in spite of his protestations to the contrary), but he will most assuredly alienate many of the disinherited who will feel that he has "sold them out." The attrition in his support resulting from the alienation of many who constitute his political base will similarly doom his candidacy to defeat at the polls. Thus the very structure of an at-large election severely reduces the chances that a real representative of the poor and the nonwhite will take a seat in the council chamber.

The partisan/ward structure can be seen as enhancing the possibilities that the poor and the blacks will have at least some political presence in the following manner: the poor in American cities—and particularly the nonwhite poor who are overrepresented among them—are characteristically congregated in ghetto-like residential districts. This fact of our "urban demography" finds political translation when the polity of the cities in which they live is structured according to the *partisan/ward* principle. Given sufficient numbers the poor can be expected to be the dominant segment in the electorate of some of the city's councilmanic districts unless, of course, such districts have been gerrymandered to reduce the potency of the poor as a segment of the district's electorate. This has been true of a number of American cities. To the extent that candidates for the city council in such districts find it necessary to be responsive to the needs of their constituents, it can be said that at the very least the poor will have some of their needs articulated (if not necessarily acted upon) in the legislative deliberations of the municipal council.

Beyond having ostensible representation in the municipal legislature, the poor and the nonwhite can attain political presence in other ways when the local polity is structured according to the *partisan/ward* principle. District structure virtually guarantees that there will be at least one organization capable of sustained political mobilization in these areas where the disinherited are forced to congregate. The presence of such an organization—a subunit of the city-wide party—

increases the probability that there will be individuals within the city's poverty areas who have organizational experience and tested political skills. This increases the probability that the disinherited will be politically visible within the community and, in particular, that they will be visible to those professional politicians who, not representing them, would otherwise ignore or pay little attention to their needs. In a manifestation of the exchange process, the local political organization gets out the vote—and a successful mayoral candidate who has received solid electoral support from the poverty areas and who hopes for continued support from the voters in these areas can little afford to ignore the interests of people living there. He is likely to develop a symbiotic relationship with the political organizers in the poverty district, and even if he actually does very little in response to the needs of the poor, he will eschew policies that publicly demean them.

In addition, the district subunit of the city-wide party can also make life a little more endurable for some of the poor in ways that have become the traditional stock-in-trade of the urban political machine. Because the district organization produces for the city-wide party, its leaders have some claim to favored treatment for a constituent when and if they request it (another manifestation of negotiated exchange). In Chicago, perhaps the prototype of the *partisan/ward* structured city, poor blacks on the South Side have for a long time come to rely on the district organization that was the preserve of the late Congressman William Dawson.[8] The Dawson machine—as it still is called—was a major subunit of the Democratic city organization controlled by Mayor Richard Daley, and while Dawson and his lieutenants were less than sanguine about the interests of the black poor *in the abstract,* they were assiduous in pressing claims on behalf of constituents with the party and the governmental apparatus that the party controlled. The following description of their efforts is quite apt.

Almost every weekend [Dawson] flies to Chicago to sit in a shabby ward office in the midst of the slums and to listen to all who come to him. Where the direct material interests of his constituents are at stake he and his organization are ready to help, they will get a sick man into the county hospital, find out why a lady's welfare check has not arrived . . . and go to the police commissioner, and if necessary the Mayor, to see to it that a case of alleged police brutality is properly investigated.[9]

It is important to avoid the very real temptation to idealize what

8 William Dawson died in 1969, but his district organization is still operative in Chicago politics.

9 Banfield and Wilson, pp. 304–305, cited in footnote 7.

actually transpires as a result of district organization and ward politics in a partisan urban polity. While it is true that as a result of the trade-off between the district machine and the city-wide party organization *some* of the disinherited benefit by having *some* of their problems attended to—problems that in the nonpartisan situation would go unattended—it is also true that the basic evils of poverty and racial divisiveness, the deprivation and the stigmatization, are rarely if ever challenged by those who manage or run the district machine. The specific favors for specific constituents are part of a covert politics and are themselves a facet of a political logic calculated to avoid an explicit confrontation with basic issues. If party solidarity is taken to mean that the district organization will "go down the line" with the policies of those who control the city-wide organization, and if those policies underplay or even avoid the facts of widespread victimization of the poor and the blacks, then the exchange process that trades solidarity for attention to specific grievances as they are passed on by the local machine is, in fact, a major impediment to the kind of social and economic reform for which the condition of the urban disinherited cries out.

A few may benefit in the short run as a result of this process, but in the long run the many are victimized because those who theoretically represent their interests fail to articulate them in the arena of public debate and policy deliberation. In all its long tenure as the dominant political force on Chicago's South Side, the Dawson machine—its assistance to many constituents notwithstanding—has done little, if anything, to change the basic life conditions of those it ostensibly represents. Chicago's black poor were disadvantaged economically, politically, and educationally when William Dawson came to power some 30 years ago, and thus they remain today when he has passed from the political scene. It may even be suggested that under a system of partisan/ward politics those who control the district subunits in poverty areas have a vested interest in ignoring the basic issues of poverty and racial disadvantage. Consciously or unconsciously the ward leaders know that the circumstances of their constituents can be used to keep them in line. It is the poverty of a constituent that turns him into a supplicant in the politician's office; it is his poverty that breeds his dependency and that insures his loyalty to the machine. Given this circumstance, it is hardly surprising to discover that the ostensible representatives of the poor are uninterested in *poverty as an abstract issue,* for reforms alleviating poverty might very well put them out of business.

In sum then, while it may be that the partisan/ward structured polity simplifies the problems that the disinherited have in achieving political presence within institutionalized parameters, it also tends by its very nature to minimize the *issue-relevance* of that presence. In an urban polity structured in this manner the disinherited do indeed become a factor, but rarely are they able to generate a politics that is truly responsive to the community conditions that create and sustain the awfulness of their experience.

Whether the community polity is *non-partisan* or *partisan/ward* in its structure, the nature of the disinherited population, in particular their numbers, in a given city will have a decided impact upon the kind of political presence they are able to generate within the range of acceptable institutional expression. The greater their proportionate number in the local electorate, the greater the probability that public rhetoric and public policy will *appear* (if nothing else) to take cognizance of their needs and interests.[10] In those cities where the poor and the nonwhite have come to constitute a substantial segment of the electorate, it has become more difficult to manipulate their interests without at least paying some public attention to their legitimate grievances. In such cities the old machines can no longer sweep the issues of the poverty experience and racial disadvantage under the civic carpet by relying upon the covert politics of trade-off. Even in Richard Daley's Chicago the treatment of the poor and the black "in the abstract" is a publicly contested issue. And in those cities where the old machines are or have grown relatively weak while the poor (usually the nonwhite poor) have increased their numbers on the electoral rolls, one can be sure that political aspirants will replace the stick with the carrot when poverty becomes a campaign issue. Few candidates in cities like Cleveland, Detroit, Gary (Indiana), and Newark (New Jersey) can expect to be elected by taking a "hard line" on poverty and race, particularly if they are running for city-wide offices.[11]

It should be noted, however, that numerical strength at the polls does

10 For example, see James Q. Wilson, "The Negro in Politics," *Daedalus*, Fall 1965, pp. 949–973.

11 At this writing, Gary and Newark have black mayors whose electoral successes have depended in large measure on their ability to capture an overwhelming majority of the votes cast by the nonwhite poor. Detroit almost elected a black mayoral aspirant, and while his successful opponent had something of a "law and order image" it cannot be said that he is a "hard liner" with regard to the poor. The successful candidates in Gary and Newark were able to win by attracting a solid black vote, among which the poor are overrepresented, and a smattering of white liberal votes.

not mean that the poor and the nonwhites will have their grievances acted upon in a manner sufficient to rectify the wrongs visited upon them. Numerical strength assures a reduction in the degree to which the disinherited are stigmatized in the politics of the community; it can assure the disinherited that those who govern them will *appear* to be sympathetic to at least some of their interests, but in the making of decisions that will really advance their interests, they are more likely to be disappointed than satisfied with the outcome.

The reasons for this are manifold, not the least of which is the fact that the municipal polity is often without the resources to really do anything about the conditions of poverty. Even the enlightened leadership of so mighty a metropolis as New York City does more gesturing about poverty than actual reforming of conditions in its midst. The city has neither the resources nor the necessary powers; it must depend upon state and federal auspices in order for its political leadership to initiate reforms of sufficient scope to make serious inroads against the poverty experience. The government of New York City cannot of itself reform the city's welfare system; it cannot of itself wage war against slum housing; and any real improvement of the schools that serve the poor is highly improbable without a massive input of state and federal funds.

But even were there no structural and resource impediments to municipal reform, it would be rare for urban political leaders to commit themselves to serious efforts on behalf of the disinherited. Without doubting their ostensible sincerity, we may nevertheless call attention to the fact that politicians, like their fellows among the nonpoor citizenry, are also subject to the constraints that emanate from the peculiar experience and functionality of social inequality in American society. If it is true that the poverty of others (particularly of the nonwhites) protects *us* from the awful awareness that our personal "distinction" and "self-worth" is in fact invidious and meaningless, we can expect public officials to be subject to the same psychic dilemma —even with the variations in community characteristics that we presume indicate a corresponding variation in the intensity in which the need to "keep the poor and the nonwhite in their place" is experienced. And if this is so we should not then expect public officials to take action that might very well destroy the meanings that poverty and racial difference has for the white nonpoor. The political significance of the disinherited in a given community will no doubt check the politicians' urge to maximize the psychic usefulness of their disadvantage, their urge to maximize the imputation of stigma where the poor and the black are concerned, but we should hardly expect that these same politicians will, as a rule, be able to rise above the logic of their culture in order to undermine the psychic functions of poverty and racial disadvantage in American life.

In an earlier chapter of this book (see Chapter 2) we came to the tentative conclusion that different types of urban communities were likely to be characterized by differences in their "power structures," or the manner in which *power* is generally distributed within them. On one hand, we argued that a monistic power structure dominated by a ruling economic elite was likely to be found in relatively homogeneous urban communities where fewer competing interests exist in the polity, and where fewer problems of such complexity exist that demand the kinds of expert attention that tends to distribute power among a multiple of discrete hierarchies. On the other hand, we argued that relatively heterogeneous urban communities—because of the complexity of their economies, the conglomeration of their disparate population segments each competing for a share of the civic pie, and the variety of problems that are generated by the need to coordinate and articulate the needs of disparate segments—tend to have a pluralistic distribution of power, a distribution characterized by a multiple of power (or decision making) hierarchies, each attending to a specific aspect of life within the community. If there are such characteristic differences in the way power is allocated from one community to the next, then we must inquire about any implications that this circumstance holds for the disinherited in their efforts to resist stigmatization and to reform the conditions of their lives.

In those communities where power is monistically structured the poor and the nonwhite will likely have little or no institutionalized political resonance. A monistic power structure is likely to be dominated by an economic elite that determines policy on major issues facing the community. If we correctly assume that the need to stigmatize the poor and the nonwhite is of significance to the white nonpoor of the community in their residual search for meaning and self-worth, then the elite will dominate public policy on the poverty and race issues, and public policy on these issues will hardly reflect the interests and needs of the disinherited within the community.

Of course it is not true that in *every* community where such a monistic structure of power exists the disinherited will find their interests totally neglected. In some communities the elite, following a tradition of noblesse-oblige, may provide for "their" poor. Nevertheless, where local elites dominate the community polity the disinherited will have little political presence of the institutionalized variety and, as such, their potential for limiting the extent to which they are publicly stigmatized (or conversely, their potential for maximizing public sensitivity to their interests) through the practice of institutionalized politics will be limited indeed.

In those communities where power is pluralistically allocated over a range of relatively specialized decision-making hierarchies the disinherited may have a better chance of developing the kind of political presence that, however limited, does nevertheless exert a moderating influence upon those who would otherwise cause them to suffer public ridicule or would ignore their just claims. In such a complex heterogeneous polity the politics of trade-off is likely to be the means by which public policy is created and executed. Since no interest group is likely to possess enough power to dominate all the others and to exert its will whenever it wishes, each interest group must be willing to support others on particular issues in order to claim support in return for positions and policies that it favors. Therefore, to the extent that the poor and the nonwhites have an organized voice in the community, they are likely to have some minimal claims on other organized components of the local polity. And while they are likely to be subject to limitations on their political resonance (or presence), relative to the disinherited in those communities that are characterized by monistic power distributions, they are more likely to be able to resist the most damaging forms of public stigma—and perhaps in some instances they are able to effect some policy decisions which are responsive to some of their needs.

There are—as we have seen—very real limitations to what the disinherited may accomplish through the practice of institutionalized politics in any community. Therefore, if the poor and the nonwhite are to be able to reform the conditions that result in their victimization and in particular their public stigma it would seem that they must turn to strategies and tactics that go beyond those available to them within the constraints of institutionalized politics. They have done this in community after community where *noninstitutionalized dissidence* has been employed to dramatize the inequities of their lot. In such communities the poor (and in particular the nonwhite poor) have rejected the political party, the ballot box, and the covert politics of trade-off for the active dissidence of radical reform and revolutionary intent—the sit in, the boycott, the disruptions of bureaucratic routine and, indeed, the violence of massive insurrection—that forces a recalcitrant citizenry to confront the issues of poverty and racial disadvantage. It may well be that the disinherited achieve their greatest political resonance when they forsake the ballot box for the street, which is not to say that recourse to noninstitutionalized dissidence will always result in the changes they seek. The obstacles to the successful use of the tactics of dissidence are many; but even in failure those who employ such tactics know that the nonpoor who continue to victimize them can do so only at some cost to themselves.

As noted earlier, noninstitutionalized dissidence can be focused and executed in rational pursuit of specific ends, or it can be a spontaneous eruption of collective disaffection. Of the two variants the former is political both by intention and implication, while the latter, having obvious political implications, has an expressive origin in the unalleviated frustrations and indignities of stigmatized daily living. To a considerable degree, noninstitutionalized dissidence (radical reform in particular) has been the strategy of the nonwhite (and particularly the black) poor in our cities. Here let us examine the conditions that lead the poor into dissidence and the qualities that portend either success or failure for such political action.

It is important to remember that noninstitutionalized dissidence is—chronologically speaking—always a *second politics,* a second choice by the disinherited of the means by which they hope to alleviate or reform the conditions of their experience. One will not find a community in which the poor have been moved to dissidence without a history of unresponsiveness to initiatives that fall within the boundaries of institutionalized or "legitimate" political expression. That this is so is not difficult to comprehend. In the first place, there is no reason to assume that the poor and the nonwhites start out by being any less committed to the ideals of the American polity than the nonpoor. It may be that the disinherited by virtue of their preoccupation with immediate personal needs and troubles (such as making a living, keeping the family together, and staying out of trouble with the law or with the Aid to Dependent Children caseworker) tend to be less than sanguine about politics in general.[12] However, there is nothing to indicate that, when made politically aware, they just "naturally" reject institutionalized political forms and the values of electoral democracy. The first political impulse of the disinherited—whether in Harlem, on the South Side of Chicago, or Watts—has been to go the route of the established political parties. Even today the majority are loath to move from institutionalized politics to noninstitutionalized dissidence as a means of establishing their political presence. Thus, it is only after confronting a series of disappointments—disappointments emanating in the legitimate polity—that some of them turn to dissi-

12 Wilson and Banfield, pp. 292–296, cited in footnote 7.

dence as a political tool. To those who would quarrel with this observation by citing the propensity of the young to join the dissidents, we would point out that the young are capable of reading the disappointments of their elders and of appreciating the apparent duplicity that so often seems characteristic of the behavior of the "legitimate" decision makers.

The decision to embrace noninstitutionalized dissidence, moreover, is not made lightly even by those who are acutely aware of the limitations of institutionalized politics. There are real personal costs involved in taking the role of the political dissident (radical reformer or revolutionary). Engaging in disruptions of the civic order by any means involves risks. The dissident must be prepared for counteraction on the part of those whose interests he is attacking, and their agents. Perhaps he will be attacked physically or even jailed. He may lose his job; his relatives may lose theirs or otherwise suffer from discriminatory acts because of his political dissidence. One can readily understand why it is that dissidence is a "second politics," entered into only after a profound alienation from "politics as usual." The disinherited, even though they have little to lose, do not readily risk the loss of what little they do possess.

If *noninstitutionalized dissidence* is a second politics for the poor and the nonwhite, we must try to understand the community conditions out of which it emerges. What are the qualities of community polity that lead to the kinds of unresponsiveness that in turn moves otherwise conventional men and women into the politics of dissidence in spite of the very real risks involved in such a course?

We have, to some degree, answered this question in our discussion of the structural limits on the efficacy of institutionalized politics where the interests of the disinherited are concerned. But let us extrapolate a bit from this earlier discussion. The structural variations in American urban polities in conjunction with the psychocultural need to stigmatize the poor and the nonwhite that is endemic to American society, notwithstanding variations in intensity, eventuates in three types of political disappointment for the poor. In communities where a monistic allocation of power and/or a nonpartisan-at-large organization of the polity deprives the poor and the nonwhite of any real political presence, the need to stigmatize will meet little resistance. In such communities (usually small or middle sized cities) the disinherited who wish to reform the conditions of their lives often find that their petitions for change do not even get a respectful hearing. They are the community's undesirables and unreliables who justly deserve their lowly station and no matter how well they document their grievances, no matter how well reasoned their arguments, or how moderate their proposals for change, they are publicly branded as troublemakers, freeloaders, and Communist conspirators threatening the "American way of life." At best such a polity is "unresponsive"; at worst it turns even the most moderate of public petitions into "reasons" for extended victimization of the petitioners.

In cities where partisan/ward politics and a pluralistic distribution of power predominate, the disinherited, as we have seen, are capable of developing political presence—although it is a presence that, while alleviating the intensity of their public stigmatization, does little in a positive way to reform the conditions of their experience. For those among the poor and the nonwhite who envision an end to poverty and racial disadvantage rather than the discrete advantages won for a minority of their number by means of the covert trade-off, institutionalized politics must seem little more than a sellout of their real interests.[13]

Finally, there has occurred in the cities a disappointment of comparatively recent vintage. In those communities where the poor and the nonwhite have achieved some political presence, however minimal, and where the established political machinery has recognized the need to assuage the disinherited because they constitute a relatively significant segment of the electorate (communities where in general there is a pluralistic distribution of power), there has been in the last decade a proliferation of aid programs ostensibly intended to address and reform the conditions of poverty. These are the programs that have been generated by the federal government's mobilization of resources to wage a "war on poverty." On the surface, it would seem that these programs—Model Cities, Head Start, the Domestic Peace Corps, Community Action and the like—represent a significant development within the boundaries of institutionalized politics with regard to the needs of the urban disinherited. In point of fact, however, this has not been the case and the most politically aware among the poor have come to recognize this. The disappointment generated by the failure of such programs to make significant inroads against the depradations of the poverty experience must be particularly bitter for those activists committed to real reform. They promise so much and deliver so very little. They are often sponsored and staffed by well-meaning people who claim sympathy for the needs of the disinherited, or by people in the community who are among the most

13 For documentation of this circumstance see John R. Fry, *Fire and Blackstone*, J. P. Lippincott Co., Philadelphia and New York, 1969, pp. 37–38.

outspoken and articulate in their moral outrage at the maintenance of poverty amidst plenty. Their statements of intent promise a new tomorrow in which the disinherited, having become masters of their own destiny in possession of themselves, will escape from the victimizing conditions of their lives. But for all the clamor, all the high hopes and grand beginnings, the conditions of the poor and the nonwhite in American cities have not been significantly improved. That the politically aware among the disinherited are increasingly estranged from even their former allies among the nonpoor, should not be surprising in this context of great expectations and unkept promises. If those on your side cannot come through for you, then whom can you trust? Who indeed but yourself and those who suffer with you? The War on Poverty? O.E.O.? Literacy programs? Head Start? Model Cities? Nothing but politics as usual, old vinegary wine in new bottles. So to hell with playing by the rules.

A distinction must be made between those conditions leading to political disappointment and the consequent propensity on the part of the disinherited to embrace the strategies and tactics of dissidence, and those conditions in urban communities which make the development of dissident politics a realistic possibility. It is one thing to believe that the salvation of the poor and the nonwhite depends upon their ability to disrupt the civic order that victimizes them; it is another to organize and sustain a movement committed to such direct action.

Because dissidence involves very real risks to the dissident and those closely associated with him, it is unlikely that there will be a one-to-one relationship between dissident intentions and dissident behaviors. It takes more than the mere desire for action to become actually committed to the realization of one's intentions. The street corners and other places where the embittered poor of our cities congregate are alive with dissident talk and insurrectionist proposals. If one tenth of these ever came to pass, a condition approaching civil war would exist in our cities, but most of the disaffection never gets beyond the talking stage for few potential dissidents are willing to take the risks which their fantasies imply.

In order to actualize dissident intentions, and in order to turn wishful thinking into a commitment to act regardless of the personal dangers that such a commitment entails, a catalyst must be present, a vitalizing agent so compelling that it can mobilize ordinary people to undertake extraordinary tasks. In those instances where noninstitutionalized dissidence has manifested itself in large scale riots—those paroxysms of violent insurrection—the catalytic agent seems to have been a cumulation of indignities over a relatively short period of time that, having occurred against a background of deprivation and disappointment, sparks a collective rage that sweeps aside all personal caution.[14]

The more focused and disciplined commitment to radical reform or revolution, however, cannot depend upon the idiosyncracies of victimization for its actualization. The catalyst that makes a sustained commitment to act out of the fantasies of shared anger is a quality of *leadership* that, in its combination of charismatic magnetism and organizational acuity, is all too infrequently encountered.

The leader possessing charisma—a Martin Luther King, or before him, an A. Philip Randolph or, indeed, a Marcus Garvey—is a man larger than life. In his person he amalgamates all the hopes and aspirations of his potential followers while he seems to be unaffected by the fears and insecurities that cause other and lesser men to hesitate in pursuit of these aspirations. By deed and by manner he seems to personify the certainty of success. His presence inspires in those who would follow him a willingness to suffer the risks and uncertainties of the present because the future he envisages for them seems undeniable.

Such a manner in itself may be counted a rarity among men while in combination with a high degree of organizational skill it is rarer still. But organizational skill may be as important as charismatic magnetism when it comes to sustaining a dissident politics. In fact, without it the magic of the leader's charisma may itself be fleeting. If the enthusiasm and the commitment generated by the person of the leader is not put to use in a manner that confirms even minimally his prophesy (reading of the future) his followers may begin to doubt, to drift away, to split into factions. Organization can prevent this from occurring by employing the energies and skills of adherents to the cause in activities that, at the very least, appear to signify progress towards that promised tomorrow. Some may be regularly assigned to recruitment activities where each new convert to the cause signifies progress. Some may be assigned the task of maintaining the movement's propaganda apparatus, and as they strive to convince others that their definition of a just future must ultimately prevail, they succeed in sustaining their own certainty of that future. Others may be assigned to the planning and execution of dissident demonstrations, and if the leadership has the wisdom to avoid objectives that cannot possibly be realized in the circumstances that they confront, the exhilaration of taking part in active protest and the rejection of the

14 See *The Report of the National Advisory Commission on Civil Disorders,* Bantam Books Edition, pp. 117–118.

present can be enough to sustain the enthusiasm of the majority of the rank and file.

Of course, winning some battles, no matter how small, goes a long way toward sustaining a commitment to dissidence; and a leadership that picks attainable objectives and organizes effective protest in pursuit of these contributes immeasurably to the viability of the movement. Given the fact that in any community the eradication of poverty and racial disadvantage will not be immediately accomplished, the *certainty* generated by the charismatic leader can only be sustained by interim activities that have an aura of success or progress. Such activities, it would seem, are largely if not entirely a function of organizational acuity on the part of the dissident leadership.

If the combination of charismatic projection and organizational savvy is a prerequisite for those who would lead a movement for radical reform or revolution, they must either possess these qualities in combination (a rarity as we have noted) or, possessing one quality and not the other, they must work out a stable collaborative relationship with those who have the complementary skill. Some people are possessed of dynamism that attracts others and fires dreams. We cannot say that such a man or woman is more likely to be found in one community as opposed to another. Moreover, the charismatic leader does not necessarily have to be a local figure to spark dissident enthusiasm among the local poor. He may very well be a national figure whose renown is itself a charismatic advantage because it appears to support his claims to a vision of ultimate victory. Martin Luther King's *dream* resonated through every ghetto in the United States, stirring many who had never seen him in person. Local dreamers of that same dream could never hope to have an equivalent impact upon their poverty-stricken brethren. Thus, while such a dramatic presence has an impact upon the local poor, such presence need not be generated from within the community. Consequently we may discount (though not totally) the importance of community characteristics with regard to the function of charisma in the genesis of radical reform or quasi-revolutionary movements.

On the other hand, community characteristics are probably quite significant with regard to the extent to which organizational acuity is to be found among local dissident leadership. The chances of finding organizational savvy among dissident leaders are greater in *larger* as opposed to relatively small urban communities. In the first place, numbers alone would increase the probability that such a characteristic will be found. The greater the pool of leadership resources, the larger the population from which dissident leadership can arise, and the greater will be the probability that at least some aspirants will possess the acuity necessary to sustain a dissident movement.

Second, larger urban communities are more apt than smaller ones to afford opportunities to the leadership of the poor for developing organizational skills. It is in the larger communities that one finds the partisan/ward electorate; and if this form of institutionalized politics does not seriously address itself to poverty reform, it does afford some among the disinherited opportunities for organizational experiences encompassing many of the activities (such as, recruitment, mobilization, and propaganda) that are also important to a dissident politics. If some of those having such experience turn to dissidence out of their disappointment with the failure of "politics as usual" to reform the conditions of urban poverty, they are likely to provide the organizational acuity necessary for its sustained viability.

There is another characteristic contributing to organizational acuity among dissident leadership that, although not strictly a function of community size, is found extensively in larger cities. In cities where manifestations of the "war on poverty" have emerged on a relatively large scale, many leaders among the poor and the nonwhite, through their involvement in such programs, develop organizational skills that can be put to good use in the service of a dissident politics. If nothing else, the "establishment programs" of the poverty "war" may be contributing to poverty reform in the cities by providing leadership training experiences for activists who, when alienated from these programs, turn to dissidence as a means of establishing political presence.[15]

In sum, then, it would seem that viable political dissidence among the poor is most likely to be sustained in those communities where (1) there are large numbers of the disinherited, (2) where some have had organizational experience within the context of institutionalized politics, and (3) where federally supported programs of "establishment reform" have afforded leaders among the disinherited the opportunity to develop their organizational skills. Each of these community circumstances contributes to an increasing probability that dissident leaders will possess the organizational acuity necessary to sustain a dissident politics. Thus it would seem that the probability of sustained dissidence within a community is increased by the cumulation of these circumstances. It is highest where all three obtain and lowest where none are characteristic of the community in question. At least two of three circumstances are more likely to prevail in large, as opposed to rela-

15 For a discussion of the ancillary effects of the "War on Poverty" see Bachrach and Baratz, pp. 97–103, cited in footnote 5.

tively small communities, (while the third—federally supported "establishment reform"—is also likely to be found in large cities, although not exclusively). Therefore it may be suggested that insofar as organizational acuity is a key factor in sustaining dissident politics—size of community may be used to predict the likelihood of sustained dissidence among the disinherited. The larger the community, the greater the probability that it will house a sustained dissident politics on the part of the poor and the nonwhites.

VARIETIES OF MANIFESTATION: A JUXTAPOSITION OF ECONOMIC AND POLITICAL FACTORS Any attempt to characterize the manner in which the experience of poverty and racial disadvantage is dramatized from one community to the next must ultimately juxtapose the economically engendered variations in the intensity of the need of the white and the nonpoor to stigmatize nonwhites and the poor, against those variations in the political presence of the nonwhites and the poor that are determined by the characteristics of the local polity. In any given community the nature of the experience will be a function of the interplay between these two institutionally based factors.

As a general rule we have suggested that the larger the community, the greater the probability of social class devaluation, the more potent the status-market[16] and, therefore, the more intense is the need for the whites and nonpoor to stigmatize the nonwhites and the poor. All other things being equal, it should follow that the experience of poverty and racial disadvantage will have its most severe manifestation in the largest cities and will tend to decrease in potency as the size of the community decreases. All other things are rarely equal, however, and variations in the extent to which the nonwhites and the poor are able to develop political presence within their respective communities must lead us to modify the foregoing projection.

Any alert individual who has spent some time in, let us say, New York City, would observe the following: on one hand, New York houses some of the worst slum ghettos in the world. The nonwhite poor who are confined to these areas of the city live lives of desperation. Their slum apartments are overcrowded with people, rodents, and vermin. Broken windows let in the winter cold, the summer heat, and street noises all year round. Because doors are often in disrepair the public life of the street extends into the presumably private space of the home. Privacy is more than scarce, it is all too often nonexistent. Because of high rates of unemployment the streets are populated by

16 As corrected for type of community.

bored and listless men whose personal disorganization can hardly inspire the children of the ghetto to strive for the rewards that adulthood should bring. The police, presumably there to protect the law-abiding, often behave as though they were an occupying army, for they are afraid (often with justification) of what awaits them around the corner. In their eyes everyone is a potential criminal simply by living in the neighborhood, and people are treated that way.

Let there be no mistake about it, the threat of crime is a very real one. No one feels safe in Harlem, the Lower East Side, the West 80's or Bedford-Styvesant. Drug addiction has turned many a young man into a mugger, many a young woman into an aggressive hooker, and many a child into a purse snatcher. The threat of violence is ever-present, a fact of life that weighs heavily upon those who have been consigned to the city's nether reaches. New York City's nonwhite poor do indeed exist in the desperate circumstances we would expect where the poor are intensely stigmatized and, consequently, rejected by their more fortunate fellow citizens.

On the other hand, however, our alert observer would recognize that the poor—particularly the nonwhite poor—do seem to possess a distinct measure of political presence in New York. The disinherited are anything but silent in this metropolis. They have their representatives in the councils and agencies of the municipality. The patrician mayor projects himself as their champion. Perhaps in no other American city is there so robust a noninstitutionalized politics of dissidence as exists in New York.

The fact of this political resonance (or presence) should not surprise us. New York has a partisan/ward electoral structure, a sizeable nonwhite poverty population, historic claims to an ethos of humane liberalism, and considerable experience (and disappointment) with "establishment" programs for the remediation of poverty and racial disadvantage. But the fact of this resonance suggests that we must modify our sense of the desperation that seems so manifest in the experience of poverty and racial disadvantage.

It is indeed true that the conditions that confront New York's nonwhite poor are oppressive almost beyond belief. And, if the logic of our thesis on residual self-worth and the need to stigmatize poverty is accurate, it is probably also true that for the nonpoor in New York there is a great need to sustain this oppressiveness. (This in spite of the ethos of humane liberalism.) Nevertheless, in this context of intense and highly visible political activity on the part of the nonwhite and the poor the impact of the poverty and racial experience in New York must be somewhat mitigated. Even if this politics has produced few tangible results—even if the movement out of poverty as a result of such activity has been minimal—few among the poor remain untouched by the positive possibility for redress and reform (illusory though it may be) that such political clamor generates. Thus it may be that in New York City the experience of the disinherited, desperate though it may be on objective grounds, does allow for some hope, for some belief that change is possible.

The New York case is not unique. In one very large city after another we find that the experience of poverty and racial disadvantage is characterized by this somewhat contradictory mix of desperate conditions and hopefulness born out of highly visible political activity that—major disappointments notwithstanding—seems to generate an aura of possible progress, of changes in the offing. Thus the irony: it would seem that as far as urban poverty and racial disadvantage is concerned, one can expect to find the worst conditions coexisting with a regeneration of hope among those who must make their way in daily contact with these conditions. In large cities, where the need to stigmatize the nonwhite and the poor is greatest, and where the conditions wrought by this need are intensely oppressive, it is also very likely that the structure of the local polity will be such that the poor will be able to maximize their political presence. The net result is hopefulness often generated among those who live in the most deprived and, indeed, the most depraved circumstances.

If the character of what might be termed the *racial-poverty politics* of a community is crucial in determining the impact that poverty and racial conditions have on the poor and the nonwhite within the community, we should expect that even the most negative circumstances (or conditions) can be mitigated (if not remedied) somewhat when the political presence of the disinherited is maximized. The exact pattern of such maximization is difficult to project with any confidence. However, some reflection on certain factors that we have already identified as being important in determining the probability of the disinherited in any given community having political presence should allow us to speculate on the nature of the pattern.

We have suggested that such factors as partisan/ward electorates, pluralistic power distributions, large pools of organizational talent, and sufficient opportunity for the disinherited to gain organizational experience all serve to maximize the probability that the nonwhite and the poor will have a noticeable political presence—whether institutionalized or dissident—within a community. Taking these factors into account, it would seem that *community size* may be the variable that best organizes the variations in the extent to which the disinherited can realize their political presence within the community. We have already noted that the nonwhites and the poor are likely to maximize their political presence in very large urban communities. We should like to suggest—thinking in terms of a continuum—that the factors that account for such maximization are more likely to be characteristic of larger, as opposed to smaller, communities. Consequently, it should follow that the larger the community, the greater will be the potential of the disinherited to generate a visible politics and, consequently, the greater will be the chance that the deleterious impact of racial-poverty conditions will be somewhat abated—even if these conditions are not actually remediated or reformed.

That size of community is a crucial dimension can be seen in the following: larger communities tend to have larger nonwhite poverty populations from which necessary organizational talent can be recruited. Similarly, such communities, by virtue of their size, are more likely than smaller communities to provide individuals possessing such talent with opportunities to gain organizational experience. Because size is likely to be correlated with degree of internal differentiation and heterogeneity, and because larger cities are more likely than smaller ones to possess those complexities that result in the need for specialized competence vis-à-vis policy and decision making, size is also likely to be positively correlated with increased probabilities of pluralistic power allocations. The larger the city, the more likely will it be characterized by a pluralistic distribution of power. Finally, as far as partisan/ward as opposed to nonpartisan at-large electorates are concerned, there is some indication that very large cities (500,000+) are more likely than middle-sized cities (25,000 to 500,000) to have partisan organization of the electorate,[17] although very small cities (25,000 or less) are also likely to have partisan organization of the electorate. On this factor the picture is mixed. Granted that these are approximations of what the reality is, it would nevertheless appear that conditions that make for maximum political visibility of the dis-

17 The reasoning behind this assertion is as follows: middle-sized cities are more likely to have a council-manager form of government. Very large cities are more likely to have a mayor-council form of government. Council-manager forms are more likely to be associated with a non-partisan at-large organization of the electorate. Mayor-council forms are more likely to be associated with a partisan/ward organization. Therefore, middle-sized cities are more likely to have a non-partisan at-large organization of the electorate, and very large cities are more likely to have a partisan/ward organization of the electroate.

For support of this line of reasoning, see Robert R. Alford and Harry M. Scoble, "Political and Socio-Economic Characteristics of American Cities," *The Municipal Yearbook,* 1965, pp. 82–97, particularly page 83.

inherited are more likely to emerge as one proceeds from smaller to larger urban communities. Consequently we would suggest that the larger the community the greater will be the chances of a racial-poverty politics emerging, which mitigates to some extent even the most damaging poverty conditions.

We must pause to note an interesting facet in our analysis. We have suggested that as size of the community increases social class as a meaning context *decreases* in potency and the status market increases in importance. Consequently, we have argued that the need to stigmatize the poor and the nonwhite—to keep them in their place—which is a function of these two occurrences, will increase with increased size of the community. We have, however, also suggested that as size of community increases, so too does the probability that a visible and vigorous poverty and racial politics will emerge. Thus we should expect the most vigorous urban protest to exist where the need to stigmatize the poor and the nonwhite is greatest and, conversely, we should expect the least visible and vigorous urban protest in those communities where the need to stigmatize is manifested less intensely. While we suggest that such a pattern is likely to obtain, we are not thereby suggesting any dynamic or causal relationship between the need to stigmatize the poor on one hand and the urban protest (the disinherited's political response to stigma and its corollary conditions) on the other.

Intense stigmatization and its consequences do not engender a vigorous political response on the part of the disinherited. Conversely, less intense stigmatization cannot be linked causally to a less intense and visible political response on the part of the poor. The projected positive correlation between intense stigma (relatively speaking) and intense political response (and vice versa) is an artifact of two independent social logics, (1) economically based structural variations from community to community that operate to vary the intensity of stigmatization, and (2) the variations in community polity and demography that result in concomitant variations in the intensity of urban protest.

Some may see an inconsistency in this view. After all, have we not argued that a vigorous urban protest is capable of mitigating (at least to some extent) the effects of the need to stigmatize the poor and the nonwhite? If this is so then should it not follow that a dynamic relationship does exist between the urban protest and the extent to which the need to stigmatize the poor and the nonwhite is expressed in public policy? The answer to such a query is quite obviously *yes*. However, we must not mistake the extent to which the need to stigmatize has public implications for the intensity of the need itself. A vigorous urban protest of the disinherited can lessen the public implication of the need to stigmatize but it cannot render the need less potent among those, the nonpoor, in whom it is engendered as a result of the social and economic conditions of their lives. As long as the conditions that foster and sustain the need of the whites and the nonpoor to stigmatize the poor and the black remain operative in American life, the need itself will remain present among the whites and the nonpoor.

There is one final issue that should be addressed regarding the variations that we have suggested occur in the manner in which the experience of poverty and racial disadvantage is manifested in different urban communities. If the pattern we elucidated does in fact exist—if, as one proceeds from smaller to larger urban communities, there is both a concomitant increase in the need of the whites and the nonpoor to stigmatize the poor and the nonwhites and the ability of the disinherited through the mechanism of political resonance to mitigate the implications of this need—then how does the experience of poverty and racial disadvantage actually vary in the context of the pattern? From the perspective of the poor and the nonwhite what does this pattern mean? If one is so unfortunate as to be afflicted by poverty and racial disadvantage, in what situations is one likely to be better off? Worse off?

It is, of course, difficult to come to grips with this issue in any precise manner. One can only speculate and hypothesize, for the necessary research has yet to be done. With this *caveat* in mind, let us indeed speculate. In the logic of our analysis thus far we have come to conclude that the larger the urban community, the greater the probability that the disinherited will be able to mitigate to some extent the conditions of stigma that are the products of an increasingly intense need on the part of the whites and the nonpoor to keep "them in their place." Thus in larger, as opposed to smaller, communities we would expect to find the disinherited in a greater state of mobilization and even though their life conditions are likely to be more severe these conditions will exist in a milieu that holds some promise of redress and reform (even though such promise may be illusory).

In smaller communities we would expect to find a less intense need to stigmatize the disinherited. However the disinherited are unlikely to have a significant political presence in such communities, so that the need to stigmatize will likely be manifest in the public life of the community with little or no resistance. Thus the smaller the community, the greater the likelihood that the poor and the nonwhite will feel the full brunt of whatever stigmatization occurs, and the greater the likelihood that the conditions of poverty and racial disadvantage such as they are will be experienced with little mitigation and little or no hope of redress.

Whether the disinherited are better or worse off in larger or smaller cities, in cities where the likelihood exists that the effects of more intense stigmatization will be resisted, as opposed to cities where the likelihood exists that the consequences of a *less* intense stigmatization will meet with little or no effective resistance is, of course, a matter of conjecture.

In this chapter we have attempted to model the variations in manifestation of the experience of poverty and racial disadvantage as they occur in different urban contexts. In doing so, we conclude our diagnoses of the national cultural *malaise*—the emphasis upon noninstitutionalized inequality and its concomitant, the need to find personal value or self-worth residually—that underlies the problematic parameters of so much of the contemporary urban experience.

A POSTSCRIPT

Chapter 8
The Failure of Professionalized Reform: A Thesis on Establisment Response to Urban Problems

It may very well be true that most Americans are without peer in their optimism about problem solving. And it may also be true that this optimism is well founded in some respects. Certainly the very real successes of American society and culture—the technological increments of remarkable sophistication, the extensive provision of public education (uneven to be sure but extensive nonetheless), the relative stability of our political system, and the emergence of an industrial economy more potent in its productive might than any other in the world—certainly these are in large measure attributable to our historic zest for solving problems, our belief that once we intend something, no obstacle is insurmountable.[1] It is moreover the genius of our problem solving that we have *professionalized* it. We value highly those among us who presumably possess the skills and special competence to construct the solutions to our most complex problems. We devalue the amateur probings of those who have not, in our eyes, been thoroughly trained to confront the problems that they are so presumptuous to address. They are dilettanti and we have little patience with them.

We have *two* valued models of professional problem solving and they may be described as follows: first, as a result of our technological successes we have come to value what may be termed the *engineering model* of problem solving. The engineer is a highly trained specialist who, within a narrowly defined field of attention, is expected to arrange available elements in innovative combinations in order to

1 For a succinct evocation of this spirit see Sigmund Diamond, "Introduction," *The Nation Transformed,* ed. Sigmund Diamond, George Braziller, New York, p. 3–22.

actualize an intention or goal at a level of cost that can be borne by those who will presumably benefit from these innovations. The engineer is a creator of mechanisms, a designer of systems whose efficiency or success is measured by the ratio of reliably intended outputs to the costs of operation. The engineering model of problem solving operates on the assumption of intense specialization of training and competence spread over a great many problem areas. Thus, while the engineer is often a highly creative individual, his professional creativity is also highly specific. His work is focused on a single problem or set of problems while his colleagues are specialized in other areas.

As we have noted the engineering model is a product of our obvious success in the realm of creating new technologies. It has, however, been applied in the social sphere as well. Perhaps because of its visible success in the area of technological problem solving, it has been adopted by those who regularly attend to *policy planning* in areas such as education, welfare, housing, and general urban affairs. Whatever its source, it is certainly true that the engineering model has been in vogue in social policy determinations for quite some time now, for at least 35 years. (The New Deal under Franklin D. Roosevelt may be looked upon as having inaugurated this style on a grand scale.)

Where once educational problems were addressed by the likes of John Dewey, they are today characteristically attended to by specially trained bureaucratic functionaries, each with his own pet program to develop, in virtual isolation of overriding philosophical and pedagogical issues. Where once the problems of social welfare were a cause for the likes of Jane Addams and her settlement house compatriots, they have today fallen to the professional ministerings of social engineers such as Daniel Patrick Moynihan and his colleagues who are retained by the government to design new mechanisms ostensibly intended to reduce the suffering of the poor. There was a time when the problems of housing and of urban conditions in general stimulated the voices of such giants as Frank Lloyd Wright, Daniel Burnham, and LeCorbusier to articulation of visionary schemes; but today, with the exception of such nonprofessionals as Paolo Soleri, Buckminster Fuller, and Jane Jacobs, the policy response to the problems and conditions of our cities is to be found in the quiet memoranda of officials who have been trained in the techniques of the properly certified urban planner. The visionary, the philosopher, the activist—all of them are on the outside looking in as the policy engineers, under the glare of their fluorescent lamps, presume to create the devices that will bring us more serviceable futures.

The action counterpart of the engineering model, and the second of our highly valued professional problem solving approaches, is the *therapeutic model.* The therapeutic model stands on the assumption that, on the one hand, there are those people who are possessed of a certain problematic condition, and on the other there are trained professionals who possess the skills necessary to rid the troubled of their particular affliction. Medicine is the prototype of this approach to problem resolution. Patients represent a class of afflicted individuals requiring the skilled attention of physicians who are competent to restore their good health. Patients may be able to provide their physicians with valuable assistance when they describe the symptoms of their afflictions, but it is assumed that their fate depends upon the diagnostic and healing skills of the physicians. They are incapable of self-diagnosis and they certainly are in no position to minister to themselves.

The therapeutic model has been adopted in many problem areas besides medicine. It is the preferred action style in social work and education where it is assumed that the problems to be solved—the difficulties that threaten to immobilize the individual as well as the learning problems of the child—are products of conditions that are personal and which, therefore, must be treated by properly certified experts who, like the physician, can administer appropriate "cures."

When the caseworker deals with an A.D.C. mother, he assumes that she is economically dependent because the personal circumstances of her life have rendered her incompetent to "cope." He thus sets about to find ways to improve her ability to "cope" so that she may eventually be returned to economic self-sufficiency.[2] When educators are confronted with children who have difficulty learning to read, they are turned over to experts in learning disabilities because it is assumed that these practitioners will apply their expertise to overcome the impediments that are part of the personal makeup of these children.[3] Without belaboring the point, it is sufficient to note that the therapeutic model of action against problems has become so well-entrenched in the fields of social work and education that those who challenge its efficacy are commonly regarded as heretics. Those who dissent often do so at great risk to their professional standing.

Whether we are speaking about the engineering model or the therapeutic model, this fact emerges clearly: *the basic social arrange-*

2 See M. Elaine Burgess and Daniel O. Price, *An American Dependency Challenge,* American Public Welfare Association, Chicago, 1963, pp. 155–157.

3 See Samuel A. Kirk, *Educating Exceptional Children,* Houghton-Mifflin, Boston, 1962.

ments that characterize social life and urban life in particular in America remain unquestioned. The social engineer will tinker with the system, and will generate what appear to be new mechanisms to get the system to work better, but in the narrowness of his focus he rarely thinks to question the efficacy of the system itself. He has what has been described as "a trained incapacity" to analyze the system as a whole, and therefore he is unable to develop plans for broadly based social reconstruction. The social therapist is most comfortable when he can assume that the difficulties he addresses are localized in a given individual or identifiable group of individuals. He too is trained to ignore the possibility that the social ills he confronts have their source in social arrangements that confound our notions of maximum human serviceability. Because we have committed ourselves to these approaches the larger questions about the efficacy of extant institutional arrangements and the social psychology that pervades our experience are rarely raised.

The inappropriateness of professionalized social reform for improving the quality of urban life must be clear to those who have read the preceding chapters of this book. Given the complexity of our urban institutions and the social-psychological investment in inequality that pervades so much of our urban experience, it is difficult indeed to have confidence in the productivity of an approach to change that is largely insensitive to the implications of such phenomena.

Shall we have confidence in the engineering approach that ignores the political realities of urban America? No mechanism, no plan for social reform can become effective in a community if that community does not possess the power to put it into effect. Time and time again the structural dependence of local polities upon higher-order polities (particularly at the state level) confounds the best intentions of the social engineer. Improvements in public transportation, education, public health, and public welfare must often await state action—an increase in state aid or a legislative go-ahead with regard to an imposition of new local taxes—before they can become reality. Often enough the necessary state action does not come through, and the social engineers are left to rhapsodize about what might be if only the communities they serve had the power to transform intention into reality.

Even when structural dependency is not an issue the social engineer may, and often does, find his intentions going unrealized because they offend the interests of the politically powerful within the community. It is one thing to plan an imaginative housing program for the poor, and certainly another to get the necessary zoning approval from local authorities who rarely represent the poor and who, consequently, tend to be relatively insensitive to programs initiated in their interests. It is one thing to design educational programs that might conceivably enrich the learning experiences of the community's young, and quite another indeed to get approval from a school board that clings tenaciously to the traditional wisdom of reading, writing, and 'rithmetic.

And how effective will the social therapist be when he ignores the political context of his work? The social caseworker attempting to improve the nurturant behavior of a black A.D.C. mother tells the woman she ought to provide a more balanced diet for her children even while the state department of welfare is cutting back on the funds she will have available for the purchase of food. The caseworker goes on to encourage this mother to keep her apartment cleaner without recognizing that in its overcrowded condition cleanliness, while desired, is nearly impossible to attain. The client responds that she would be better able to keep a clean house if she could move to a more spacious accommodation. The caseworker chooses to ignore the fact that such a move is not possible, for there is little housing available to poor blacks in the community, and instead maintains that if the client would only "try harder" some improvement in the physical appearance of the apartment could be achieved. Can we really expect such political insensitivity to be productive of positive change in the lives of those whom the social worker ostensibly wishes to help?

The sincere remedial reading teacher tries to improve the cognitive skills of her so-called culturally disadvantaged charges even while she ignores the fact that the school in which she labors is understaffed and overcrowded, and even while the school board has failed to allocate sufficient funds for materials that would conceivably give her a reasonable chance to succeed. Should she become sensitive to the fact that teaching reading is not simply a technical problem but a political one as well, her training and narrow professionalism will likely prevent her from undertaking a crusade in behalf of her pupils for better learning conditions. At best, she becomes resigned and continues on in an effort that can only result in sustained frustration and failure. At worst, she begins to blame her charges for the inadequacy of their performance, an inadequacy for which they bear little or no responsibility. In any case, her failure to become active in changing the political context of her work can only render her efforts ineffective, and once again we can have but little faith in the productivity of the therapy that she administers.

Often the social engineers and social therapists—the professionals—

do not have the confidence of those they seek to help. This tends to be so because the professionals refuse to consider the political context of their efforts and the political conditions that lock those in need of assistance into poverty and disadvantage. When the radical reformers and the revolutionaries take to the streets, and when they employ the tactics of direct action, their targets may very well include the social engineers and the social therapists themselves. It is the professional reformers who are regarded as the enemy, as representatives of retrogressive forces in the community. Their accomplishment does not match their rhetoric and, as a consequence of this, a ghetto's-eye view finds them no better and perhaps worse than those who are explicit in their opposition to change. Shall we be optimistic about the productivity of an approach to social reform that not only makes a principle of political naïveté but also alienates many of those it is intended to serve? Can we really have confidence in its efficacy? Try as we may to avoid it, the answer to such a query must be "no."

The reader may wish to argue the point: after all, it may be claimed that our critique attacks the professional reformers where they are most vulnerable, in the political sphere, and this is less than fair. Granting their characteristic political naïveté, is it not true that professional reformers can produce intended positive change when they focus upon those problems about which there is general consensus within the community and that, consequently, do not require sensitivity to the uses and abuses of power? Are there not areas of reform that demand technical and professional expertise in the place of political ardor? Let us see.

It is difficult to find many urban problems about which there is likely to be such general consensus within any particular community. Even those problems that seem to evoke consensual recognition from the populace (for example, there is a widespread sense that a problematic condition exists that needs to be remedied) often turn out to evoke a considerable amount of dissension when the community considers what ought to be done to remedy them. Nearly everybody in "Mill City" recognizes that this community of 50,000 has a severe economic problem, that with the migration of the textile mills out of its environs the economy is well on its way to becoming moribund. But what should be done about it? One faction wishes to encourage the state to build a prison in the area—a plan the state favors—and thus provide stable employment for a large number of local residents. Another faction opposes this for fear that a prison located in or near the community will devalue the locale so that new income producing enterprises in the export sector will not wish to locate in "Mill City."

From this point of view the presence of a prison only stigmatizes the community, and although it is true that a state facility would assure sustained employment for a considerable number of people, it is also true that its presence could effectively limit the growth potential of the community. In such a situation as this the professional reformer will find that in spite of the consensus about the problem in need of solution, his proposals, whatever they may be, will be endorsed by some and opposed by others. Thus his proposals will not be evaluated merely in terms of their presumed technical proficiency but will ultimately have to face a *political* test.

The downtown of "Havensburg," a city of some 100,000, is in need of revitalization. It is old, shabby, and crime-ridden and many residents of this community no longer wish to go there for shopping and entertainment. But how shall the downtown area be revitalized? Some argue for an urban renewal program that will clear the area and its immediate environs for massive physical reconstruction. Others argue that this will deprive the poor who live on the periphery of the downtown area of the only housing available to them in the community. For those who take this position, urban renewal is not the answer. What is needed, they maintain, is a full blown Model Cities program replete with an increase in the amount of social services available to those who are forced to live in the slum-ghettos that abut onto the downtown area. Urban renewal, in their view, is a mask for the removal of the poor, and for their continued victimization at the hands of the rich and powerful. Clearly the problems of "Havensburg's" downtown will not be solved merely because most of its citizens agree that there are problems to be solved. Beneath the thin veneer of consensus, it is dissension and conflict that defines the situation.

Where are those problems that really do evoke a more than superficial consensus? Where are those problems that do not involve some dissension, some conflict that makes considerations of power absolutely necessary to any plan for reform? Perhaps we ought to seek such areas of agreement on a more limited scale. Perhaps problems that are less visible to the community as a whole are less likely to generate dissension and consequently are more likely to be amenable to the ministrations of the professional reformer.

While this may be so, it is not *clearly* so. For example, a recent study by the Rand Corporation, done at the behest of the City of New York, indicated that the city's fire protection would be improved as a result of redeployment of firemen and a relatively minor reorganization of the fire department. The result of such redeployment and reorganization, the study concluded, would be a reduction in the time it should take for firefighters to respond to calls for assistance. Few New Yorkers were aware of the recommendations and certainly it is difficult to believe that anyone cognizant of them would object to the intent that the proposals were supposed to realize. It would be difficult to conceive of a more fortuitous situation for the application of the professional style of problem solving. But some of those who *did* know of the Rand proposal did object—and quite vigorously at that. It seems that the firemen who had a collective bargaining contract with the city perceived the intended changes as implying a violation of their agreement with the city. The proposed redeployment would change the rules under which they were working, and because they believed that these work rules were personally advantageous as well as technically sound, they did not wish to see the proposal become operating policy. They argued that, contrary to the Rand assertions, the proposed changes would not improve their efficiency and they refused to go along with them. The Rand consultants, the professional problem solvers, naively assumed that "rational" or systematic analysis was all that was needed to come up with an improvement. They neglected to take account of the fact that the firemen had an interest or stake in the existing organization of their department and that they would, of course, view any proposal to improve their efficiency from the perspective that that stake implies. Moreover the consultants neglected to take account of the fact that the firefighters, by virtue of their functional importance with regard to the well-being of the city, possessed some determining power with regard to their jobs. Once again the assumption of consensus proved false, and a proposal that was based upon this assumption ran into considerable difficulty.

Allow me to offer yet another example that confounds the professionalized approach even when it is being used to attend to problems on a limited scale, an example which I relate from firsthand experience. A number of years ago, several social welfare agencies operating in Harlem, in New York City, agreed that they would be of greater assistance to the people of that locality if they set up a coordinated office. It was assumed that if social workers from these agencies worked together in a single center, they could pool their expertise for the benefit of those people who came to them for assistance. The center was set up with workers from the Department of Welfare, The Youth Board, The Bureau of Attendance of the Board of Education, and the Juvenile Court.

When a worker from the Welfare Department had a client whose son or daughter was in trouble it was assumed, for example, that the worker would join with his Juvenile Court colleague to arrive at a helpful disposition of the child's case. When a Bureau of Attendance worker found that the mother of one of the children with whom he was working was having economic difficulties, it was assumed that he would collaborate with his Welfare Department colleague to arrange for adequate support for the family. Close collaboration, it was hoped, would bring about a more efficient and felicitous solution to the problems presented by Harlem residents.

Unfortunately, this hope was not realized and within a few short years the coordinated center ceased to exist. The center failed for the following reasons: not everyone in the parent agncies agreed that the coordinated effort would be a good thing. Some believed that the "center" concept would only dilute the services that their particular agency and their agency alone could provide. Others were threatened by the centralization of service that the coordinated agency implied, seeing in it the possibility of a reallocation of resources that might ultimately reduce the availability of funds for their own particular approach to therapy and problem remediation. In any case the parent agencies turned out to be less cooperative than had been assumed. The center was never adequately staffed, for the parent agencies claimed they simply could not assign more workers to it. And workers at the center often found that they could not elicit the cooperation they needed from their own agencies in order to make collaboration reasonably effective.

This organizational reform failed because the planners failed once again to take into account the fact that *consensus on intent does not necessarily imply consensus on means or method*. Since virtually everyone agreed that improvements in social services for Harlem residents were necessary, it was easily assumed that there would be consensus with regard to the means by which that improvement could be effected. This latter assumption was unfortunately in considerable error.

There are, no doubt, instances when the professional approach to social reform and remediation works reasonably well. There are times when the therapist can be of real assistance to his "client." To say that the therapeutic model is *largely* inappropriate is not to say that it is *always* so. People in slum-ghettos like Harlem, Roxbury (Boston), the South and West Sides in Chicago, Hough (Cleveland), and Watts (Los Angeles) do need and benefit from the ministerings of a social worker, just as, it might be added, do some of the more affluent and advantaged suburban Americans. There *are* children who *do* need special attention from experts in the field of learning disabilities.

Similarly, to say that the engineering model is largely inappropriate to urban social reform is not to say that it is always so. While it would seem to be a totally inadequate approach to the big problems of American urban life, there are times when a suggestion from the technical expert can improve the quality of urban life, albeit in a very limited way. The centralization of emergency communication is a case in point. By means of such centralization, citizens in trouble are able to receive assistance more speedily than would otherwise be the case. In many communities when an emergency occurs all one needs to do is dial 911 and report the circumstances that require assistance. This eliminates the necessity for separate communication to the police, the fire department, or the hospitals and, consequently, it represents a small but real increment in efficient response to emergency situations. Such centralization represents engineering change; it represents the design and adoption of a *mechanism* for improvement, and while there has been some resistance to its adoption, such resistance has been minimal and of little or no consequence.

The main thrust of our criticism of professionalized social reform has not been to rule out the possibility of its effectiveness in discrete instances, but rather to note that *on balance* or *in general* the engineering and therapeutic models are not likely to be productive of significant progress in dealing with those issues that inhibit the maximization of human serviceability in the social life of our cities. The thrust of our criticism has not been intended to demean or undermine the efforts of sincere professional practitioners as they work to improve our lot in specific instances, but rather to warn against placing too great a faith in their efforts overall. The complexities of urban life in the contemporary United States make continued confidence in an approach that is largely insensitive to these complexities foolhardy indeed, and we need to be aware of this if we are to have any real hope of maximizing the serviceability of our urban communities.

At this point the reader should be somewhat perplexed. There is a disturbing question that lurks in our discussion thus far. If urban Americans are distressed and discontented with their lot, and if the professionalized approach to reform does not appear to be very productive, why is it that this approach continues to command support? Why is it that professionalized reform is still the dominant pattern of response to the issues that trouble the lives of those whose personal destinies are played out on the urban scene? There is, of course, one obvious answer. Social habits die hard. Given the fact that the engineering and therapeutic models have been employed with great success in the technological and medical fields, and given the fact that the engineering model in particular was employed with some success in dealing with the disaster of the Great Depression during the 1930s, it may be argued that Americans, particularly urban Americans, have become fixated on the possibility of great success in dealing with their problems by means of these styles of reform and remediation. Thus one would argue that in spite of the shortcomings of professionalized social reform most Americans are simply unprepared to recognize these shortcomings. And if they do, in their desire to believe in the ultimate success of this approach, they interpret such inadequacies as being indicative of a relatively undeveloped social technology—a condition that can be remedied by continued work within the boundaries of the engineering and therapeutic models.

Doubtless most urban Americans *are* unprepared to recognize the shortcomings of professionalized social reform. But is it simply a matter of habit dying hard? Is it simply a matter of believing that if engineering and therapy have worked so well in other spheres of problem solving they can be effective in the area of social problems as well? If this were so we would certainly have some grounds for optimism about the reform and remediation of the troubling contexts of urban life. With a little patience we could foresee a time when even those most desirous of proceeding in the direction of the professionalized approach would lose confidence in its efficacy, and begin to search for new ways to make urban life more serviceable.

This interpretation, of course, assumes that there is a genuine desire on the part of most urban Americans to solve their problems, that they will soon become aware that current attempts to solve those problems are inadequate, and they will seek other avenues of reform. But suppose this is unlikely? Suppose that genuine desire for problem solution, for reform, is not so widespread? What if there are those people—their general uneasiness with urban life notwithstanding—who do not wish to have specific problems solved, who in terms of their personal interests (no matter how narrow) perceive themselves as benefiting from the persistence of certain conditions that give rise to the problems in need of solution? Then what grounds do we have for patient optimism about the future of reform and remediation in our cities?

But surely this circumstance is farfetched. After all, how many people living amidst the troubling contexts of urban life would *not* wish to see those contexts rendered less difficult? The question is a good one. Nevertheless the circumstance posited is not at all farfetched. It is not that people do not wish to see the troubled or problematic contexts of their lives rendered less difficult; but instead, that granting this they remain personally wedded in their immediate situation to the perpetuation of those conditions that would have to be remedied if urban life were to be made more humanly serviceable.

Wishing, however sincerely, that things would get better is quite a different matter from relinquishing the immediate advantages derived from pursuing that which seems to be in one's own interests. The citizens of a particular community might agree that upgraded education would help to improve the quality of life in that community, but how many of them will be willing to have their taxes raised in order to accomplish this? How many slum landlords, concerned with "crime in the streets," will be willing to make improvements in their buildings, improvements that could create a more habitable residential atmosphere for the poor, thus replacing the decay and deterioration that contributes significantly to tenants' frustration and anger? How many members of those unions, which by their discriminatory membership policies control the local labor supply so that the demand in exceeding availability drives up the salaries of their members, will be amenable to ending these policies so that qualified blacks can have an equitable share of work and rewards? How many will support such a move even if it helps to ease racial tensions? How many politically powerful people are going to support changes in the electoral structure of the community that would ensure equitable representation of the less powerful on the decision making councils of that community? And if we consider the residual self-worth thesis developed in Chapter 5 of this book, how many of the nonpoor are going to support programs that will effectively reduce poverty and the stigmatized visibility of the poor even when their immediate material interests are not threatened by such programs?

No, it is not farfetched to question the extent of the desire to make real improvements in the troubling contexts of urban life. And consequently, while some of the persistent support for professionalized reform—in spite of its demonstrable inadequacy—may be accounted for by die-hard social habit and wishful thinking, there is another interpretation that may be offered to account for its persistence, an interpretation that is far less optimistic in its implications.

While it is probably true that most of those involved in pursuing the engineering and therapeutic models of social problem solving are sincere in their belief that these models will bring about positive change, it is also paradoxically true that *the popular support which these approaches continue to command derives from the fact that they are unlikely to be very successful.* In contemporary urban America we have seen that we are frequently confronted with conflicts between our values (such as equal opportunity and equal justice) and our narrow interests (such as keeping the blacks out of our union and out of our neighborhood), and between our desire to improve the human serviceability of our communities (such as bringing peace to the streets to make the city a good community in which to live and grow) and our perceived interest in pursuing a course that impedes such improvement (we do not wish to have our taxes raised, we do not wish to have the slum-ghettoes disappear, and we do not wish to change the electoral structure to ensure equitable representation). It may be suggested that these conflicts are themselves a major fact of our discontent with urban life. We want things to get better, we cannot escape the importance of such normative ideals as equal opportunity and social justice; but we often find ourselves behaving in ways that, while personally useful or profitable, also violate our ideals and contribute to the troubling nature of the way "things are." To the extent that we are conscious of the conflict between our ideals and our behaviors, between our desire for reform and our investment in those very conditions which inhibit it, we are likely to be troubled by the contradictions within ourselves, and this sense of moral dilemma can be profoundly disquieting.

If this be so, the continued support of professionalized social reform can be understood as a function of the need to reduce the psychological dissonance and consequent discomfort arising from the sense that we are not doing what we ought to be doing about those conditions that render the cities less than habitable for many and minimize their serviceability for almost everybody.

Endorsing the professionalized approach accomplishes the following things: first, by asserting that the problematic conditions of the urban communities can only be solved by the application of professional expertise, we divorce these problems from our own sphere of personal responsibility. In effect, we tell ourselves that problems, while affecting us, cannot be solved through our own efforts, for we simply do not have the expertise to deal with them. No one would hold a layman responsible for doing little to correct a medical, mechanical, or legal difficulty—these are beyond the scope of his competence. Therefore, if social problems demand expert attention no one should hold us responsible for doing little to correct them. Second, by supporting or endorsing the efforts of the professional reformers we convince ourselves that within the limits imposed by our own lack of expertise we are, in fact, doing something about urban problems. We may not be able to take direct action, but our commitment to the efforts of the professionals indicates (at least to ourselves) that we are doing that which is within our power to improve the quality of urban life.

Finally, we support the endeavors of these individuals because their efforts rarely, if ever, put us in the unhappy position of having to relinquish the personal gains we derive from the persistence of a problem-generating condition (for the professionalized approach is largely insensitive to this dimension). In its style of largely abstracted planning and direct therapy with those who have a problem, in its penchant for locating the source of a problematic condition among those who are victimized by it, the professionalized approach allows us to deny that our personal interests have anything to do with the persistence of the problems that trouble the urban experience. The slumlord, by supporting the efforts of the family caseworker who deals with the tenants in his building, can convince himself that the rundown condition of his property is the fault of disorganized life-style of these tenants. He is not to blame: those people are neither able nor willing to care for the place in which they live. They need help; they need a social worker. By supporting special education programs for the so-called culturally disadvantaged the white "middle-class" parent can deny that the segregated schools that he would like to see maintained have anything to do with the educational problems of the nonwhite poor. Those children need not be transferred to his child's school—they need special help to compensate for learning deficits that derive from their culturally impoverished life-style. They need special teachers who know how to educate them; integrating the schools will not accomplish the task. By supporting the belief that incompetence is the source of unemployment or underemployment, and by asserting, therefore, that job-training programs are needed, the member of a union that excludes certain minorities can deny that he supports and benefits from economic discrimination. By supporting therapeutic efforts of various types focused on the poor the nonpoor can deny their responsibility for poverty. By such support they can convince themselves that the poor remain poor of their own volition (particularly when these programs provide an opportunity for some among the poor to rise out of their impoverished circumstances), and in doing so they can confirm *in residuum* their own sense of personal value or self-worth.

In sum, continued support of the professional approach to reform and remediation is support for the absence of success that nevertheless removes or reduces the discomfort that arises out of an awareness of the conflict between our values and hopes for better communities and the behaviors that serve our narrow self-interests. By continued support of the professionalized approach, we delude ourselves into believing that there is little we can do about the problems that trouble the urban experience, except to support the notion that these problems should be left to the ministerings of those who are professionally trained to deal with them. We convince ourselves that the problems in need of solution and the conditions in need of change have little or nothing to do with the manner in which we pursue our interests. By such support we are able to deny the conflict between what we ought to do, or not do, and how we actually behave. We sustain in our communities and in our society a condition that may be termed *progressive-status-quoism* whereby change and progress are apparent but the status quo is real.[4]

It is not that we do this consciously. We do not sit down and deliberately attempt to delude ourselves. We do not ask: "How may I relieve this moral tension that troubles me?" Doing so would defeat the purpose or function of progressive-status-quoism. If we were conscious of what we are doing we could no longer delude ourselves; to *understand* the process is to render it ineffective. It is simply that history has provided us with two ways out: the existence of the engineering and the therapeutic models of problem solving and, in our collective need to avoid the contradictory implications of our behaviors juxtaposed against our values and intentions, we have invested these approaches with a potency that has no basis in fact.

If this is indeed so, then there is little ground for optimism when we consider the future. If our support for professionalized reform springs from a need to delude ourselves, a need to protect ourselves from an awareness of our own responsibility for conditions that render the urban experience so troubling, and from an awareness that we shall have to sacrifice some of our narrow self-interests to effect progressive change within our communities, then in all probability we shall continue to blind ourselves to the inadequacies of that approach. Time alone will not erode such support, nor will continued lack of success in its use. Indeed, such *lack* of success is one of the ingredients which elicits our defense of professionalized reform.

The consequences of continuing on in this present course will—in my view—only exacerbate already trying conditions in American cities, and render the urban experience increasingly troublesome. The problems of local economy will continue unabated, proposals for educational improvements will more often than not remain unrealized, and even problems of limited scale, problems having to do with the

4 This formulation was originally developed in Bernard Farber, David Harvey, and Michael Lewis, *Community, Kinship and Competence,* Research and Development Program on Preschool Disadvantaged Children OE6-10-235, *III,* U.S. Department of Health, Education and Welfare, Office of Education, Washington, D.C., 1969, pp. 211–214.

organization and efficiency of public services, will remain with us. In other words, continued support for professionalized reform as the dominant response to urban problems will mean little or no improvement in the conditions that constitute those problems. But it will mean something more as well: the mutual estrangement between the "haves" and the "have nots" in American communities will increase, and as a consequence of this, life in many of our cities will become even more threatening than it is presently.

On poverty related issues in particular the following scenario does not seem beyond the limits of reasonable prediction: the disinherited, those for whom the professionalized reform programs are intended, do not seem to benefit very much from such efforts. The indicators of their disadvantage remain. They are poor, their children drop out of school, they have a high incidence of family disruption, and the crime rate in their neighborhoods continues to rise steadily. The solid citizens of the community, having supported the professional reform efforts, interpret these indicators as meaning that the disinherited have not responded to sincere attempts in their behalf. Given their endorsement of professionalized reform the solid citizens are hardly likely to interpret these indicators to mean that such efforts are ill-conceived and inappropriate. They blame the victims for the continuing conditions of their victimization.

The disinherited for their part, lose patience with the social workers, educational specialists, and program planners in their midst. They respond with increased vigor to the militants who stand for a radical reconstruction of American life. This increased militancy on the part of the disinherited serves only to reinforce the opinion of the solid citizens that the disinherited are disreputable. "Those people," they say, "want something for nothing. We've tried to help them but they had to meet us half way, they had to exert some effort to help themselves, to improve themselves. They did not, and now they blame *us;* now they want to tear things down and take from us the things we have worked so hard for. They want what we have but they do not want to work for it. They want it on a silver platter." Judging the disinherited to be almost totally without merit the solid citizens withdraw much of their support for the professionalized efforts intended ostensibly for such people. Instead, they increase their clamor for greater control measures, for more police protection, and for a hard line in dealing with the militants. The disinherited see in this "call to arms" an expression of the solid citizens' implacable hostility to their just aspirations and, as such, become more militant than ever. In this calculus of estrangement, our communities are polarized to the point where rapprochement is all but impossible, and where the disinherited as well as the solid citizens become parties to a state that can accurately be described as bordering on internal war.

For those readers, appalled by such a prospect, who react by saying that "it can't happen here," we would suggest that they take a more careful look at circumstances now existing in their communities. Not only can this unfortunate scenario come to pass, it has probably begun.

Thus, in sum, we conclude that professionalized social reform and remediation is not only inadequate to the task of maximizing human serviceability in American cities, but that it may be contributing to a marked increment in the troubled quality of urban life.

A TROUBLED EPILOGUE American sociologists, it seems, will go to great lengths in order to avoid a pessimistic conclusion. Lewis Killian has noted that sociologists will often present analyses that are bleak indeed, but when they turn to the task of drawing conclusions from these analyses they find some ray of hope that, before they are finished, becomes a hymn to optimism.[5] In closing this study of urban America, I am tempted to "find" that ray of hope, that silver lining, to seize upon it and say to my readers: "No matter how bad things appear there is reason to believe that the problems of American communities will be solved." I am tempted to do so because that is what I wish to believe, that is what I want to see. But wishing will not make it so and my analyses in this study do indeed lead me to some pessimistic conclusions about the future of urban America.

Our institutions are beset by problems, our daily experience is troubled, and our characteristic modes of response in community after community (with variations duly accounted for) seem inappropriate. The established response of professionalized reform keeps us from really facing up to the sources of our discontents, while the dissidents in our midst do not seem capable of "winning the war" even if they do manage to win a few battles. The reform-radicals and the revolutionaries are important insofar as they have given many of those locked in the ghettos of poverty and discrimination hope, and a sense of legitimacy in organized resistance to further victimization; they are important because they have made continued inattentiveness to the claims of the disinherited costly. But for many the cost is not so great that it cannot be borne—particularly when there are gains to bearing

5 Lewis Killian, "Optimism and Pessimism in Sociological Analysis," *The American Sociologist,* 6, No. 4 (November 1971), 281–286.

it. The increased militancy among the disinherited only confirms their disreputability in the eyes of those who feed their sense of self-worth by that image.

No, I find little reason for optimism. Our cities will not crumble and our communities will not become uninhabitable, but it does seem to me that we will continue on as we have been doing, and that is hardly comforting.

No deus-ex-machina descends here, no silver lining shining through. Only in a concluding statement, a possibility: if we develop an *awareness* of how our urban institutions function and of the problematic nature of that functioning, if we come to recognize the ways in which our self-interests—economic, political and most profoundly psychological—operate to generate the conditions that trouble contemporary urban life, and if we can discern that our proposed solutions are often protections of the *status quo,* then perhaps, stripped bare of our illusions—whether in New York, Champaign, Illinois or Beaumont, Texas—we will begin to do all that cries out to be done in order to maximize the human serviceability of urban America. This book has offered no solutions, only diagnoses. The solutions must wait until we are truly motivated to create them. The first step to effect positive social change in our cities must be an *unmasking,* and this book has been a small effort in behalf of that undertaking.

A Selected Bibliography of Materials for Further Study

The following bibliography is not intended to be exhaustive. It is instead a purposive selection of materials that readers, interested in continuing their study of urban America, are encouraged to consult. Some of the items included in this bibliography are particularly relevant to aspects of the analysis developed in the body of this book. Where this is so, it has been noted in the annotation that accompanies each listing. Some items in this listing have been cited in the text (although all text citations are not listed in the bibliography); others, while not cited in the text, appear here because they should be useful and stimulating to students of those conditions and problems that characterize the urban American present. The citations are listed alphabetically within three distinct substantive classifications: (1) *Sociology and Social Improvement,* (2) *Institutional Analysis,* and (3) *Problems of the Urban Experience.*

SOCIOLOGY AND SOCIAL IMPROVEMENT

Gouldner, Alvin W. *The Coming Crisis of Western Sociology.* New York: Basic Books, 1970. This book is Gouldner's controversial critique of contemporary academic sociology. The work of Talcott Parsons, a major contemporary general theorist in American sociology, is singled out for extensive criticism. Gouldner is particularly sensitive to what may be termed the political sources and contexts of social theory. In large measure he sees the work of Parsons and other theorists of the "functionalist school" as being inherently conservative of the status quo in society. Theirs is a sociology incapable of generating a thoroughgoing reconstruction of society, a sociology that at best strives to serve the conventional welfare state, American style. Students of sociology with a good background in theory should find this volume useful in their consideration of the possibilities for a sociological analysis that measureably contributes to the improvement of society.

Kaplan, Abraham. *The Conduct of Inquiry: Methodology for Behavioral Science.* San Francisco: Chandler Publishing Co., 1964. In this wise and comprehensive volume Kaplan takes the reader through a host of problems characteristic of contemporary social science. Eschewing doctrinaire formulations, Kaplan creates a clear sense of the possible with regard to the promise of social inquiry, while at the same time he establishes realistic limits to the expectations we might have about that promise. Of particular relevance to readers of *Urban America* are his incisive discussions of the uses and limits of formal models in social science and the fallacy of conventional distinctions between "basic" and "applied" scholarship. In particular, Kaplan sensitizes the reader to the possibilities of a mutually beneficial relationship between the practice of social science and the development of social policy. This discussion is pertinent to issues discussed in Chapters 1 and 8 of *Urban America.*

Lynd, Robert S. *Knowledge for What?* Princeton: Princeton University Press, 1939. In this volume Lynd makes an impassioned plea for a social science that does not shirk its responsibility for providing an analytically intelligent basis for social improvement. Although this book was first published 34 years ago, its thesis remains instructive for those who are thoughtful about the role of social science in contemporary society. Readers will find it a useful supplement to the discussion in Chapter 1 of this volume, which develops a rationale for an historically specific sociology of urban life.

Mills, C. Wright. *The Sociological Imagination.* New York: Oxford University Press, 1959. This book contains a critique of such themes in modern American sociology as empirically unsubstantiated "grand theory" and the naive concern for the measurement of social minutiae, as well as a positive paradigm for a sociology that illumines the relationship between personal biography and historical setting. The task of the sociological imagination, according to Mills, is to create for men and women "lucid summations of what is going on in the world and of what may be happening within themselves." Mills' argument is useful for an in-depth consideration of the rationale for an historically specific urban sociology that has been developed in Chapter 1 of this volume. It is, moreover, a major source informing the intellectual purpose of *Urban America*.

Myrdal, Gunnar. *Value in Social Theory*. New York: Harper and Brothers, 1958. There are two essays in this collection that bear special note for our purposes. "The Relation Between Social Theory and Social Policy" (originally published in *The British Journal of Sociology*, September, 1953) and "Valuations and Beliefs" (originally published in Myrdal's influential study of American race relations, *An American Dilemma*, 1944) speak with considerable optimism to the role of social science in maximizing the probabilities for human serviceability in society. Myrdal is a committed rationalist who exhorts his fellow social scientists to engage in analytic efforts that can undermine false beliefs about the conduct of human affairs. In his view, enlightenment is a most powerful tool in behalf of democratic social progress. The two essays cited here are particularly pertinent to the position adopted in Chapter 1 of this book with regard to the development of an historically specific urban sociology.

Page, Charles H. *Class and American Sociology*. New York: Schocken Books, 1969. Although the central thrust of this study is the analysis of the manner in which *social class* was treated by the pioneers or "founding fathers" of American sociology, Page devotes a good part of his effort to an explication of the extent to which these scholars saw sociological inquiry as related to social improvement. This volume is particularly valuable in its demonstrations of the fact that from its inception American sociology had an intimate association with the felt need to make society more equitable and just. Thus we have Ward's commitment to social reform by means of applied sociology and telesis, Sumner's antireform "reformism" in which he envisioned social progress as the result of evolutionary competition between the classes, Small's faith in gradualism as the direct route to reformation of the excesses of capitalism and consequently to social progress, Giddings' assertion that societal engineering based on the principles of sociology would bring about social improvement, Cooley's optimistic projection to the effect that the "competitive spirit" could be directed to group betterment and social justice, and Ross' contention that the "over-mastering purpose" of sociology is to "better human relations." Readers concerned about the relationship of contemporary social science to the remedial needs of urban life will find this study a useful introduction to important formulations on the issue of societal guidance in American sociology.

INSTITUTIONAL ANALYSIS

Adams, Bert N. *Kinship in an Urban Setting*. Chicago: Markham Publishing Co., 1968.

This is a study of kinship in Greensboro, North Carolina, a middle-sized city. Using survey data, Adams presents descriptive findings on such topics as the importance of kin, the character of young adult-parent contacts, and sibling relationships and contacts with secondary kin. While this study is limited with respect to its representativeness, it is a good example of the kind of work that contemporary sociologists are doing on urban kinship.

Adrian, Charles R. and Charles Press. *Governing Urban America*. New York: McGraw-Hill Book Co., 1968.

This is the most recent edition of Adrian's standard text on urban government. The usefulness of this volume derives from its comprehensiveness, as it covers such topics as local government ideology, municipal elections, urban political organization, forms of municipal government, intergovernmental relations, municipal revenues and expenditures, public utilities and transportation, and public health and welfare. Adrian's work is a useful introduction to urban government, and can be used to supplement the discussion of the urban polity developed in Chapter 2 of *Urban America*.

Banfield, Edward C. and James Q. Wilson. *City Politics*. New York: Vintage Books, 1963.

This is a straightforward descriptive treatment of urban politics. It is a handy reference, particularly for newcomers to the study of urban affairs. This volume contains easily understood discussions of urban electoral systems, forms of governmental organization, the urban polity in relation to the federal system, the urban "machine," and the role of interest groups in the polity, as well as a number of other topics. Readers of *Urban America* will find it a helpful supplement to Chapter 2 of this book.

"City Bosses and Political Machines," *The Annals of the American Academy of Political and Social Science, 353,* May 1964.

This is a special issue of *The Annals* containing a series of articles on urban government forms and political participation. It is a useful resource for material on the social basis of the decline of traditional urban political parties, factions within urban political parties, the new ethnicity and party representation, organized labor and party politics on the local level, citizen leadership in nonpartisan council-manager cities, leadership and city-county consolidation, and the effect of state politics on municipal politics. This collection is supplementary to our discussion of the urban polity in Chapter 3 and may be of some use as a supplement to our discussion of the urban protest of the disinherited in Chapters 6 and 7.

Dahl, Robert A. *Who Governs: Democracy and Power in an American City.* New Haven: Yale University Press, 1961.

This is the study in which Dahl purports to find a pluralistic distribution of power in New Haven, Connecticut, with regard to issues in such areas as urban renewal, party nominations, and the schools. Dahl's work has been thoroughly reviewed in Chapter 2 of *Urban America.* It is sufficient to note that students of community power cannot consider themselves informed on the matter if they are not familiar with Dahl's formulation and analysis.

Farber, Bernard. *Family: Interaction and Organization.* San Francisco: Chandler Publishing Company, 1964.

An excellent analytic treatment of family and kinship in contemporary American society (inclusive of urban society). In this volume Farber develops his "Permanent Availability versus Orderly Replacement" model as well as a number of family typologies. His distinctions among efficiency welfare and conservative family orientations have been used in Chapter 4 of *Urban America.* Those seeking an analytic framework for the analysis of family and kinship in urban communities would do well to consult Farber's work.

———. *Kinship and Class: A Midwestern Study.* New York: Basic Books, 1971.

This is a study of kinship among the lower strata of a middle-sized city in Illinois. Rather than simply focus upon the usual problems of kinship affiliation and mutual aid in an urban setting, Farber develops a sensitive treatment of the relationship of kin organization to socialization and the development of competence. Readers will find this volume a useful resource when they consider our arguments in behalf of differential personalization and the character of the socialization process as they appear in Chapter 4 of *Urban America*.

Farber, Bernard, David L. Harvey, and Michael Lewis. *Community, Kinship and Competence,* Research and Development Program on Preschool Disadvantaged Children, *III,* U.S. Department of Health, Education and Welfare, Office of Education OE 6-10-235, May 1969.

This monograph contains three studies that are particularly relevant to the study of lower-strata family and kinship. Harvey's work is particularly useful for its exploration of interpersonal styles in the lower-class family. It is a helpful supplement to the discussion of personalization that appears in Chapter 4 of *Urban America*. Lewis' study also contains materials on the scale, degree of bureaucratization, and functioning of a school system in a middle-sized city, which can be used to supplement the discussion of urban education in Chapter 5 of this book.

Firey, Walter. *Land Use in Central Boston.* Cambridge: Harvard University Press, 1947.

Along with his study of the determinants of land use in one area of Boston, Firey has developed a systematic critique of the type of ecological analysis that does not recognize the importance of cultural factors in determining land-use patterns. Attacking the mechanistic formulations of those he designates as rationalists, Firey develops an argument that gives primacy to values and what he terms the symbolic society-space relationship in defining the character of urban space and the uses to which it is put. Although this book was published in 1947, it remains today the single most systematic statement on social as opposed to human ecology. It is recommended for those who would like to explore land-use problems in urban communities, a subject that is not explicitly treated in *Urban America*.

Gittell, Maralyn, and T. Edward Hollander. *Six Urban School Districts: A Comparative Study of Institutional Response*. New York: Frederick A. Praeger Publishers, 1968.

A study focusing on the organizational characteristics of school systems in urban areas, it concludes that in large cities a small core of professionals, protected by elaborate bureaucracies, controls the decision-making processes of public education. This is a particularly important conclusion in light of the continuing struggle for control of the schools in urban communities. Readers will find this study a useful supplement to our discussion of bureaucratization in urban school systems in Chapter 5.

Gottman, Jean. *Megalopolis: The Urbanized Northeastern Seaboard of the United States*. Cambridge, Mass.: The M.I.T. Press, 1961.

This is Gottman's encyclopedic study of the most intensely urbanized area in the United States. It is an important source, not only for its detailed description of the conditions in that area, but also for its conceptualization of a new type of urban form (one that diminishes the importance of discrete communities) that may very well become characteristic of a number of areas in the United States. Readers may find the chapters on the megalopolitan economy particularly useful. Students of urban affairs would do well to give this volume a careful reading, particularly with an eye to the emerging need for interurban coordination.

Hawley, Amos H. *Human Ecology: A Theory of Community Structure*, New York: The Ronald Press, 1950.

This volume is the classic formulation of the ecological perspective in the sociology of communities. Its range extends far beyond the discussion of urban communities. It is particularly relevant for readers of *Urban America* in its treatment of (1) the relationship between demographic composition and organizational characteristics, (2) the role of corporate and categoric groups in the day-to-day life of the community, (3) the city as a dependent territorial unit and, in particular, as an economically dependent unit, (4) the economic competition for space, (5) the temporal organization of community activity as based on the routines of economic organization, and (6) the patterns and processes of urban growth. It should be noted that the ecological perspective is not employed to any great extent in *Urban America*. For this reason alone, readers may find it useful to consult Hawley's volume. Hawley's *Human Ecology*, moreover, may be a useful supplement to our discussion of the urban economy in Chapter 3.

Hunter, Floyd. *Community Power Structure: A Study of Decision Makers*. Chapel Hill: University of North Carolina Press, 1953.

In this volume, Hunter purports to have found a monistic distribution of power operating in the city of Atlanta, Georgia. This study is a major demonstration of the elitist position on community power. Like Dahl's work (cited above) Hunter's work has been thoroughly reviewed in Chapter 2 of this book. And as is the case with Dahl's work, no informed student of community power can afford to ignore Hunter's research.

Levy, Jr., Marion J. *The Structure of Society*. Princeton: Princeton University Press, 1952.

This book is a very rigorous treatment of functional analysis in sociology. While *Urban America* is not inspired by functional analysis, it does make use of a conception of institutions that is similar to that used by many functionalists (see Part 1) and by Levy in particular. Students wishing to acquaint themselves with the conceptual apparatus of functional analysis and its underlying logic would do well to consult Levy's book.

Moore, Wilbert E. *The Conduct of the Corporation*. New York: Random House, 1962.

Moore's dissection of the modern American corporation is a particularly useful source for those who wish to explore the relationship between large scale business enterprise and the economies of urban communities. Moore analyzes the structure of large scale enterprise and the behavior that routinely occurs within the context of that structure. Readers will find Moore's work helpful in understanding our discussion of the bureaucratic component of local urban economies and, in particular, the implications of trans-urban economic organization for the viabilty and local control of urban economies.

Parsons, Talcott, and Robert F. Bales. *Family, Socialization and Interaction Process*. Glencoe: The Free Press, 1955.

This book contains theoretically sophisticated work on the family in urban-industrialized society. Of particular importance are Parsons' conceptions of the structural isolation of the nuclear family and the character of the socialization process in the nuclear family. The treatment of the latter of these two concerns informs some of the discussion of socialization in Chapter 4 of *Urban America*.

The Quarterly Digest of Urban and Regional Research. Bureau of Community Planning, Urbana: University of Illinois.

This digest is a useful source for anyone doing research on contemporary urban affairs. It contains short summaries of research in progress as well as completed work. Because it monitors ongoing work, it can often provide scholars with leads to the latest developments in urban scholarship. Entries are classified under the following headings, among others: Demography and Human Behavior, The Urban and Regional Economy, Social Services, Government, Land Use, and Transportation.

Rogers, David. *110 Livingston Street: Politics and Bureaucracy in New York City*. New York: Random House, 1968.

This is a case study of what may very well be the prototype of highly bureaucratized school systems in large cities. Rogers takes us through the operating bureaucracy of the New York City schools, and details the ways in which policy directives and reforms are confounded by organizational resistance. Upon reading this volume, one might conclude that the big city educational bureaucracy is worthy of Franz Kakfa's imagination. The material in Rogers' study is particularly pertinent to our discussion of education organization in Chapter 5 and our discussion of the professionalization of social reform in Chapter 8.

Sayre, Wallace S. and Herbert Kaufman. *Governing New York City: Politics in the Metropolis*. New York: The Russell Sage Foundation, 1960.

This is an in-depth study of the complexities of government in a large metropolitan city. Sayre and Kaufman demonstrate in almost painful detail how the exercise of power is diffused in a municipal political system that encompasses an extensively heterogeneous population. This book is an important case study and should be consulted by students of community power as well as by those who are interested in the organizational characteristics of municipal government. It is particularly pertinent to the discussion of the effects of heterogeneity on the character of power distributions in urban communities which appears in Chapter 2 of this book.

Thompson, Wilbur R. *A Preface to Urban Economics*. Baltimore: The Johns Hopkins Press, 1965.

This is one of the few systematic treatises in urban economics. In order to appreciate Thompson's work in its entirety, one should be conversant with the standard concepts of contemporary economics. Thompson systematically covers such topics as urban economic growth inclusive of the roles played in this process by the export sector and the local sector, income inequality, economic instability, the federal role in urban economic development, the economics of public finance, the economics of urban renewal, and the economics of mass transportation. Readers of Chapter 3 in *Urban America* will find Thompson's discussion of economic base analysis useful in understanding the relative importance of the export and local sectors in the economies of urban communities.

Tiebout, Charles M. *The Community Economic Base Study*. Research Memorandum, Area Development Committee of the Committee for Economic Development, September 1962.

This memorandum, which is generally available in university

libraries, sets out the logic underlying economic base studies of urban communities. Tiebout is an economist who believes that the export sector is the basic sector of the economy of any city. Readers with a background in economics will find this study a helpful extension of our discussion of export and local sectors in Chapter 3.

PROBLEMS OF THE URBAN EXPERIENCE

Altshuler, Alan A. *Community Control: The Black Demand for Participation in Large American Cities.* Indianapolis: Pegasus-Bobbs-Merrill, Co., 1970.

Here is a systematic consideration of the community control issue in the racial politics of large American cities. After reviewing the arguments for and against the community control option, Altshuler concludes that in the pursuit of a "peace of reconciliation," it is worth trying. Given the white resistance to black demands for inclusion, community control is, in his view, the most feasible possibility for giving blacks a "tangible stake in the American political system." This study is particularly pertinent to our consideration of noninstitutionalized inequality and the protest it has engendered (in Chapters 6 and 7) as well as to our consideration of conflicts in education (in Chapter 5).

Blau, Peter M. and Otis Dudley Duncan. *The American Occupational Structure.* New York, John Wiley and Sons, 1967.

This is an extremely sophisticated study of occupation and mobility in the United States. For the most part, it focuses on objective indicators of mobility as opposed to the social meanings of mobility as experienced subjectively by modern Americans. This work will be most appreciated by those who are conversant with advanced statistical techniques such as path analysis. The Blau and Duncan book is pertinent to our consideration of noninstitutionalized inequality in Chapter 6 of *Urban America.*

Duhl, Leonard J., ed. *The Urban Condition.* New York: Basic Books, 1963.

This is a collection of papers focusing, for the most part, on the development of policy for reform of urban conditions. Some of the papers report the results of empirical investigations. Other papers assess the role of professional planning in urban revitalization. The papers are of varying quality. "Part Four: The Strategy of Intervention" provides some materials which can be used in the context of our discussion of the failure of professionalized social reform which appears in Chaper 8 of *Urban America.*

Edelman, Murray. *The Symbolic Uses of Politics.* Urbana: University of Illinois Press, 1964.

Things politic are not what they seem! In a closely reasoned and provocative study, Edelman examines political interplay as a system of symbols serving the persistence of order in society. Edelman sensitizes us to the social-psychological dimension of political behavior, a dimension that, if understood, can account for the regularity with which "exceptions" to ideal expectations for political behavior occur. This is a sophisticated book that develops a useful framework for considering some of the issues we have raised in Chapter 8 with regard to the failure of professionalized social reform. Readers may wish to consider our discussion of *progressive-status-quoism* in light of Edelman's theoretical formulation.

Friedman, Laurence M. *Government and Slum Housing: A Century of Frustration.* Chicago: Rand McNally Co., 1968.

This book is a thorough study of the formation of housing policy as it has been expressed in law. It contains a critique of urban renewal policy and a critical history of federal and state involvements in the development of public housing in urban areas. Friedman distinguishes between social cost and welfare ideologies as the rationales for government involvement in urban housing, and indicates the variations in housing programs that result from the application of one ideology as opposed to the other. Friedman's work is particularly useful as a supplement to our discussion of the failure of professionalized social reform which appears in Chapter 8.

Jacobs, Jane. *The Death and Life of Great American Cities.* New York: Vantage Books, 1961.

This is Jacobs' response to the decay of the great urban centers in American society. She attacks the revitalization schemes of the professional city planners whom she perceives as practitioners of a pseudoscience. She argues that the professional planners are really antiurban in their approach to the problems of the great cities. Jacobs advocates the encouragement of mixed land use, concentration, small blocks and, in general, physical and social diversity as the salvation of the urban present. Aside from its general interest as a tract on urban revitalization, Jacobs' book should also be of interest to those who are concerned about the professionalization of social reform. See Chapter 8 of *Urban America.*

Killian, Lewis M. *The Impossible Revolution? Black Power and the American Dream.* New York: Random House, 1968.

Killian examines the interplay between the black protest and dominant white society. The conclusion he comes to is troubling in its pessimism. The black minority may indeed make a revolution but in doing so it can only evoke a reactionary and repressive response from the white majority. The police state is not so remote as we may like to think. Readers of *Urban America* will find Killian's work of interest, with particular reference to our analysis of the protest of the disinherited.

Liebow, Elliot. *Tally's Corner: A Study of Negro Streetcorner Men.* Boston: Little, Brown and Co., 1967.

This book contains a detailed analysis of life in a large city as it is lived by the black poor. Liebow graphically describes, and then analyzes, the relationship of the streetcorner men to the limited economic opportunities that are afforded them, the nature of their conjugal interaction, the character of their cross-sexual relationships in general, and the structure of their friendship networks. Liebow's work is particularly relevant to our discussion of personalization in Chapter 5 and to our analysis of what it means to be a member of the disinherited in the cities of the American present.

Lubove, Roy. *The Professional Altruist: The Emeregence of Social Work as a Career* 1880–1930. Cambridge, Mass.: Harvard University Press, 1965.

Lubove offers us a history of the emergence of social work as an aspiring profession. Among other things, Lubove traces social work to its American origins in the Charity Organization Movement. He notes its early association with the fear of revolution in the United States, and its consequent emphasis upon social control of the poor. Lubove chronicles the bureaucratization of social work and, in its emphasis upon character regeneration, its growing commitment to therapy and the medical analogy. Social work has, of course, become a familiar endeavor on the urban scene. For this reason alone Lubove's book is a useful source. Those who find the arguments on the professionalization of social reform, presented in Chapter 8 of *Urban America,* persuasive, should consult Lubove's work for insight into the historical background of professionalized social welfare efforts.

Malcolm X. *The Autobiography of Malcolm X.* New York: Grove Press, 1964.

This is a remarkable book written by a remarkable man. It documents the nature of the black protest in the cities from the perspective of a committed militant and evangelical of resistance. Beyond this, it brings the reader into close contact with the life of the ghetto as it has been lived and continues to be lived today. It is not sociology but it is the stuff of which a perceptive urban sociology must consist.

Mills, C. Wright. *Power, Politics and People.* New York: Ballantine Books, 1963.

This is a collection of Mills' major papers prepared by Irving Louis Horowitz. Of particular importance to those who are interested in the problems of the American urban present are: "The Structure of Power in American Society," "The Political Gargoyles: Business as Power," "The Trade Union Leader: "A Collective Portrait," "The Labor Leaders and the Power Elite," "The American Business Elite: A Collective Portrait," "The Big City: Private Troubles and Public Issues," and "The Professional Ideology of Social Pathologists." Mills was an extremely insightful commentator on social life in modern America. Right or wrong, he always seemed to be able to get to the core of the issue he was examining. Students of the contemporary scene would do well to study his formulations on American power. To the extent that Mills was correct about power in the society in general, he was also correct (by implication) with regard to the distribution of power in American cities and its problematic manifestations. Those readers of *Urban America* who find the discussions of power and its problematic implications in Chapters 2, 5, 6, 7, and 8 of interest will find Mills' work to be of considerable importance.

Poverty Amid Plenty: The American Paradox. The Report of the President's Commission on Income Maintenance Programs. Washington: U.S. Government Printing Office, 1969.

This report contains useful descriptions and statistics on the poverty experience in the United States—urban as well as rural. It also includes a review of existing government programs giving aid to the poor, and concludes with a recommendation for an income maintenance program that would offer direct cash payments to all in proportion to their need. It should be noted that the recommendations of this commission are far more liberal than the so-called welfare reform programs that, at this writing, are being considered by Congress. The main report is accompanied by a published volume of technical studies that should prove useful to those who are reasonably conversant with the economics of poverty and welfare.

Report of the National Advisory Commission on Civil Disorders (The Kerner Commission). New York: Bantam Books, 1968.

This is the Kerner Commission investigation into the riots or insurrections which struck American cities in the middle 1960s. It is a valuable descriptive source, containing data on the racially based disorders in Tampa; Cincinnati; Atlanta; Newark; Northern New Jersey; Plainfield, New Jersey; New Brunswick, New Jersey; and Detroit. Beyond such coverage there is an historical outline of the black experience in the cities, and a depiction of contemporary conditions in urban ghettos. The report is particularly pertinent to our discussion of the emergent protest of the disinherited in Chapters 6 and 7.

Ryan, William. *Blaming the Victim*. New York: Vantage Books, 1971.

This book is an analytic polemic that attacks our conventional wisdom and, consequently, our conventional remedial efforts where the disinherited poor of American society are concerned. Ryan argues that we blame the poor for their poverty because we suffer from a conflict between our altruistic values and our less praiseworthy interests. We approach the poor as though they were responsible for their sorry condition. We see their way of life as a cultural design that must itself be reformed, rather than look at poverty conditions as situational adaptations to economic exclusion and discrimination. It is, maintains Ryan, the victimizers who need to reform—not their victims. Readers will find this book an excellent supplement to the discussion of noninstitutionalized inequality that appears in Chapters 6 and 7 of *Urban America*.

Seligman, Ben B., ed. *Aspects of Poverty*. New York: Thomas Y. Crowell, Co., 1968.

This is a collection of pieces previously published in other formats. Of particular importance are (1) Seligman's study "Poverty and Power," which is a critical review of the assumptions and strategies associated with the "War on Poverty" and the development of the Office of Economic Opportunity, (2) Richard Elman's "The Poorhouse State," which sharply criticizes the administration of public welfare programs that he views as victimizing the poor, and (3) Loren Miller's "Race, Poverty and the Law," which documents the disadvantages suffered by the poor and the black before the bar of justice. These selections are particularly pertinent to the discussions of stigma and noninstitutionalized inequality that appear in Chapter 6 of *Urban*

America, and the discussion of the failure of professionalized social reform which appears in Chapter 8.

Youth in the Ghetto: A Study of the Consequences of Powerlessness and a Blueprint for Change. New York: Harlem Youth Opportunities Unlimited, 1964.

The HARYOU Report is included here as an example of an extremely ambitious "War on Poverty" proposal. Put together by a coalition of local groups, the report made farreaching recommendations in such areas as education, employment, family, and community organization. The HARYOU program was eventually funded, but most of its intended goals were never realized. This document is generally available in university libraries and should be consulted by those who are interested in the problems of federally sponsored reform in the cities. It is highly probable that much of HARYOU's failure stems from the fact of its political ambitiousness, a fact that was threatening to the entrenched status quo politicians in the area.

Index